KU-187-931

A Personal Narrative
of the
Irish Revolutionary Brotherhood

JOSEPH DENIEFFE

A Personal Narrative of the IRISH REVOLUTIONARY BROTHERHOOD

Introduction by
SEÁN Ó LÚING

SHANNON IRELAND
1969

Published serially in *The Gael* New York 1904
First Edition New York 1906

This IUP reprint is a photolithographic facsimile of the first edition and is unabridged even to the extent of retaining the original printer's imprint

SBN 7165 0044 2

Irish University Press Shannon Ireland
DUBLIN CORK BELFAST LONDON NEW YORK
Captain TM MacGlinchey Publisher

PRINTED IN THE REPUBLIC OF IRELAND AT SHANNON
BY ROBERT HOGG PRINTER TO IRISH UNIVERSITY PRESS

INTRODUCTION

Joseph Denieffe's personal narrative, *Recollections of the Irish Revolutionary Brotherhood*, first appeared serially in the New York monthly *The Gael* from May to October, 1904. It was followed in November 1904 by a selection of some dozen letters from the extensive Fenian correspondence in the possession of O'Donovan Rossa. The narrative with its useful footnotes was re-published in book form in 1906 with an Introduction by Stephen J Richardson, editor and publisher of *The Gael*, and an Appendix consisting of a greatly enlarged selection of Fenian letters and documents not only from the Rossa papers but also from those of John O'Mahony, General T W Sweeney and Dr Denis Dowling Mulcahy.

Documents were also supplied by John Quinn, the New York bibliophile and collector. As the editor points out in his *Foreword* to the Appendix, they supplement and corroborate Denieffe's narrative. In the result, the Narrative and Appendix form a compendium of primary importance for a study of the Fenian movement between its beginnings and 1867.

It is significant that some of the best accounts of the Fenian movement come from the United States. Devoy's *Recollections* which spreads a canvas of immense and informative detail, and O'Donovan Rossa's *Prison Life*, telling of the fierce protest of one of Fenianism's great individualists, were originally published in New York. From the United States came Thomas Clarke Luby's manuscript *Memoirs* (now in the National Library) which, in addition to their serious historical content, include some fascinating chatter and gossip. They all point to the complementary nature of Irish and American Fenianism. Denieffe's narrative, to quote his own words (p 151)

> is a personal one and deals only with the matters with which I was closely connected, and the facts which I can vouch for as being absolutely true.

Denieffe, a native of Kilkenny who emigrated to New York in 1851, was a tailor's cutter and representative of the finest type of tradesmen who joined the Fenian movement in such numbers as to form one of its principal sources of strength. That he was a man of keen intelligence and perception is clear from his narrative, which is of considerable value in giving us a first hand account of the introduction of the Fenian movement into Ireland and of its early fortunes and development. It is interesting to note that the movement as initally introduced was called not the Fenian movement, but the Emmet Monument Association.[1] Denieffe naturally made his first contacts in his native Kilkenny and, nationalist reasons apart, it is important to note that he ascribes solid economic and social causes for the origin of Fenianism, 'business crushed, industry paralysed . . . the Emigrant Ship . . . The Poorhouse . . . The excessive taxes extorted from the poor farmers and other taxpayers. . . .'[2] The belief that the continued attrition of her population owing to emigration would reduce Ireland to inconsequence was one of the motivating forces of American Fenianism.[3]

The lack of satisfactory and informed communication between the revolutionary elements in Ireland and the United States was a bedevilling factor during the first phase of the Fenian movement. Denieffe came up against this experience in Dublin at the meeting in Peter Langan's timber yard, 16 Lombard Street,[4] where he was introduced to a group of republicans which included Philip Grey, Thomas Clarke Luby and Garret O'Shaughnessy. Langan and Grey who, like Luby, were 1848-49 men and linked with the land reformer Fintan Lalor,[5] joined the Emmet Monument Association. Luby, who did not join the new movement at once, thought it strange that he had never even heard of the Emmet Monument Association. Denieffe confessed himself equally surprised at finding no revolutionary organisation existed in Ireland as he had been led to believe.

Should anyone have doubts about the value of James Stephens's services to the Fenian movement Denieffe's narrative will remove them. Here we see Stephens at his magnetic best. His cheerfulness, his belief that Ireland was never in a better condition to be organised for revolution, his earnestness and his optimism, communicated themselves to others, and the description of his labours and influence, as given in this book, go far to bear out the claim he later made:

> I had found the cause of Ireland dead. . . . I awaked the dead and gave it action and power[6].

One cannot help but admire, even if critically, his dramatic notion of establishing Ireland's university in the spectacular setting of a Killarney scenic region, and though we can well understand why the level-headed Denieffe dismissed it as savouring of dreamland, we are left with the tinge of regret that he omitted to record the plans for the project which Stephens detailed with such earnestness. We are enabled to review the movement and the men who made it through the keen and perceptive eyes of the author. His precision of mind is revealed to effect when he says, with regard to Stephen's failure to order a rising at the moment when destiny appeared to demand it:

> I concluded then and there that Stephens's work was done, and his usefulness ended on that night of November 26th, 1865.[7]

Denieffe's view is one of sharp and clear definition, both as to events and personalities. With Peter Langan he was a witness to the unfortunate clash in 1860 between John O'Mahony and Stephens, and considers it his final analysis that neither man was equal to the responsibilities he had undertaken. Although Denieffe takes no sides in controversy, O'Mahony's capacity for revolution suffers heavily at his hands.

His active, inquiring mind views life and art with appreciation, when more serious cares are for a moment set aside. He writes a better description of Killarney than many a tourist brochure. Paris obviously delighted him. He never fails to give honour to valour. The romantic circumstances of his engagement are treated with a brevity which does not impinge on a narrative of revolution. In Dublin his reputation as a loyal and conservative citizen began with his employment in the quality tailoring house of Ammermann and Reid and became firmly established when he attracted to his own excellent business at South Anne Street the custom of some of Her Majesty's most devoted servants. Who would think of looking there for Fenians, or ever suspect that over his shop Denieffe had a room which became one of the most important centres of Fenian rendezvous in Dublin and virtually the headquarters of James Stephens, Chief Executive of the I.R.B.

Few great revolutionary movements can have been organised with such economy as the I.R.B. When Joseph Denieffe remarks, briefly and casually, (p 17), 'We had no funds, in fact we never had any', he states something which will be obvious to readers of this book as the plain truth and puts to rout the entire legion of detractors who spoke much gusty rhetoric to the contrary. Even the meagre £80 which he brought as a help from America in March 1858 took two months to raise.

Research indicates that the meeting which brought the Irish Republican Brotherhood into formal existence took place most probably in Maginess's Place in a district of Dublin rich in Fenian associations.[8] On that historic occasion Stephens, Luby, Langan, Garret O'Shaughnessy and Denieffe, all of them 'supremely joyous and anxious for the work', took an oath of allegiance to the Irish Republic, and the fortunes of the movement in its seminal first decade are recorded in the present narrative from the author's special knowledge.

Of the men stated by Denieffe to be present in Stephens's room when the I.R.B. was inaugurated he was himself the last survivor. Peter Langan, who is mentioned with profound respect by John O'Leary and Denieffe and whose home in Lombard Street was a centre of the I.R.B. in its early days, died in 1863.[9] Garret O'Shaughnessy of Dublin who gave the I.R.B.

his generous aid of purse and personal endeavour, died at the age of 65 in September 1898, in Bellevue Hospital, New York, and is buried in Calvary Cemetery. He had been confidential agent to Stephens and his principal duty at one stage was to convey the revolutionary funds from France to Ireland. His great colleague O'Donovan Rossa writes:

> Forty years ago I came to know Garret O' Shaughnessy in Dublin. I met him in the house of Peter Langan, 6 Lombard Street. Peter and he were two of the first men in Dublin who in 1858 joined the I.R.B. movement that James Stephens started. . . . I went to his wake. Very few people were at the wake. He died poor; he had been out of employment a long time. . . . His trade was that of an iron moulder and in his particular branch of it, the march of machinery and modern inventions had almost paralysed manual labor entirely.[10]

Stephens died in Blackrock, Co Dublin, on 29 April 1901 and Luby in Jersey City on 29 November the same year.

Denieffe's career to 1867 will be found in this book. After the failure of the rising that year he returned to New York, where he lived for some years before moving to Springfield, Ohio. From there we find him corresponding with John Devoy in January and February 1887, about Irish national matters. Throughout his American career he took an active part in these and a letter of his[11] indicates that his influence in Irish national affairs was strong in Springfield, Cincinnati and Indianapolis. At that time he was preparing to move to Chicago, which he pays the attractive compliment of saying it was the only city outside of Dublin he would like to make his home.[12]

In Chicago his active interest in Irish affairs continued. When O'Donovan Rossa escaped serious injury in an accident towards the end of 1902, De nieffe sent him a message of warm regard:

> I think you believe in prayer, for you are certainly under the protection of some good Providence (else you would be amongst the missing long ago) who is preserving you for some noble purpose. We may differ on trifles, but you will always command my esteem and admiration.
>
> Yours sincerely
> Joseph Denieffe.[13]

Denieffe died in Chicago on 20 April 1910 at the age of 77, 'true to the principles of Fenianism' till the last, as stated in his obituary in the *Gaelic American*.[14] There could be no epitaph that man of integrity would value more.

The Appendix, running to over 130 closely printed pages, consists of a series of documents the study of which is essential for anyone who wishes to become acquainted with the Fenian movement both in its American and Irish contexts. The letters printed here from the hand of James Stephens help us more than any amount of commentary to understand the character and essence of the man who led and controlled the I.R.B. from its origins to its zenith. The very first letter setting forth his claim to lead the movement as

> a provisional dictator. On this point I can conscientiously yield nothing,

displays the autocratic touch characteristic of him, which might have been his great strength but, combined with later adverse factors, became his great weakness. In fluent and discursive correspondence he shows us the tensions that operated behind the scenes at the MacManus funeral, which under I.R.B. control turned out to be a decisive factor in advancing the republican movement. He reports with authority and assurance on the condition of the movement following the seizure of the *Irish People* and the arrest of the chief leaders. His voyage of escape in the collier *Concord,* as narrated by the master of the vessel, Captain Weldon, brings us in contact with that sense of adventure which is never absent from the story of the I.R.B.

Important and copious documentation on phases of the American movement is supplied mainly from the papers of Major General T W Sweeny, Secretary of War to the Fenian Brotherhood. Much of this relates to the preparation for the invasion of Canada in 1866. Resources, armament and transport problems occupy considerable attention. A new dimension of the Fenian movement appears in the dispatch, dated 7 June 1866, from Samuel P Spear, Brigadier General, I.R.A., announcing that Irish troops crossed the Canadian border at 10 a m that morning and took a strong position. General Sweeny's report on the invasion is illuminating. Although a failure, the threat to Canada represented an early chapter of the formidable movement of the American Irish which for the six succeeding decades, manifesting itself in many different ways, became a powerful arm of Irish nationalism and an influence the potency of which became much respected in London.

Great names contribute to the correspondence. John Mitchel, busy in charge of the Fenian funds in Paris, is plagued with spies and robbers. An appeal from Charles Kickham for funds discloses the ever tenuous state of the I.R.B. exchequer. John Boyle O'Reilly writes on many matters as engagingly as we might expect from a mind so rich and human as his. There is much else, of great interest and value, to make this volume a source which any evaluation of the Fenian movement must of necessity take into account.

Seán Ó Lúing

Aibreán 1968

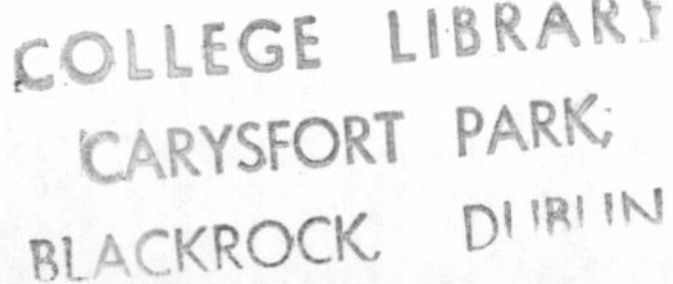

A PERSONAL NARRATIVE

OF THE

Irish Revolutionary Brotherhood

GIVING A FAITHFUL REPORT OF THE

PRINCIPAL EVENTS FROM 1855 to 1867

WRITTEN, AT THE REQUEST OF FRIENDS,

BY JOSEPH DENIEFFE,

To which is added, in corroboration, an Appendix containing Important Letters and Papers written by JAMES STEPHENS, JOHN O'MAHONY, JOHN MITCHEL, THOMAS J. KELLY and other Leaders of the Movement.

NEW YORK:
THE GAEL PUBLISHING CO.,
140 NASSAU STREET,
1906.

DENIEFFE'S RECOLLECTIONS WERE PRINTED SERIALLY IN THE GAEL (S. J. RICHARDSON, EDITOR AND PUBLISHER), NEW YORK, 1904.

ILLUSTRATIONS.

INTRODUCTION.

THE years between 1855 and 1867 cover a period of Irish history which has been much misrepresented by current English writers and those who seek to justify England in her course in Ireland. We think it is time now that the whole truth should be told, and justice done to the memory of those brave and sincere patriots who took up Ireland's cause at a time when everything looked dark and hopeless.

At the time the Irish Revolutionary Brotherhood was founded in Ireland the country was after passing through a most terrible ordeal. During the ten years from 1845 to 1855 she lost over two millions of her population, more than half of whom were killed by a manufactured famine, while the rest were reduced to the direst poverty, with the emigrant ship and the poor house staring them in the face.

On April 9, 1855, Archdeacon Fitzgerald, a patriotic priest, wrote to Gavan Duffy that all hope for the poor of Ireland was dead, and the latter, who was about to quit Ireland in despair, thus wrote in his farewell address:—

"It may be thought I despair too soon of the present time. If there be any who honestly think so, let them try to do better, and may God prosper them. For me, I have tried. For seven years I have kept the green flag flying alone or with but a handful of friends; for twice seven years I have thought, written and acted to one sole end. In these five years I have been five times prosecuted by the English Government, and wasted thirteen months of my life in English prisons. I have 'spent and been spent' cheerfully in fortune, health, peace, the duties of home and the rights of my children; always in exhausting personal conflict with a hired press and all who lived, or hope to live, by corruption. It may be the result is small and I am an unprofitable servant, but I have done my best."

The author of our history, Mr. Joseph Denieffe, a native of the City of Kilkenny, was then a resident of New York, and a member of the Emmet Monument Association. He was called to Ireland by the serious illness of his father, and on the eve of his departure was given a commission to found the organization in that country.

It is here Mr. Denieffe takes up his narrative, and from that time until 1867—when all hope was temporarily abandoned—he took a leading part in the movement, and was twice sent as a delegate to this country by the men in Ireland. He is, therefore, in a position to speak with authority on the subject of which he writes. He was always in close touch with James Stephens, the Chief Organizer of the Irish Revolutionary Brotherhood, and his place of business in Dublin was for many years the headquarters of the Organization. He was one of its most useful, loyal and enthusiastic workers; nothing was done or contemplated without his knowledge and counsel. His story is a graphic "inside" history of the movement, and can be accepted as the exact truth.

Of all men now living Mr. Denieffe is the most competent to deal with the events which transpired in Ireland between 1855 and 1867. He does not claim to be a great writer or a possessor of literary style, but he tells his story in a clear and entertaining manner, while sincerity and truth are stamped on every line.

Mr. Denieffe is now a resident of Chicago. During his long life he has devoted himself to the betterment of his people, and has made many sacrifices in their behalf. He has been through the fire and not found wanting, and well deserves the repose and honor due a good and faithful servant.

In order that our readers may clearly understand the graphic story told by Mr. Denieffe, we deem it advisable to give a brief review of Irish affairs in America previous to his time, and of the events which gradually led up to and finally crystallized into the most powerful secret revolutionary society that ever existed.

After the abortive rising in '48 whatever opinions

were entertained regarding the cause of the sudden, and to Americans, inexplicable, collapse and failure which took place in Ireland, it was pretty generally recognized and conceded that it was mainly owing to a lack of military knowledge in those engaged in the revolutionary movement. The Irish peasantry had been led into revolt without arms or military training or even a commissariat. Their leaders, without material means or scientific knowledge, had failed to provide these indispensable requirements to a successful rising, and in consequence, the insurrection became a dismal failure.

While preparations for the '48 revolt were yet being made in Ireland, a military organization known as "The Irish Republican Union" had been set on foot in New York by a few sterling Irish patriots, chief among whom were Michael Phelan, James F. Markey and John G. Fay, all well-known citizens at that time. Mr. Phelan financed the organization and to his energy and liberality the rapid progress made by the new organization was mainly due. To Mr. Markey belonged the honor of raising and disciplining the first military company for this new organization. It was the first military body organized in America for Irish Revolutionary purposes. It was called the "Irish Fusileers," and subsequently became the Mitchell Guards, Co. C, 9th Regiment, New York State Militia. Mr. John G. Fay was an active worker in the movement and became Adjutant of the organization.

Towards the close of 1849, the Irish Republican Union was organized into companies according to accepted military regulations and was regularly officered preparatory to its becoming incorporated into the New York State Militia. Michael Doheny, who had fled from Ireland the year before, was elected captain of one of these companies. In May, 1850, the Irish military organization was formally admitted into the service of the State and thenceforth became known as the Ninth Regiment, N. Y. S. M. The military spirit evoked among Irish-born citizens of New York by the appearance of a State regiment wearing their "immortal green" on St. Patrick's Day, 1851, soon led to the formation of a second Irish Regiment, the "Sixty-ninth." Col. Charles S. Roe was its first commander, and Michael Doheny was Lieutenant Colonel, which position he held until November, 1853, when he resigned. He subsequently became Colonel of the "Seventy-fifth" (or Irish Rifles), the third Irish regiment incorporated into the State Militia.

COLONEL MICHAEL DOHENY.

The most fame came to the Sixty-ninth through its first war colonel, Michael Corcoran. At the outbreak of the Civil War it was the most talked about regiment in the United States. Colonel Corcoran had been ordered to parade the regiment in honor of the visit of the young Prince of Wales, now King Edward, of England. The regiment was then as distinctively and pronouncedly Irish in its organization as at any time in its history. Corcoran flatly refused. He was placed under arrest and relieved from command. Charges were preferred against him for disobedience of orders, insubordination and disrespect to superiors. A court martial was ordered, but pending its first sitting Fort Sumter was fired on and President Lincoln made his first call for troops. Horace Greeley, Richard O'Gorman and others interceded with Governor Morgan, pointing out that the regiment was needed to defend Washington, and the charges were dismissed. Colonel Corcoran was restored to the command and the regiment was at once sent to the front.

No regiment of the militia acquitted itself with more honor in the Civil War than the Sixty-ninth. It was cut up and recruited eight different times. Three regiments were in the war as representatives of the Sixty-ninth. These were the original Sixty-ninth militia, another Sixty-ninth which became part of the Irish brigade and a third made up after the other two had gone into the field and been cut to pieces.

At the close of the war Colonel Corcoran was thrown from a horse and killed. He had ridden down to a station near Washington to see General Meagher off for the North. He rode Meagher's horse back. The general was a fine horseman and had spirited animals. Corcoran was not used to such a horse, and the animal ran away, throwing his rider.

Towards the close of 1853, the certainty of England becoming involved in a war with Russia filled the hearts of Irish Nationalists in America with hope; and the arrival of John Mitchell and John O'Mahony about the same time gave fresh impulse to the existing Irish military organizations and soon led to the formation of another—a secret military organization, which was called into existence for the special purpose of preparing for the opportunity which all expected would be soon afforded them.

This new revolutionary society was known as the "Emmet Monument Association," and was ostensibly organized for the purpose of erecting a monument to Robert Emmet. According to tradition, no monument can be erected to Emmet "until Ireland a nation can build him a tomb," therefore, the work of the Emmet Monument Association presupposed the freedom of Ireland as a necessary preliminary.

The new organization spread rapidly until it numbered within its ranks the greater portion of the organized Irish Nationalists throughout the chief cities of the Union.

Its leaders entered into confidential relations with the representatives of Russia at Washington and New York as other Irish leaders of the present day have done within the past few months—a case of history repeating itself.

The representatives of the Emmet Monument Association apparently satisfied the Russian gentlemen of the power and influence of the Irish element in America and of the expediency of Russia's aiding their project of creating a revolution in Ireland and thus striking at the British Empire in its most vital part, so that the Consul held out to them the strongest hopes of their obtaining from the Russian Government all the material aid they required—namely, the means of fitting out an armed expedition for Ireland.

The muster-roll of one of the companies composing "The Emmet Monument Association" is still in existence. It is dated exactly fifty years ago and few of its members are now alive. There were one hundred men and two officers in the company. In order that their names may be preserved and handed down the muster-roll is given herewith.

"THE EDWARD FITZGERALD GUARD."

ORGANIZED APRIL 7TH, 1854.

Captain—JOHN O'MAHONY.

First Lieutenant—MICHAEL F. NAGLE.

John Barnade.	John D. Hughes.	Mich. O'Boyle.
Michael Barry.	Peter Ivory.	W. O'Callaghan.
C. Boobidge.	Chas. J. Jackson.	Pat. O'Donnell.
James Boyd.	F. A. Jackson.	Thos. O'Higgins.
Denis Brown.	Charles Jones.	Owen O'Neill.

Edward Brown.
R. J. Brown.
Thomas Burke.
Edw. K. Butler.
John C. Byrne.
Patrick Carr.
B. J. Casey.
James Connor.
Joseph Corlies.
Andrew Cullem.
Edw. Cummins.
John Curry.
William Curry.
Owen Dermody.
William Dooley.
John Duane.
S. Fannon.
Francis Farrell.
James Farrell.
John G. Fay.
John C. Foley.
Pat. Gallagher.
Peter Gaughran.
John Geoghegan.
Michael Hannon.
David Hinds.
Patrick Hogan.
Bryan Holland.
Dan'l S. Howley.
J. H. Kelly.
M. A. Kelly.
Louis Kenyon.
Wm. E. Lalor.
James Lanigan.
Thomas Leddy.
John C. Lynch.
Patrick Lynch.
Thomas Lynch.
Frederick Lyster.
John McAllister.
Chas. McCarthy.
H. McConnell.
P. McIntyre.
J. W. McManus.
J. McNamara.
W.S.McNamara.
William Maynes.
Pat. J. Meehan.
Samuel Mitchell.
Michael Mullin.
B. P. Murphy.
C. Murphy.
Edw. Murphy.
Patrick Murphy.
Richard Murphy.
Wm. Murphy.
Peter Murray.
Rich. J. Nagle.
Rich. O'Neill.
Chas. O'Reilly.
F. O'Ryan.
P. O'Ryan.
H. S. Persse.
M. H. Power.
W. F. Power.
Edward Price.
Michael Price.
Philip Reid.
Jas. Riordan.
Michael Ryan.
Patrick Ryan.
Edw. F. Sinnott.
Wm. T. Sinnott.
Edward Sisk.
James Skehan.
Michael Skehan.
William Tierney.
L. Verdon.
Maurice Wall.
Patrick J. Wall.
J. S. Walsh.
Michael Walsh.
William Walsh.
John Warren.
Edward White.

For various reasons the help promised by Russia never materialized; delay and proscrastination seemed to be the rule until finally the Crimean war came to an unexpected close, thereby ending all hopes of assistance from their new ally. At this juncture it was deemed expedient by the directors of the E. M. A. to formally dissolve the association and release the members from their pledges. Before this course was taken, however, they took the precaution of first forming a permanent committee, consisting of thirteen men, representatives of the several divisions of the society. This committee was empowered to resuscitate the organization whenever they deemed the proper time had come for taking such a step.

It may be remarked here that when the Emmet Monument Association was in existence there were more armed, disciplined and determined Irishmen in New York pledged to the cause of Ireland's freedom than there have been at any time since.

After an interregnum of two years, the ever watchful patriots composing the committee came to the conclusion that the time had again arrived for renewing preparations for an Irish revolutionary movement on a large scale and accordingly summoned the members of the E. M. A., and from its members commenced the formation of a new organization, which they designated the Fenian Brotherhood.

Mr. Denieffe joined the Emmet Monument Association in 1855, while hope for Ireland was still strong on account of the European war. He spread the organization in Ireland on the same basis as it existed in America until the arrival of James Stephens, when, on St. Patrick's Day, 1858, the Irish Revolutionary Brotherhood was launched into existence, the old organization being incorporated and continuing under the new name.

EDITOR THE GAEL.

RECOLLECTIONS OF THE
IRISH
REVOLUTIONARY BROTHERHOOD.

RECOLLECTIONS

OF THE

IRISH REVOLUTIONARY BROTHERHOOD.

CHAPTER I.

EARLY in June, 1855, the Emmet Monument Association of New York was steadily organizing, and its members were drilling once a week. The object of the Association was the invasion and freedom of Ireland. Only those were admitted to membership who were free from family obligations, such as having a wife, mother, or others, depending upon them for support. Each and every member should be ready to serve at a moment's notice. This was the organization from which sprung, a few years later, the great Fenian Brotherhood.

Michael Doheny (1), John O'Mahony and other exiles of the Forty-eight movement were its organizers. As soon as I became aware of its existence I spoke concerning it to my friend, Patrick Mackey, also a Forty eight man, who had been a student in St. Kyran's College, Kilkenny, preparing for the priesthood at that time. After the failure at Ballingarry, in which he was engaged, he was obliged to leave Ireland and go to the

---

(1) Michael Doheny and John O'Mahony made good their escape from Ireland after Smith O'Brien failed in his efforts to create a revolution. The latter was captured, sentenced to be hanged, drawn and quartered, but his sentence was commuted to exile for life in Tasmania. After serving five years he was pardoned and allowed to return to Ireland.

Michael Doheny was a lawyer in New York, a Colonel of

United States. His family, selling out their property, followed him. He was a particular friend of mine.

I suggested that we join the organization, and it was arranged that I should join first, and inform him if there was an oath or any obligation which would prevent him from joining, as he had some conscientious scruples in that regard. In that case I could let him know when the invasion was to take place, when he would join us as a volunteer.

I became a member of the Association, but found I could give no information to my friend. It was the old story of the man joining the Free Masons. If his friends wanted to know anything of the order they would have to become Masons themselves.

About this time I received a letter from home, informing me of my father's illness, his death being expected at any moment. This letter, written by my youngest brother, was very brief, and showed signs of deep sorrow. I immediately went to my employer, Mr. Wm. H. Stewart, then under the St. Nicholas Hotel, Broadway, and showed him the letter. I told him I wished to leave for home at

---

one of the Irish regiments, and was sent as delegate to Ireland with the remains of Terence Bellew McManus. He was an orator of great ability and was the author of "The Felon's Track," a book descriptive of his escape from Ireland, and a "History of the American Revolution." He died in New York in 1861.

John O'Mahony, after '48, escaped to France and lived there for two years with James Stephens. It was during this period that they formed the plan of creating a great organization, with branches in Ireland and America, for the liberation of Ireland, Stephens agreeing to take charge in Ireland and O'Mahony in America. In 1856, after the Crimean War was over, the Emmet Monument Association was allowed to wane, but out of its remains, two years later, was organized the Fenian Brotherhood, which rapidly grew in numbers and influence. John O'Mahony was its Head Centre or Chief Executive. He was also Colonel of the Ninety-ninth New York Volunteers during the Civil War, was editor of the Irish People Newspaper and Sunday Citizen, and translated Keating's History of Ireland from the Irish. He died in New York in 1877. His body was taken to Ireland for interment and his funeral, like that of T. B. McManus, was made the occasion of a great national demonstration. He rests in Glasnevin Cemetery, Dublin.

once, and asked him to excuse me for leaving on so short a notice.

"It is hard on both of us," said he. "I don't like you to leave, but hope you will soon return and report to me."

At this time travelling by steam was very expensive, but there were some fast sailing clipper ships, boats that made the passage inside of eighteen days. I engaged passage on one of these, the "Emerald Isle," belonging to the Tapscot Line. I met in the office of the Company a Dublin friend I knew very well, who was going across on a different purpose to mine. He was going to be married.

After securing my passage I went to see Col. Doheny, told him of my unexpected departure, and asked him who I was to report to on the other side. "We have no one there as yet," he replied. "So we give you carte blanche to do what you can for the organization and yourself."

I was amazed at this announcement, as I understood a descent was to be made on Ireland early in the following September. John O'Mahony was present, as was also James Roche, formerly editor of the Kilkenny Journal.

I asked what time or date could I announce to any friends I might organize as the time they expected to move on Ireland.

"You may assure them," was the reply, "the time will be September. We have thirty thousand men ready now, and all we need is money, and arrangements are under way to provide it. We propose to issue bonds and some of the wealthiest men of our race are willing to take them."

That was my commission, and I went with a cheerful heart, although I had no one in Ireland to report to. Oh, what a charming period is youth, when nothing seems impossible.

Next morning I met my Dublin friend at Tapscott's Office, and two others with him, one of whom was going across to receive a legacy left to him by his father, in Kingstown. The other would like to come, but had no money; he was expecting some every day. He, like his friend, had also fallen in for some property, and was desirous to be with us. We arranged that he could also come.

We had plenty of everything necessary for a long voyage—given us by friends. Tom, my first acquaintance, had three cases of wine, given by his employers, besides some more potent beverage, and I was also well supplied. After some hand shaking and other manifestations of affection by our friends, we got on board, and sailed out of New York Bay.

It never looked so beautiful to me as it did on that day. There was not a cloud to be seen in the sky. A good stiff breeze in our stern, which caught us after passing Sandy Hook, kept up all the way across until we came abreast of Cape Clear. The whole passage was pleasant, and nothing occurred to mar our enjoyment. There were but few passengers, all of them belonging to the middle class, excepting one, who was constantly in the company of the Captain.

After the first day was passed all became pretty well acquainted, and seemed as if they had known each other for a lifetime. We were all of the same race, without a single exception. Tom became a great favorite. It was he who started all our amusements, and when any one felt down hearted, or was thinking too deeply, he would stir them up. If he found them too gloomy he would take them to our quarters and give them some solace.

During the trip an interesting event took place which to some was very amusing, and which after those most concerned were well and out of danger brought consolation to the one most interested. A lady was confined and gave birth to a fine boy. It was the intention of the father to have him born in Ireland. The poor dear woman felt disappointed and could not account for it; she looked as if she accused herself of some mistake, and couldn't get over it. However, as soon as the condition of her ladyship permitted a visit from the quartet it was made. We congratulated her on her good luck, and how providential it was that the boy was born on the "Emerald Isle." We had an impromptu christening. As the boy was strong and healthy we had no formal baptism, but every feature of the ceremony was duly celebrated and observed with respect and decorum. Thus the time was passed. How it flew over us!

On the seventeenth day, about 4 o'clock in the morning, we heard the watch call out "Land ahead." Tom jumped into his clothes and was on deck in a few minutes. He soon came tumbling down the companion ladder shouting, "Boys, we are in sight of Cape Clear!" We all got into our clothes as soon as we could. Tom, bringing the last bottle of champagne, mounted on deck. The Captain and his friend were already there. Tom broached the bottle, filled the cup and with eyes full of gladness drank to the land of his love. All followed, each in turn repeating the sentiment in raptures of thanksgiving. The Captain and his friend approached us, and complimented us in very nice terms; he wished he had on every voyage four passengers who took such an interest in making others happy.

Very soon we came abreast of the Old Head of Kinsale, and steered down channel. What a day to me! We kept close to the land all the way to the County Waterford. We could see the green fields and the people moving along. The hills, so sacred to Irishmen, were smiling a welcome to us. We gradually lost sight of them, as we made for Liverpool.

We arrived in Liverpool the next day, and after some delay passed the Custom House. We found we had a few hours to spend before our boat left for Ireland, so we took a stroll through the city, seeing nothing worthy of notice, except the docks, which are very extensive.

We were glad when the time arrived to get on board our boat, which we did in the nick of time. When we entered the cabin we were surprised to find our friend, the Captain's companion, sitting alone awaiting supper, which he had ordered.

As soon as he saw us he beckoned us to him, shook hands and ordered supper for all, insisting that we should be his guests for the evening.

He was evidently glad to see us, and later told us of an experience with a Customs Officer.

While in the Custom House his trunks and mine lay close together. He was apparently in haste to get away, and hailed one of the inspectors who was standing a little way off, and asked him to pass his traps. One of these was a square, seafaring chest, on which lay a sovereign, which the inspector put in his pocket. He put his official mark on each of the trunks, did the same to mine and we passed out. "You saw that sea chest," said he. "It is full to the lid with plug tobacco." Beating a British Custom House he thought was an act to be commended. In this case we heartily agreed with him. He then told us that this was his first visit to Ireland, since he left it, a boy, from Youghall, County Waterford, for America, where he spent his years coasting around South America, Mexico and the United States. He did not expect to meet any one he knew on his return, as he had not heard from any of his friends for many years.

We spent the night pleasantly, and arrived at the North Wall in due time, where we put our friend in a cab, and directed the jarvey to take him to the Shelburne Hotel, where the proprietor, Martin Burke, would give him all the information needed during his stay in Dublin.

We wended our way to Terry McCabe's, near Carlisle Bridge, where Tom was well known. I would have gone direct to Kilkenny, but could not get away from Tom. He wanted me to see his father and his best girl, so I concluded to stay over night with him. He didn't care to go home right away, so we went to the Theatre Royal, in Hawkins street. We took seats in the pit, close to the orchestra. Between the first piece and the last the orchestra struck up "God Save the Queen." All took off their hats in that part of the house. I did not understand the thing, and did not remove mine. All around me shouted, "Take your hat off!" I paid no attention to them. One fellow near me said if I didn't he would remove it. He made an attempt, and I knocked him over a seat. Immediately the gods on the top gallery shouted, "Bravo," "Jump on him," etc. All was turmoil in a moment. I was ordered out. "I will go," I said, "but hope the next time I come I shall not be annoyed with this anthem, as you are pleased to call it. I call it an insult to the Irish people, who have not as yet become slaves." I must say the majority of those present were on my side.

We got home safely to our hotel. Next morning before we got out of bed, Tom's father, hearing of his arrival, called, and after some greeting and scolding took us to his house for breakfast. After a little while we went to see Tom's fiancee and friends. I was obliged to spend another night in Dublin.

Next day, Sunday, I left for home, and arrived in Kilkenny at 9 o'clock in the evening. Although a fine bright night, very few people were at the depot. I passed through John street and over the bridge, which commands such a fine view of Ormond Castle, and on through the centre of the city, which appeared to me to be deserted. I met but one or two persons, until I reached my father's residence. I found my father, recovered from his illness, had retired for the night. My mother and two sisters were sitting together when I was admitted. They did not know me, nor I them. Five years had elapsed since I left them, and the changes that had taken place in that short time baffled us. I did not at once make myself known, but said I was a friend of Joe's (myself), and called, according to promise, to see them. While telling them how he was, etc., I could not but admire their affectionate interest. Their anxious eyes told how each of them felt. When I declared myself, the maternal feelings gave way, in the joy of the moment. My father came down stairs half dressed to add to the already strained emotions of the group. In a few minutes the room was filled with our neighbors, who flocked in to greet and welcome me, amongst them a dear friend and classmate, John Kavanagh. After a time, when greetings had been exchanged, questions asked and answered, and all had become calm and cool, John and I started out to take a stroll, and see some old places dear to both of us. Even at night I could see that a change for the worse had come over the little town. The woolen mills that were working when I left home were all closed up and deserted, gloom and sadness prevailed all over; no improvements, everything seemed going to the dogs!

Within a day or two I called on John Haltigan, at the "Journal" Office, who, next to Dr. Cane, was then one of the most popular men of the city, and was foreman in the printing department of that paper. After making arrangements to meet him that evening at his house, where we could talk with more privacy and without interruption, I left him, pleased with our interview.

JOHN HALTIGAN
Foreman Printer "Irish People" Newspaper.

We met accordingly, and talked matters over. He was enraptured with the prospects ahead, as he considered that everything was going from bad to worse, and something must be done to check the impending destruction of our people. We got together all the intelligent young men that we knew, and in a few weeks had all we desired for the present.

Haltigan at this time was in good circumstances, and had a nice little farm on the borders of the town. His wife, like himself, was a good, sincere Nationalist, whose counsel infused prudence and courage into many. He had two fine greyhounds, and we went hunting every Sunday to the Tullaburn Mountains, where he knew a great many men of the right stamp, all of whom he initiated into our movement. (1)

There was another fertile spot in the southern part of the county where friend Haltigan was well known, the old town of Callan, almost under the shadow of Slievenamon. We arranged to pay a visit to this burg on the following Sunday. On our arrival we were met at the Bridge by Edward Coyne and James Cody. Coyne was the most popular young man in the town, and Cody, who was a draper, had many friends in the adjoining section and in the County Tipperary. Both were genial, hearty men. After hearing our message, both rejoiced at having something to do to which they could give their hearts and all their energies to work out. The conversation of the afternoon showed they were well aware of the state of the country—business crushed, industry paralyzed, not a ray of hope around. Apathy, and the continuous flight of the best bone and sinew of our race to the Emigrant Ship were becoming a settled conclusion in all minds. No effort was being made to avert the impending desolation that must follow. The poorhouse was the only last refuge in sight for those who couldn't get away. The excessive taxes extorted from the poor farmers and other taxpayers reduced them to a condition that left them no choice between becoming inmates of those institutions or the Emigrant Ship. Such were the logical deductions made from the policy that prevailed all over Ireland.

---

(1) John Haltigan was afterward made foreman of the Irish People newspaper, the official organ in Dublin of the Irish Revolutionary Brotherhood. On its seizure and suppression he was arrested and sentenced to seven years' penal servitude, after serving four of which in Pentonville and Portland prisons, England, he was pardoned, completely broken down in health. He came to New York in 1873 and acted as foreman printer for his son, James, who was then editor and publisher of the Sunday Citizen, and who afterward founded the Celtic Monthly. He returned to Ireland in 1877 and died in the City of Cork in 1884. He was taken to his native city for interment, his funeral being attended by thousands of his fellow-countrymen. A beautiful Celtic cross, erected to his memory by his fellow citizens, marks his grave in St. Patrick's churchyard, Kilkenny. Patrick J. Haltigan, editor and publisher of the National Hibernian, Washington, D. C., is his youngest son.

We were delighted in finding two men who so thoroughly understood the situation, and were ready to stake their lives to do away with such a state of things. Petitions and remonstrances had been scoffed at and thrown aside. It was time we should work with a will, with all our might, night and day, and unite the manhood of our race for one grand struggle, and be done with it. Sentiments like these took possession of us and filled us with hope, as we wended our way back to the city, confident that Callan was in good hands.

We did not meet the poet, John Locke, on this trip, nor Heffernan Dunne, the nailor, but were glad to hear afterwards that both were afield in the good work. Later on those men distinguished themselves. Heffernan Dunne, in pure derision of parliamentary agitation, ran for Member of Parliament, while Locke won world-wide fame as a National poet.

Our next move was to get into communication with the men in Dublin, of whom Haltigan knew the address of but one, a Mr. Farrell, a master chimney-sweep. We arranged that I should go next day and find them.

I started accordingly for Dublin, and in due time found Mr. Farrell's place. He was not in, however, but his wife expected him to dinner every minute. She made me await his coming.

He came punctually at the noon hour, just from his work, as black and sooty as a man could well be.

I told him my errand, which was to procure through him an introduction to the leading Nationalists of Dublin. "As soon as I eat a morsel," he said, "and change my clothes I will go with you." After his meal he was going to dress himself, but I objected, as he was going back to work again. I told him his garb made no difference to me if it didn't to himself. He laughed and we left his place.

After a short walk we arrived in Lombard street, and stopped at a lumber yard, well stocked with articles of manufacture for building purposes. I was introduced to a sunny-faced, good-looking man, the proprietor, Mr. Peter Langan. I handed him a note from Mr. Haltigan. Mr. Farrell took his departure and left us together.

After he had read the note of introduction, I told him my business and all the particulars relating to it. He was surprised, but rejoiced, and said if I would remain that evening in Dublin, he would send for a few friends, who would be glad to meet me. I agreed to do so.

At eight that evening I attended a meeting of Nationalists and tried friends of Ireland, who had been called together by Peter Langan for the purpose of hearing what I had to communicate. They were surprised and pleased to learn how far the movement had advanced in America, and readily promised to assist and co-operate with the American organization.

At that meeting I first met Garrett O'Shaughnessy (2), whom I shall have occasion to mention again as I go along. He died about ten years ago. I also met Philip Grey there for the first time. He was one of the tried and trusted men of '48 and a confidant of Smith O'Brien. He was a bookkeeper by profession and held a good position at Smithfield. He died about six months after. Peace be to him; he left no honester nor better man behind him.

Both joined the organization, as did also Peter Langan. (3) Thomas Clarke Luby was present, and thought it strange that he had not even heard of the existence of the Association.

I told him he was not more surprised than I was when told they had no organization in Ireland, but nevertheless

---

(2) Garrett O'Shaughnessy was one of the most faithful men the organization produced. He escaped arrest and came to New York only after all hope had fled. He was engaged in the iron manufacturing business in Dublin and his purse was ever open when funds were required.

(3) Thomas Clarke Luby belonged to a noted literary family in Dublin. He was educated in Trinity College, Dublin, in which his uncle was one of the chief professors. He became a leader in the movement and one of the editors of the Irish People. He was arrested and sentenced to twenty years' imprisonment. He was exiled to this country in 1871, where he continued to live until his death in 1902. He was married to the daughter of the Irish poet Frazer. One of his sons, Mr. James Luby, of Jersey City, is an able newspaper man, and another is an officer in the United States Navy.

what I stated was true. He did not join then, but Gray told me not to mind—he was all right.

After arranging matters with them and establishing a mode of communication, I returned to Kilkenny. Haltigan was well pleased with the results of my trip, and next arranged a meeting between Dr. Cane and myself. I shall never forget the warm, unostentatious way he received me. He impressed me with the idea that he was a most perfect model of a man, physically and mentally, the truest type of the Irish gentleman I had yet met. I knew his career as Mayor of Kilkenny, as a citizen, orator, lecturer and patriot. He opened the conversation, by saying my friend Haltigan told him I had just returned from New York, and that I had some good news from there. I told him all I knew, at which he was well pleased. He gave us every encouragement, and said he would help us in his own way. At this time his friend, Charles Gavan Duffy, was about leaving Ireland for Australia. Haltigan told me afterwards that Duffy had postponed his departure for some time, in consequence of Dr. Cane writing to him.

The only way we had of getting news from our friends in America was through "The Citizen" (once belonging to John Mitchell, who sold it to McClernan (1) his manager). I received it every week. About the time we expected to hear something of our friends an article appeared on the editorial page signed "From One Who Would Go." This article called on all Irishmen in the United States not to contribute to or buy any scrip from any self-constituted body acting in the name of Ireland until there would be a responsible committee appointed to receive it, etc., etc.

This evidently referred to the issue of bonds which were being prepared when I was leaving New York, therefore Haltigan and I concluded that all was up for the present.

---

(1) The Citizen was started in New York by John Mitchell and Thomas Francis Meagher on Jan. 7, 1854, after their escape from the convict settlements of Austrália. Owing to ill health Mitchell retired on Dec. 31 of the same year, and thereafter the paper was continued by his business manager, James McClernan.

We waited until the appointed time, September. It came, but brought no sign of the intended invasion. We still hoped on, but alas, our first impressions were right.

CHAPTER II.

About this time I was getting very short financially. All the little money I had was gone, and I must get back to America. I wrote to a friend in New York, Michael Fitzpatrick, to send me enough money to take me back. I received it in due course. This man did not belong to the movement.

In the meantime I was looking out for something to do, and had a letter from an old friend in Dublin, asking me to come up, as he thought he had something that would suit me.

I took a position that was offered in the North, and stayed there until '57. I was all this time in communication with my Dublin friends, and with Haltigan, but finally got tired of waiting, and becoming anxious to get back to New York went to Dublin for that purpose. I found a letter from John Haltigan awaiting me at Langan's, which informed me that James Stephens had arrived in Kilkenny, and being told of my mission was anxious to see me. He was coming to Dublin, and hoped I could wait his arrival. I wrote him saying I would wait to meet him, although I had all my arrangements made to start for America.

He arrived next day, and I saw him at Langan's, where all were glad to meet him. He was fully informed of everything up to date in relation to Irish affairs, both in Ireland and America. When he saw I was determined to leave for America he plied me with questions, and said I ought not to go back if I could get a living in Ireland. If I would stay, he promised he would stay, and wait events. He had spent all his time in Paris since '48, and came over to Killarney to finish some work he had in hand. He was to see John B. Dillon next day, about starting in as a

French tutor. (2) He saw him, and the project was favorably received, Dillon's two sons becoming his first pupils, and through these he secured more pupils, which placed him in a position of comparative independence. I went back to the County Antrim as agreed upon to await events.

We corresponded regularly. I was now in a new country, yet only one day's ride from Dublin. Everything was different, accent, feeling, customs, so far as the people were concerned, but it was Ireland, nevertheless. I lived there with my Orange brothers, amongst whom I mixed considerably, until two days before Christmas of '57, when I received a letter from Stephens, requesting me to come immediately to Dublin, and if possible to break with my employer, as he had something that would suit me. This letter was a business one, well conceived as from a friend who wished to forward my interests.

After Mr. Dunne (my employer) read my letter he released me from my engagement in a truly friendly spirit, and so I hastened to meet Stephens.

I arrived in Dublin next day, and went direct to my old friends in Trinity street, where I always stopped while in the city. As I was crossing College Green, to my surprise I met Stephens coming the other way; he had called to see if I had arrived. He looked on this meeting as a lucky omen, as neither of us ever took such a course before.

I promised to come to Langan's as soon as I could after seeing my friends in Trinity street. These were people whom I had known in New York, and who had returned to spend the remaining days of their life in their native city. I was always welcome and made happy while with them. They knew nothing about my business, although both were superior in Irish feelings to the majority of the people. For many reasons I did not wish them to be aware of my proceedings—my chief reason being, if anything should happen to me, they should not suffer any inconven-

(2) John B. Dillon was one of the '48 leaders. With Gavan Duffy and Thomas Davis he founded the Dublin Nation. One of the sons, who became pupils of Stephens, was John B. Dillon, the present Irish leader.

JAMES STEPHENS
Chief Organizer Irish Revolutionary Brotherhood

ience. They were true friends, and could be trusted, as shall be seen. Stephens and friends were awaiting me at Langan's when I arrived. He read a communication he had received from Col. Doheny and John O'Mahony, asking if he thought Ireland could be organized for revolution, would he undertake to do it, and, if so, about how much money would he require.

It was to take an answer to this, to the parties in New York who sent it that I was required. It was considered too great a risk to entrust it to the mails.

Stephens read his reply to us. It stated that Ireland was never in a better condition for such a project, that he would undertake to organize the country, the amount required being only one hundred pounds sterling a month for three months. I was instructed to leave next day, and carry this reply to Col. Doheny, Chairman of the Committee; John O'Mahony, Pat O'Rourke, Capt. Corcoran, Oliver Byrne, James Roache and John Reynolds, were the other members of the Committee.

We had no funds, in fact, we never had any, so when an emergency like this occurred it fell on one or two. I had some money myself, and Garret O'Shaughnessy made up the balance so that I was enabled to pay my way to the United States.

I at once made hurried arrangements and started for Liverpool, where I engaged a second cabin on the old Asia, Captain Lott, and sailed for America.

We started from Liverpool in fine weather and in good spirits, but, inside of forty-eight hours experienced a sudden and complete change in the weather conditions. A terrific storm sprung up that severely tested the seaworthiness of the "Asia" and the seamanship of its captain and crew. The storm lasted for a week, and its effects followed us all the way across, rendering the trip the most tempestuous and dangerous ever experienced by Captain Lott, who was a veteran seaman.

We were obliged to put into Halifax for repairs, where I left the ship and took passage on a coasting steamer for Boston, whence I took a train for New York, and arrived in due time.

Our voyage across the Atlantic had been slow and

tedious, and naturally I was anxious that the letters I carried should be delivered as promptly as possible, therefore, on my arrival in New York, I went direct from the depot to the law office of Col. Doheny. To my great disappointment, I learned he was not in, and his son Michael professed not to know where he was.

My appearance or makeup was not very preposessing, and perhaps he thought I was one of those unfortunates who often imposed on the good-natured man. I told him the business I had with his father was very important, and he should be made aware of it as soon as possible—it was strictly personal. "Well," said he, "you may find him at the Tombs."

I thanked him and went where directed. I found the Colonel holding forth in a case before the Court. He won the case and there was a great rush for the street. The Colonel got out before I could, and as he was a good walker, I had to run to catch up. When I came up to him, he stopped, shook hands, and I handed him my paper. He tore it open and read a few lines; the tears came to his eyes; he folded up the letter and we hastened on to his office.

He dispatched Michael to the Tribune office for Pat O'Rourke (1), and then for the other members of the Committee. That evening we had all of them together. While waiting their coming, I inquired how John O'Mahony was. He said he had not seen him since the letter was sent, to which my communication was an answer, but he had heard he was organizing a colony to go West. Pat O'Rourke and Capt. Corcoran arrived, and the others soon after, and although their

(1) Patrick O'Rourke was employed in the mechanical department of the New York Tribune from the time of the inception of the paper. When Horace Greeley ran short of funds he turned the property into a joint stock company. At one period being unable to pay his employees he offered them shares of stock in place of cash, which were spurned as worthless by all except Thomas Rooker, the foreman printer, and Patrick O'Rourke. They accepted the stock and afterward realized over $2,000 per annum from each share. Mr. O'Rourke later occupied the position of superintendent of the Tribune Building, which he held up to the time of his death.

PATRICK O'ROURKE, Treasurer, F. B.

residences were scattered all over the city, all were present.

The letter which I had delivered was read and considered satisfactory, gratifying, in fact, to all. To raise the first instalment was the question of the hour. Several propositions were made, but none of them seemed practical, until Capt. Corcoran, the youngest man amongst them, proposed that each should lay on the table what money he could conveniently spare, and also say how much he could collect or otherwise raise among his friends by that day week. This was unanimously approved. A list was made out for the purpose, the amounts they expected to have at the appointed time were placed opposite to the names, and the meeting adjourned.

Capt. Corcoran (2) took me to his home, where I stopped until I was ready to return to Ireland. We went around together each day among his friends and acquaintances, endeavoring to collect his part of the sum. At that time it was extremely difficult to raise any money for such a purpose, as the people had lost all confidence in such movements, and in the good faith of the leaders. Some of the Irish-American newspapers took a special interest in decrying any active movement for Ireland. They were, for various reasons, pandering to the local politicians, and consequently, were not with us. The "Irish American," then the leading and most influential Irish paper in America was, I remember, one of them.

---

(2) Michael Corcoran was an employee in the New York Custom House and at first a Captain in the Sixty-ninth Regiment of the New York National Guard. When the Prince of Wales, now Edward VII., visited America in 1860-61, the Sixty-ninth Regiment was ordered to parade in his honor. Corcoran, who was then Colonel, peremptorily refused to obey the order. Col. Corcoran was put under arrest and was threatened with trial by court martial. A great outcry was made by the Anglo-Americans of that time, but the Civil War breaking out just then, Corcoran silenced them all by tendering his sword to the President, while his regiment volunteered to a man into the service of the United States. Corcoran was afterward promoted to be Brigadier General for bravery in the field and devotion to the Union. He was an ardent Irish patriot. He was killed by a fall from his horse before the close of the war.

CAPTAIN MICHAEL CORCORAN, 69th Regt.
(Afterwards Brigadier General)

It took two months to raise four hundred dollars (£80.) I was anxious to get back, and proposed to the Committee that I would start with that amount, and they could send the balance of instalment later, which they agreed to. (3).

A circumstance occurred at this time which is well worth mentioning here: While on the collecting tour O'Mahony saw some of the leading men of the Ancient Order of Hibernians, and solicited their co-operation. They advised him to have some of us join their organization, and then we could bring up the matter regularly for their consideration. O'Mahony, Corcoran, Roche and myself joined the Order, and were initiated. Before leaving I got a letter from the Secretary to their head man in Liverpool, introducing myself and explaining the object of my visit.

I left New York by steamer early in March, 1858. On the way over I fell in with two Irishmen, who occupied berths adjoining mine. One was about my own age and the other about 45 years old. They both belonged to the County Sligo. Tom, the youngest, and I became great friends, and I soon induced him to join the organization. He told me if I could get Barney, his elder companion, to join, he could set the whole county at work. Barney was very reserved all the way across, and in no way conversational until the day before landing. There were a good many young Englishmen returning from the United States, and in the washroom that morning some of them let loose the vials of their wrath on the States.

I resented their remarks. I said it was cowardly, now that they got on their own dunghill, to crow so vociferously, and villify a generous young nation that had benefited them. We had quite a hot time of it. Neither Barney or Tom took any part in the controversy, but I was aware they stood ready to help if there was any trouble.

---

(3) It was hard to collect money for Ireland then. The Crimean War was over, the Emmet Monument Association had suspended and the Fenian Brotherhood was not yet established. Hope for Ireland was at a very low ebb.

When we got back to our quarters, Barney asked me if I had any particular place to put up at Liverpool. I told him I hadn't, as I knew no one in the place.

"Then," said he, "come with Tom and me."

"All right," said I, appreciating this sudden change to sociability.

So we wended our way to Regent street. Barney led us into a little hotel, or tavern it might be, and up straight to the bar. The man in charge and Barney were great friends. He was a fine specimen of an athletic Irishman, smart and intelligent. We were introduced, and Barney ordered the best beefsteak to be had in Liverpool.

After enjoying our meal, I told Barney I wanted to transact a little business, which would not take me long, and that I would return and spend the afternoon with him.

"I thought," said he, "you knew no one in Liverpool."

"Neither do I," I said, "it is only a message I have to deliver for a friend."

After leaving him I made certain that there was no one following me, and soon arrived at the place where I was to present my note of introduction. It was a sailors' outfitting store, close by the shipping. My man had not come down yet, the young man who was keeping shop told me, but if it was on business I wished to see him, he could attend to me just as well.

"My business is of a personal and confidential nature," I said, "and if it does not inconvenience you I prefer to wait till he comes."

It was a small shop with a narrow stairs leading upwards. I had not long to wait. Soon I heard a very heavy step on the stairs, and an old, heavy, cumbersome man, not quite awake, made his appearance.

"This is Mr. Mullen," said the young man.

I handed my letter of introduction to him; he handed it to the young man and told him to read it. I told him it was private, and important, and intended only for his own perusal.

"Oh," he said, "never mind; he does all my reading and writing."

The young man read the letter slowly to himself. The old man did not hear a word of its contents.

"Well," said the young man, when he got through reading, "that's all ephemeral."

I reached out my hand, for I wanted the letter back; he gave it to me. I was glad he did. I tore it up and threw it into the fire. "Good morning, gentlemen," said I, and left them gazing after me.

When I got back to Barney he asked where I had been. "I know," said the young fellow behind the bar.

"If you know, why do you ask me?" said I.

"You were to see Mullen," said he.

"Right you are," said I.

"Well, you were sent to the wrong party. If you stay to-night I will bring you to see the right ones—the true ones."

"I cannot stay over night," I answered. "I must be in Dublin to-morrow. But if you give me a token, I will send some one, if I don't come myself, whom you can oblige." This was the last I saw of them.

CHAPTER III.

I arrived in Dublin next morning, Patrick's Day. I found James Stephens in his lodgings, and delivered the money and a letter from the Committee. That evening, March 17, 1858, the Irish Revolutionary Brotherhood was brought into existence. An obligation was adopted, and each in turn bound himself by it—Stephens first; Luby was second, who declared himself now ready to devote his best efforts to its fulfillment. All the others, Langan, Garret O'Shaughnessy and myself, each took the obligation. We were all supremely joyous and anxious for the work. (1) The form of oath or text which was administered and which Luby drafted, was as follows:

> I, A. B., in the presence of the Almighty God, do solemnly swear allegiance to the Irish Republic, now virtually established, and that I will do my very utmost, at every risk, while life lasts, to defend its independence and integrity; and, finally, that I will yield implicit obedience in all things, not contrary to the laws of God, to the commands of my superior officers. So help me God. Amen.

Some slight variations of this oath were made later on, but the above is, substantially, the form generally used in Ireland. The oath administered in America differed somewhat in form, but was identical in spirit.*

Stephens and Luby started South next day, stopping at different points where they were known, and likely to meet with adherents to the cause. In Kilkenny, Haltigan

---

(1) The Irish Revolutionary Brotherhood was established on a military basis, with the first four letters of the alphabet used instead of the ordinary titles. A standing for Colonel, B for Captain, C for Sergeant, and D. for private.

* See Appendix XX, Page 199.

was set to work. In Tipperary they were well received. In Templederry Father Kenyon (2), then a great friend of Luby's, had them to spend a few days with him. In Cork they found some fine material. While there, however, the funds gave out.

There was in the South a secret society which had been organized in Skibbereen in 1856 by a number of patriotic men who saw no hope for Ireland, save what could be won by force, and who had organized under the name of the Phoenix National and Literary Society. The word Phoenix was intended to signify that the spirit of Irish Nationality had arisen again from the ashes of oppression.

The majority of these men, the best in the country, became later on identified with the I. R. B. and were its mainstay and backbone in various places.

James Stephens, on his visit to Skibbereen, brought a letter of introduction from James O'Mahoney, of Bandon, to Dan McCartie (Donel Oge), whom he initiated into our Society. Donal Oge, I was told, initiated O'Donovan Rossa, who in turn initiated Pat Downing and Morty Moynahan, who in turn initiated others and in that way the organization spread.

In three or four months the southern half of the County of Cork was organized, Pat Downing, Morty Moynahan and O'Donovan Rossa becoming Centres of circles. The same spirit of enthusiasm spread to other counties and very soon the men of Munster were out nights on the hillsides and on lonely roads drilling.

During all this time no word had been received from America regarding the balance of the instalment. After vainly waiting some time, Stephens and Luby were obliged to return to Dublin, stranded.

Langan's was a great place for meeting—that and Stephens' lodgings being the only places then in Dublin. In Kingstown there was a family of four brothers, the Hickeys; John, Patrick, William and another. They were all connected with the building trades, a host in themselves. John, the eldest, was a thoroughly practical

---

(2) A patriot priest of the '48 movement.

man. He had great influence and a wide acquaintance among that class, and was the means of getting in the city a great many members in the same line. The Hickeys knew none but the best people. They were certainly among the most sterling men in the Dublin organization.

At this time Charles Beggs turned up, and joined our ranks. He, Considine and myself, took rooms at Mat Farrell's, Creighton street. A more gentle, kind hearted man than Beggs I had never met. He was an enthusiast in everything pertaining to revolution in Ireland. He wrote "The Military Resources of Ireland," had it published in pamphlet form at his own expense, but found no market for it then, so the books remained dead stock on his hands.

Considine was the courier that brought the letter from Doheny to Stephens. He was rather conceited and egotistical and clashed with the honest Beggs on nearly every subject, as he did also with Garret O'Shaughnessy, who called every evening to lighten our monotony and brighten our hopes for the future. We needed his consolation, as this period was a most gloomy one. Everything was not only at a standstill, but the outlook for the future was dark indeed. There had been no news from America since my return, and it looked as if our friends there had given up all thought of us. Stephens was after returning. He sent Considine home to his father, somewhere in Tipperary. This state of inertia was demoralizing. Stephens was unable to keep his appointments, and all engagements had to be abandoned. Each day came and passed into yesterday, but still no tidings.

At last Stephens came to the conclusion that I must go back again to America, but where was the money to take me there? We were all penniless, or nearly so. Again Garrett O'Shaughnessy came to the rescue. He had no funds of his own, but borrowed from his brother seven or eight pounds—I forget which, but it was about that much. I started again for America, bearing a hot letter to the committee.

When I arrived and delivered the letter, I found they were just after sending the balance of the first instalment, one hundred dollars (£20), and there was not another cent in the treasury. Colonel Doheny took me to his home in Brooklyn, where I stopped until my return to Ireland. O'Mahony was taken up with his Keating's History of Ireland, which he was translating into English from the original Gaelic manuscript, and had some difficulty with his publisher.

After a month, occupied in foraging around, I returned to Ireland with only forty pounds, which disappointed all our friends. I told Stephens not to depend on America for further assistance. "The Irish-Americans," I said, "will not subscribe until they are obliged to. They have been humbugged so often they have lost confidence, and at present have no faith in attempts for the regeneration of Ireland."

Thomas Davis said that we had all reason to hope as long as the Irish people were not materialists,—that they would always keep the freedom of their country in their leading thoughts. Unfortunately, too many have fallen away from Davis' ideal, and societies gotten up in the name of Ireland are often used for local or personal politics. There is not a charitable body, club, or anything in that way, that is not turned to advantage by unprincipled men. Until these hypocrites are set aside, and the eyes of the people opened to the duplicities which have been practiced upon them, there can be no help for Ireland from America.

On my arrival in Dublin, Luby was sent to the South, while Stephens and I went on to Waterford. At that time we did not make much headway in the city of Waterford, but it afterward became a stronghold of National activity. John Dillon, who kept an extensive wheelwright business, became one of the leaders, and for many years was the "Centre" of the city. He was a most prudent and conservative man, but, at the same time, an intense Nationalist, and carried on his work with such secrecy and precision that the Government remained completely in the dark regarding the existence of the organization until toward the close of the movement.

Denis B. Cashman was another of the leading spirits in Waterford. He was chief clerk for a legal firm and had a wide circle of friends, among whom he instilled his patriotic principles. He was arrested later on in Dublin and sentenced to fourteen years' imprisonment. He was sent to Australia, but was pardoned after about four years. He came to America, settled in Boston and became assistant editor of the Pilot under John Boyle O'Reilly. He died in Boston in 1902. W. K. Hearn, Terence Kent, John Kenny, John Tobin and P. J. Donohue were also prominent leaders in Waterford.

After seeing some friends in Waterford, we started for Carrick-on-Suir on foot. It was a lovely day in Summer. I never enjoyed a day's trip so much. At this time Stephens was at the highest notch in my estimation. He was grand. I would undertake anything for him. He seemed to have me under a spell. He was the only practical man I had met in the Movement up to that time. There was earnestness in his every move. He was abstemious, frugal—in fact, in adversity his greatest qualities were shown to perfection. He was all that could be desired as a leader. If he had continued so, and lived up to the doctrine he promulgated and practiced his own precepts, we would have a different state of things now. But he was not a Wolfe Tone.

Strict attention to duty, perseverance, privation, toil—no rest until the object was reached and victory achieved; these were a few of the discouragements he pointed out to all. We were willing to bear all and followed him to the end.

We arrived in Carrick that evening and called on old man Kavanagh, where we stopped that night. He had a fine lot of young fellows, and some few older ones to meet Stephens, who, after a little time, made them joyful with his remarks. He sent me on to Denis Dowling Mulcahy, who lived in Powerstown, near Clonmel, to ask him to meet him in that town next day. I spent that night with Denis and his family. His father was a fine type of an Irish gentleman, of most distinguished and patriarchial appearance. His mother must have passed away, for I saw no one there who would be likely to fill that place. His two sisters were present. One of them, the eldest, I met afterward, under changed circumstances, which shall be dealt with in the proper place, and Denis also shall be heard from again.

After spending a pleasant day in Clonmel I was sent to Kilmallock to see a friend and arrange a meeting for Stephens. I saw my man and arranged for the meeting. Thence I went to Macroom to see another. Here I had to wait until school was out, as the man I came to see was a teacher. It was a fair day there, and I enjoyed it while waiting for my man, with whom I was highly pleased, and whose name was Lucy. I strolled around the remainder of the afternoon and stopped for the night right opposite the castle in a very snug hotel kept by M. Murphy, if I remember right.

CHAPTER IV.

Next morning I left for Cork, and met Stephens and Luby at the Commercial Hotel. After resting and refreshing ourselves we took a stroll through the famous city, among other places visiting the pile from which the famous bells of Shandon send out their rapturous melody. I was captivated and satisfied I had performed a duty for neglecting which I would never forgive myself.

After seeing the places of interest inside the city, I could not help noticing that the devastating hand of misgovernment had been doing its work of destruction. Although not so bad as elsewhere it was quite perceptible. We took in the Mall, a pleasant walk, and also got a good view of the Cove. Spike Island, with its menacing and frowning aspect, kept my attention riveted for a moment or two, but what passed through my mind during that short space of time, I cannot attempt to describe. It marred the pleasure that otherwise would have been complete. (1).

We had arranged to meet our Cork friends at Carroll's

---

(1) The convict establishment of Ireland was at that time situated on Spike Island, which is located in the Cove of Cork, modernly known as Queenstown Harbor, so named after a visit of Queen Victoria. Beneath its gloomy walls many thousands of Irishmen were done to death, most of whom were imprisoned on trumped-up charges in connection with the various land agitations. One of the prisoners, named Cornelius O'Reilly, afterward a resident of New York, made his escape from there under extraordinary circumstances. He was implicated in the killing of a rack-renting and licentious landlord and enlisted in the army in order to escape from the police. While standing on St. Patrick's Bridge, Cork, as a soldier, looking with hundreds of others at a furious flood in the River Lee, a little child fell over the parapets of the bridge out of the arms of its nurse, who was among the spectators, and was being carried away by the flood. Quick as a flash O'Reilly jumped after it, caught it in his arms and, although he was

that evening. When the hour came all were on hand. Among the advanced Nationalists were Carroll, Bryan Dillon, Morty Moynahan and James Mountain. These I remember distinctly. They made a deep impression on me as they were the most advanced men I had up to that time fallen in with. It was an evening well spent and shall never be forgotten. It brought me in touch with men who were abreast of the times, and who by their efforts redeemed the city's good name, and made it the first on the roll of honor in Ireland. (2).

---

carried five miles by the rushing current, succeeded in saving its life and his own.

The child was the daughter of Michael Joseph Barry, a leading lawyer of Ireland and an ardent poet and patriot of the '48 movement. For accepting office from the British government and turning traitor to his Irish principles he was nicknamed "Judas Barry." He was Attorney General for Ireland during the Fenian trials and prosecuted his countrymen for avowing the same principles which he advocated himself twenty years before.

O'Reilly was lionized by the public generally for his noble action, but the fame he achieved disclosed his identity and he was arrested for the murder of the landlord and sent to Spike Island for life. He was there only a short time, when the warden one evening winked in the direction of a stone on the beach and told him to lag behind. Under the stone was a note telling him to watch a ship which lay in the offing. As night was closing in a boat put off from the ship, made for the direction of O'Reilly. picked him up. carried him on board, and he was brought safely to New York. It never became known who O'Reilly's savior was, but it is generally believed that it was Barry, as no one else interested had the power to bring about such an escape. Although he proved recreant to Ireland he still retained enough gratitude in his heart to rescue from a living death the man whose bravery saved the life of his child.

O'Reilly lived for many years in New York and kept a restaurant in Eighth avenue, near Twenty-third street, about a quarter of a century ago. He was known as the Commodore from his love of aquatics, and was prominent in many Irish organizations.

(2) Of the Corkmen mentioned above Bryan Dillon and James Mountain were arrested, convicted of treason-felony and sentenced to long terms of imprisonment. Mortimer Moynahan was one of the men arrested for the so-called Phoenix conspiracy in 1858-9. He was not arrested in the '65-67 movement. He escaped to New York, where he died five years after his arrival.

But we must move again—this time for Killarney, for a sight of which my heart was panting. We left next morning on a jaunting car, and, after traveling some distance, took to walking. Stephens spoke of Gougane Barra, but, as we had no special business there, we went up the side of a mountain and were soon in Glengariff. Stephens knew every point of interest, and took pride in pointing them out to us as they appeared in their most captivating aspects. We passed under the natural bridge, and were soon in the County Kerry, the birthplace of Daniel O'Connell, the Liberator. I was wrong in expecting to find conditions better there. I found the people apparently more enslaved than in any other part of Ireland which I had yet visited, and which I learned that evening, to my great sorrow.

Our first stop was at Kenmare. We put up at a little hotel and tavern, where we were to meet some of the townsmen that night. We were now in the dominion of Lord Landsdowne, governed by his Agent Trench, one of the meanest and most contemptible petty tyrants that ever held authority over poor mortals. His vigilance never slumbered, consequently there was more caution displayed here on that account. This I learned from a man who sat beside me, and who had arrived later than the others. I could not help noticing that an uneasy feeling possessed him, and asked was there anything the matter with him, he looked so woebegone.

"No," said he; "but this is new to me, and this is a terrible place."

"This house?" said I.

"No," said he; "I mean the town; you can't move without you are watched and talked of."

He then told me of the espionage that was exercised and some of the rules this agent had laid down for observance by the community. If any one should go to a wake, no matter how great the friend, or near the relative, you must first get the agent's consent. Tenants were not permitted to marry without his sanction. Such were some of the rules in this part of Kerry. This beautiful place was cursed by this haughty tyrant, blustering and crimping all the joys and comforts, social and economic all round.

'Twas here, I think, I first met O'Donovan Rossa and Dan McCarty. I know the meeting was brief. After Stephens got through, we left the place. (3).

We were now on our way to the Lakes, and arrived there in a very short time. Those intervals on the road were very interesting to me. My two traveling companions could find no equals as conversationalists in all that talkative land. It was equal to a course of lectures on history, literature and poetry, not of English only, but of all the nations that had any to boast of in ancient or modern times. I took it all in and venerated these two worthy men for the wonderful knowledge they possessed and had so ready at command on all occasions. I thanked Providence for the privilege of seeing this romantic and picturesque part of my native land in such company, and was perfectly conscious that we were on a noble mission for the sake of liberty, truth and justice. With such pleasing fancies floating around me, Killarney burst forth on our anxious eyes. Stephens had the jarvey drive in by a certain road between two slopes forming a little valley on high ground. A sudden turn in the road revealed the Upper Lake in all its glory as suddenly as an artist throws a stereopticon picture on a canvas.

Stephens had a very happy way of getting up such surprises, and this could not have been better conceived. He had kept us interested until the view broke on our vision. This is considered the best approach to Killarney for tourists. The town is insignificant, but all else magnificent. We put up at a small hotel, the proprietor of which knew Stephens well, a circumstance that brought him into trouble afterward. This hotel was a resort for those of limited means, but homely and comfortable. After refreshing ourselves, and making arrangements for a meeting in the evening, Stephens took us to Ross Island and Muckross

---

(3) O'Donovan Rossa has since achieved a world-wide reputation as an Irish patriot. He became business manager of the Irish People newspaper, Dublin, and was afterwards sentenced to imprisonment for life. He was pardoned in 1871 and came to New York, where he has resided ever since. He is now publisher of the United Irishman. Daniel McCarthy was one of the principal leaders of Cork.

O'DONOVAN ROSSA
From Photograph Taken in 1894.

Abbey, and he knew and explained so many things of interest, natural beauties, historic scenes, legends, etc., that I imagined I was in fairy land.

The object of Stephens' tour was to secretly visit and personally interview the most influential Nationalists in each town, explaining to them as far as was permissable at that time the plan and scope of the organization in America and Ireland, and what it hoped to accomplish.

He invariably succeeded in getting them interested to the extent of their becoming active local organizers and always, before leaving, instructed them regarding the expected growth and future government of the society in that section.

The meetings were carried on with great secrecy behind closed doors and in each place Stephens was given the names of reliable men in the next town, men in whose patriotism he could rely to the death; these in turn referred him to others further along and in that way the entire South was organized.

Later on other men were sent North and West, men widely acquainted in those sections who repeated the good work performed by Stephens, Luby and others in the South and Southeast.

CHAPTER V.

Next day he had a boat ready, and sent it somewhere for future use. He brought us through Lord Kenmare's grounds, then to Kate Kearney's cottage, where we had some goat's milk and mountain dew, then through the gap of Dunloe, stopping at times to hear the echoes, which were caused by the firing of small cannon by men who got a living out of this enterprise. The surroundings were different to anything I had yet seen. All nature was shut out from our view. On either side the mountains ran up perpendicularly and as the passes were of a winding nature, only the sky above us and a short glimpse of the pass before us and behind us was visible to the eye. It is a weird, lonely place. The sun has very little chance of displaying his influence in this valley.

We now arrived in sight of MacGillicuddy's Reeks, the highest mountain peak in Ireland. After resting a while and taking in all the points of interest pointed out to us, we met the renowned guide, a real knight and a very interesting acquaintance—the Knight of the Gap of Dunloe. Lord Musgrave, while Lord Lieutenant of Ireland, had visited this place, and, in one of his happy moods, conferred on this man the honor of Knighthood. It was merely an empty title, with nothing at the back of it, he remarked, and rather placed him in an awkward position, as he had no way of entertaining his friends.

We next descended the rocky side of the Black Valley. There is no vegetation here—nothing but rock, the formation of which is very peculiar. It is formed as if an ebbing tide on every receding ebb left an effect like a stairs, some of the steps being wider and deeper than others. Mrs. S. C. Hall, we were told, was the only woman who had made a descent of this valley. We now reached the head of the Upper Lake and the boat that was dispatched in the morning was found waiting us there. We got on board and steered for Arbutus Island. In a few minutes we were there. The boatman had a nice lunch spread out for us—another of Stephens' surprises. Never was a meal more thoroughly enjoyed.

But, as in all terrestrial affairs, there were some drawbacks. At certain times of the year, the midges come in great swarms. This island is their home—at least they make it appear so, for they never cease to make war on all intruders. We did not remain long; finding we were not welcome, we departed and left them in peace. In this island the Arbutus tree reaches perfection. Its bright green leaves and red berries make it a picture in itself. We embarked again and steered for the Middle Lake, the scenery all around us increasing in beauty and grandeur, the hills and mountains thrown up so fantastically that they were utterly beyond my powers of description.

On we went through this maze of wonder, until the boatman ran us on a little strand, right opposite the Eagles' Nest. We all jumped on shore and found Gillespie, the cornetist, there. He gave us an entertainment never to be forgotten. He played "The Last Rose of Summer" a bar at a time, stopping until the echoes died away, and then continuing. Every note he played was echoed and re-echoed a thousand times in the promontory of the Eagles' Nest. He then went around a rock close by, concealed himself and resumed playing. It appeared to me that he had been wafted by some mysterious and unseen power to the Eagles' Nest, the echoes reverberating from there being the only sound we heard.

We regretted having to leave this enchanting place, but were compelled to, because of the rapidly approaching close of the day, and the necessity of keeping engagements at the hotel. I will refrain from mentioning the names of those we met there, fearing that, even though they have passed away, their offsprings might be harassed by the relentless tyrants who rule there yet.

Next day, we visited Glena, took a peep into "O'Sullivan's Library" and examined with great interest everything said to have been identified in the past with the chieftain of that name. The "Devil's Punchbowl" was next on our list, a mountain with a lake on the summit. Both command the attention of the visitor and are worthy of a pilgrimage. Some important work was to be done by us on the following night and then we were to leave the place. This left us all next day for sightseeing, and Stephens told us to prepare for a long journey on the morrow on foot.

We started early next morning, taking refreshments along, as there was no likelihood of our being able to obtain anything to eat until our return. We wended our way up the Esk River, a little mountain stream, so narrow at some places one could jump across it. The route we took to Glen-na-Coppal or the Horses' Glen is one seldom used by tourists.

This day's journey affording the opportunity, my companions began discussing matters in their usual happy vein. While resting, Stephens, indicating a plateau on an adjoining hill affording a view of the lakes and mountains, which we had seen the day previous, said: "There is where we will build our University." Then he described his plan for the proposed structure. Previous to this the conversation had been on the past, its heroes, great men of literature, thinkers, artists, etc.; but now it turned to the future. The idea of the University to me appeared to belong to dreamland, but then I thought it was Fancy taking a little recreation or amusement, but I would rather not have heard it expressed in so earnest a manner.

We ascended a mountain, and when we came down on the other side Luby was quite beside himself at the feat we had performed. If Hannibal, after crossing the Alps, felt more elated, he must indeed have been a proud man. It was one of the funniest experiences we had, except the crossing of Cromwell's Bridge, which excelled the event at Lodi, in our estimation.

We came at last to the Lake, a lonely spot with nothing but its solitariness to recommend it to any one. The day being excessively hot, and all around quite still, with no one in sight or likely to be, we—Luby and myself—made up our minds to have a dip in the Lake. Its nice sandy beach looked quite inviting. Although I cannot boast of my swimming, I knew my friend could not swim a stroke, so we went carefully along, treading within our depths and with antics worthy of happier days, enjoying our refreshing amusement, when suddenly down I went over a ledge into the depths. I could feel the side of the abyss until my feet touched bottom. When I arose to the surface, I found my friend within an arm's length of me. Another jump of his would have brought him to the edge and put both of us in a precarious position, so I rushed on him and knocked him over. It took some time to convince him of the danger we were in. He was like a boy full of fun and excitement all through our bath. Stephens, stretched on the grass, was laughing at us, but did not know at the time the danger we were in.

We dressed and partook of the refreshments we had brought with us, but had no goat's milk. Stephens knew of a cot convenient, so we went there. Leaving the woods and groves behind us, we ascended a slight eminence and found ourselves in prairie land.

The cot was at some distance, standing alone, like a place forsaken; but, on nearer approach, we found it comparatively cozy and cleanly kept. On entering, an old man came to greet us, and Stephens told him of our need. In a few moments a young woman came out of an adjoining room, barefooted and very thinly clad. Her unexpected appearance struck us with surprise; her beauty, grace and gentleness, appearing so unexpectedly, silenced us for a minute or two.

We had not the slightest idea of finding such a pleasing hostess in this remote habitation. She brought us some fresh sweet milk and bade us make ourselves at ease. She said: "So seldom are we visited, that it makes us glad to see anybody."

If Davis' girl at Lough Dan excelled our heroine in any feature, she must have been an angel. After paying our devoirs to her and her father, we retraced our steps, having new food for contemplation in the varied trifles that made up the day. We arrived at our hotel and finished business in Killarney, for that time at least.

Next morning we started for Dublin, passing the two lovely hills called the Paps, an adjunct of Killarney. We had a few minutes' stoppage at Limerick Junction, where we had some most excellent coffee, a rare thing to find at a railway station.

In Dublin we found no news from America. About this time Luby had important business in the County Meath, and as I knew the party he was to see, he took me along with him. We went by way of Navan, where we called on Thomas Masterson. Thence by jaunting car to Drumcondra, where we were to see our man. It was Sunday morning when we arrived and we found him at breakfast. He was the parish schoolmaster, and also acted as sexton to the Chapel, which stood nearly opposite his house. His name was Reilly. He invited us to be seated and wait awhile, as he had to ring the chapel bell for mass, and would return in a short time.

After he had left, Luby and I took a walk northwards, intending to return in time to meet our friend. A short distance outside the village we met a man I knew well—a respectable farmer, on his way to mass. When he saw us he jumped off the jaunting car, took me aside and asked me if that was Luby with me. I told him it was, and introduced them. He advised us not to go back to the village, for Reilly had sworn to him he would have Luby arrested the first time he saw him. He told us to go on as we were going until we came to the railway station, and take the next train for Dublin.

I wanted to return to the village, as I thought there must be some mistake, and knowing Reilly, I could not believe he would act as we were told, but my friend remonstrated and assured us it was true, and gave reasons for avoiding Reilly. We hastened to Gormanstown where, after waiting a short time, we got a train bound for Dublin, where we arrived in good time.

We received news of our trip to Drumcondra a few days later through a friend engaged in the pawn office business, who showed us a copy of the "Hue and Cry," which contained a description of Luby and myself, with an order authorizing any policeman to arrest us on sight. The facts in the matter were, Reilly told Father O'Brien there were two emissaries of a Secret Society

THOMAS CLARKE LUBY.

from Dublin in town. His Reverence after the Gospel, told his hearers to beware of them and advised them on that head. The Sergeant of Police and his squad being members of the congregation, left the chapel at once and had all the roads leading out of Drumcondra guarded, while they searched the place for us. They arrested two tramps, and after putting them through an examination, let them go.

In consequence of this, Luby was obliged to leave home, and took temporary lodgings in the North Suburbs. I remained where I was, but kept very close, not stirring out until night, when I would visit Langan's. My residence was not known, nor myself, only among a few friends.

For about two months we were kept in this seclusion, which was a very severe strain on Luby, who lived among strangers. I called on him as often as possible, and had a pleasant time listening to his daily vexations and surprises which were unavoidable under the circumstances.

James Stephens left for America and everything remained practically at a standstill, or nearly so. It was arranged that he would return by way of Paris. About this period the Government seemed to become aware for the first time that a powerful secret Revolutionary society was being propagated throughout the country, and became much alarmed thereat.

At this juncture "The Nation," of Dublin, then in the hands of A. M. and T. D. Sullivan, published an article on the evils of spreading an illegal society in the south and declaring it would be the duty of that paper to expose those engaged in such reprehensible business. I kept the paper for Stephens, and showed it to him on his return. On reading it he denounced the Sullivans as "felon setters," a name which was publicly applied to them soon after and which stuck to them for a generation.

It has often since been a source of surprise and pain to me to see good, true Irishmen engaged in fiercely denouncing some other good Irishman with whom they happened to differ on some minor question of policy or of detail.

Some men love to pose as patriots and leaders and want a monopoly of the posing. When another equally good man becomes tired of seeing them pose and accomplish nothing, and starts out to do better, then the first patriot suddenly awakens to the enormity of the offense being committed by his rival and a row ensues in which all sight of the main object aimed at by both parties is entirely lost.

In looking back on this period after a lapse of many years there does not seem to be any doubt concerning the true patriotism of the Sullivans (although I did not think so at the time), but it does seem to me they aspired to a monopoly of Irish patriotism, perhaps of Irish leadership, and could not tolerate any men or any movement that tended to infringe on their imaginary position of being the sole Irish political leaders at that time.

The inquiries instituted by the Government officials resulted in the procuring of a few mercenary informers on whose uncorroborated evidence a number of Phoenix men were unexpectedly arrested in various places. O'Donovan Rossa was arrested in Skibbereen, Dennis Riordan in Macroon, and Martin Hawe in Kilkenny. Morty Moynahan, Billy O'Shea, P. J. Dowling and others, equally well known, were also taken in and imprisoned. There was some excitement for a time, but most of the prisoners were eventually released, as no juries could be found to convict them. O'Donovan Rossa was not brought to trial, but was remanded twice without bail, thereby compelling him to suffer a long imprisonment without having been convicted. He was finally released without trial.

An informer named Warner, after he had done his infamous work in the South, was sent, under the care of the police to Ballybock Bridge barracks. This fellow was a recreant member of the Society in Skibbereen. He continued to frequent public houses around the barracks and boast he was the informer that had those fine fellows locked up. This boasting, which was done with impunity, became the talk of the neighborhood, and finally reached Dublin.

At Langan's the matter was often talked of. We thought it disgraceful to have it going on day after day. We also thought as he was the first informer, it would have a good effect morally, and act as a deterrent to others, to have that wretch summarily dealt with. We looked upon his boastings as a challenge and finally decided that one of us should see the fellow, and if he again boasted of his treachery, shoot him. There was every probability that our man would be captured, but he was to go prepared to take the consequences.

As James Stephens was still absent, Luby was in charge of affairs, and I shall never forget the effect the proposition had on him. Pacing up and down, he said, "My God, it cannot be permitted. The sacrifice would be too great—giving a good man for a scoundrel; moreover, I will not take the responsibility of such a course upon myself." The matter was reluctantly given up, perhaps, for the better. I have, however, sometimes thought if it had been carried out it might have checked the treachery and audacity of other scoundrels and perhaps saved many a good, true man, who was afterward made the victim of perjured informers.

CHAPTER VI.

According to arrangement, Luby left Dublin about the early part of March, '59, to meet Stephens in Boulogne, on his return from America. Stephens' trip was reported to have been a most successful one; at last, he had secured sufficient funds to work with and was sanguine of having a supply for the future.

In a short time I received a call to come to Paris. Dan McCartie and Owen Considine were already there, but a few days after my arrival were sent back to Ireland. It was Stephens' intention to bring over all the "A's"—that is, the centres of circles—and give them a course of instruction in military affairs. He told us he had laid the foundation of a plan that would yield him all the money required, and he would soon have a school for the purpose of preparing those whom he would select and utilize for the advancement of the cause.

It was at this time I got acquainted with Arthur O'Leary, brother of John O'Leary, who was about leaving for America, sent by Stephens on some important mission. This took place about the latter part of May, 1859. Arthur was a splendid specimen of the student class. He had been teaching English in one of the colleges, and lived with Stephens. Denis Dowling Mulcahy arrived next.(1)

(1) Dr. Denis Dowling Mulcahy, the famous Fenian, was 67 years old at the time of his death, which occurred on September 13th, 1900, in Newark, N. J.. He had resided in Newark for twenty-seven years. Dr. Mulcahy was a native of Redmondstown in the county Tipperary. He was born in 1833. He joined the Fenian Brotherhood, and soon rose to eminence in the councils of the patriots. He was arrested, tried and sentenced to a term of penal servitude. He served his term in Portland and Millbank Prisons.

His speech in the dock revealed the true patriot. It was im-

I had been in Paris nearly four months when I discovered, to my amazement, that the funds were again getting low—rent unpaid, various bills due, expenses accumulating, and everything looking blue again. As for myself, knowing how we were depending on America for remittances, I began to feel uncomfortable; in fact, almost ashamed to come to our quarters. I resolved to ask Stephens to let me go back to Dublin, and he decided I could go if he heard nothing from New York the coming week. The week expired, but

DR. DENIS DOWLING MULCAHY.

we received no news from New York, and finally, after a sojourn of four months in that beautiful city, I left for Dublin.

---

passioned, vigorous and defiant. The judge vainly said he would not listen. Mulcahy made his speech to the end.

On being released he went to France, where he lived for two years, and then came to the United States. After many wanderings he settled in Newark, and engaged in the practice of medicine.

I must tell how we spent our time in Paris. John O'Leary returned from America in September, '59. I had met him before leaving. He did not belong to the Organization, at least, he never took the obligation. He was an entirely different man to his brother Arthur, very reserved, somewhat of an aristocrat, but very genial to anyone he liked.

Paris, at this time, was in its happiest mood—the Empire being in its halcyon days. We saw the army depart for Italy and return, covered with glory. Magenta and Solferino were victories the nation was proud of. As we were laying on our oars, with little to do, we put in our time in the most profitable and best way we could—seeing everything of note.

The Captain (Stephens), knew everything that happened in and around the city, and his directions were carried out to the letter. Sometimes he came with us himself to Versailles, St. Cloud, Pere la Chaise and the Bois de Boulogne. He took great pleasure in pointing out the bas-relief—all allegorical studies—on the Arc of Triumph. Once he accompanied us to the Luxemburg, the Palace de Cluny, Sevres and St. Clotilde. These places were often visited by us afterward. Wet days were spent in the picture galleries and art studios.

Arthur O'Leary devoted one day to taking me through the Latin Quarter, which presented to me a phase of Parisian life I had not seen before. One place we visited was a pension or kind of hotel, where the students lived. As soon as we entered a large hall, there was a rush for Arthur—who was known to all and exceedingly popular—such handshaking and kicking up I have never witnessed since I came from that decorous city. He was beloved by all who surrounded him. Some were young ladies who were more reserved in their compliments, but none the less genuinely pleased to see him. Among the students were two young men from Brooklyn, N. Y., who made it very pleasant for me, as we could converse freely in English. They told me they were sometimes annoyed by the remarks and reflections of the other students on New York and America generally; to the effect that the

JOHN O'LEARY
(Editor "The Irish People") From a Painting by J. B. Yeats

United States was a receptacle for the scum of Europe, and consequently there was no society, no refinement there, etc., etc.

After a while some of the students asked me how I found the United States, and I told them they were mistaken in their opinions regarding it; that they could find as good society there as they could in any city of Europe, and after all, their remarks reflected on themselves, as the disreputable classes in America were the product of their own beautiful European civilization. We finally succeeded in removing the odium cast on America and placed it at the door of Europe. Our two American friends were so elated with the outcome of the interview, they took Arthur and myself to the Bois and we had a glorious time. In blaming Europe, I excepted Paris, as I thought there was more civil liberty to be found there than in any place I had yet seen. A person is safe and unmolested there wherever he goes, night or day.

I spent many pleasant evenings with John O'Leary. His greatest pleasure lay among the bookstalls along the Quay d'Orsie, a favorite resort of his. He gave me a souvenir the day before I left that I highly prize.

The evenings spent in our quarters were also very pleasant. Our landlord and family, the LaCours, occupied the first floor, and we a suite above them. They were from Lyons and were but a short time in Paris. We were on good terms with them and visited them frequently. Stephens was always happy on these occasions, for he seemed to be at home in French society.

Luby left for Dublin about this time. I began to be satiated with all this dazzling splendor and gaiety, and longed to see the green hills and mountains around Dublin. The dependent state in which we were placed added to my desire to get away. I was well pleased with my trip, and thanked Providence for the opportunity afforded me for so delightful a sojourn. As long as life remains, the impressions made on my mind by these charming French people will never be effaced.

My return was over the same route as I went, through Normandy to Dieppe. It was in autumn and the crops were all cut and husbanded, the orchards all stripped and their fruits put away. Abundance of everything had blessed the labors of these industrious people. As I passed along this section of the country, I was at a loss to know how they managed their herds and flocks, as there were no hedges, fences or rails seen dividing the different holdings.

One of the husbandmen, who got on the train, a very sociable person, explained all to me. Stakes set in the ground mark the limits of each one's holding, and a common pasture serves for all purposes of cattle raising, so there is no waste by these unnecessary and conservative structures. It did not appear to me so picturesque or so pleasing to the eye as the more extravagant space-occupying ditches and fences used in Ireland, nor does it appear so home-like or cosey as some well kept farms of the privileged classes in Ireland, or even those of the humbler class of farmers, who, with all the disadvantages of "tenants at will," yet have something around their homes to bind them to the place of their nativity.

I arrived in Dieppe on a market day, but found I had not much time to see this quaint old town, as I would wish to do, so I made the best use of the time I had to spare. I could not understand much of their conversation, so my inquiries were very limited.

The first thing that impressed me was the attire of the women, there being very few men to be seen. At first glance I thought it must be a religious meeting, as the women were all dressed alike, or nearly so, the only slight difference apparent to me being in the make-up of the neckwear or in the material of the dress, but invariably everyone wore the same style of bonnet or head dress. There were no filthy or dirty rags to be seen anywhere. Cleanliness, temperance and thrift seemed to be well observed by these sturdy and comfortable looking people, which impressed me very favorably. Good by, La Belle France, may your days of peace and plenty long continue.

CHAPTER VII.

After a shaky and disagreeable passage across the Channel, I arrived in Newcastle, and took the next train for Liverpool, where, after a few little naps en route and some occasional stoppages, I arrived and took the next steamer for Dublin.

It was about 8 o'clock on Sunday evening when I once more entered my welcome quarters in Trinity street. As I had not communicated with my friends while in Paris, my unexpected return was agreeably enjoyed by all. These friends, of whom I have spoken so often, as Mr. and Mrs. K., I had known in New York. They left there two weeks before I did. When they departed I had no intention of following them so soon, but did so, as I have explained before, because of a letter acquainting me of my father's illness.

On my second visit to Dublin I found time to call on a schoolmate of mine, James Grace, and spent that Saturday night with him. He had married a schoolmate of ours, who had been a good wife, but who had died a short time before this meeting, and when her name was mentioned it caused sadness and sorrow.

On going to church next morning, while crossing Wicklow street, we saw a young lady being assisted into a carriage by a young man, at which time I was asked by Mr. Grace if I ever intended marrying. I replied, humorously, "No, I intend to spend a single life; but if ever I do, I should like to wed a young lady like the one entering that carriage."

Walking through Sackville street next day, who should I meet but Mr. K., of New York, who was greatly surprised to see me, and who, after I had explained my unexpected appearance, welcomed me very kindly.. He made some inquiries about my intentions for the future, and then advised me to settle down and live in Ireland. He said he was disgusted with the feeling that was prevalent in America at that time. Know-Nothingism was then rampant and directing all its venom against the Irish Catholics. I had myself experienced some of its disagreeable annoyances, and deplored the fact of such an un-American institution. Before we parted he invited me to call and see him at his home, which I accepted, promising to call next day.

The address he gave me was, strange to say, the house from which I saw the young lady leaving in a carriage the day before. Mr. K. was expecting me, and met me at the door. Mrs. K. then came and gave me a warm greeting and introduced me to her two sisters, the younger of whom was the same lady I saw the previous day, and I learned that the gentleman who assisted her to the carriage was her brother, whose acquaintance I made a few days later.

Circumstances brought the young lady and myself together very often, but the feeling was no stronger than mere friendship until my return from Paris. Then a new and stronger feeling set in and in a short time after we became engaged.

About this time Patrick Mansfield Delany, of Kilkenny, was arrested in that town. He was a prosperous merchant and also owned and managed a large farm in the country. While Delany was in jail awaiting trial (bail having been refused), and the Government busy hunting up evidence with which to convict him, his harvest crop became ripe and ready for the sickle. (1)

Haltigan, then the head of the organization in Kilkenny, organized a corps of harvesters, all young men and women, who, with Rody Kickham, of Mullanahone, at their head, set to work on a Sunday at daylight and cut and stacked every blade of grain on the farm, so many of them being present that the work was done

(1) Patrick Mansfield Delany was acquitted, the jury unanimously declaring him not guilty. His good wife died soon after and, as he had no family, he sold his property and emigrated to America. He enlisted in the Union army and was killed in the first battle in which he took part.

in a few hours. There was a banquet arranged for at a hotel in the town of Carlow, about eighteen miles distant, to which all the leaders of the harvesters were invited. Through the courtesy of my friend Haltigan I was present as a guest, and I have been glad ever since I was present, for of all the merry makings I ever attended, that one eclipsed them all. Never had I seen a more jovial set before; they had the bloom of the harvest on their cheeks, and their eyes beamed with kindness and love, as if the work they were after accomplishing had surrounded them with a halo of blessedness.

Rody Kickham presided and did honor to the occasion. I had read of King Arthur making merry at the round table with his knights, after some chivalrous foray, but if he looked more gracious, benevolent or condescending than did Rody on that occasion, or better pleased with the patriotism and devotion of his followers, he must have been a divinity. The solemnity of the day forbade all excesses of jocularity, therefore the dance—the climax of all Irish festivities—was abandoned. Sentiment, a little music and a flow of good humor filled the place. .

Toward the end of the banquet it was suggested that, before we separated, we should go and pay a passing tribute at the shrine of the great champion of civii and religious liberty, Dr. Doyle, which was close by in a neighboring church. All went and knelt at the shrine.

"What did he do to make him so revered?" asked one of the young women on rising from her prayers. She was told he was the bishop that was summoned before a commission in the House of Parliament in London, presided over by Lord John Russell—to find out how far the allegiance of the Irish Catholics was extended to the Pope—as there was a bill before the House to have the Government pay the Irish bishops and priests a yearly salary and thereby have them under its control, and he gave all the opposition in his power to the bill.

He was asked if the bill passed and the Pope should command him to accept its terms, what would he do?

He answered: "I will remonstrate."

"And if the Pope would still insist, what then?"

"I would remonstrate again."

"But if the Pope determined that you should obey the command, what would you then?"

"I would take off mitre and stole and with the crozier, hand them back to him, and tell him that no blood-stained money will ever pollute my hands."

After the banquet we parted, hoping to meet soon again, each returning to his home. If Patrick Mansfield Delany was aware of the high estimation in which he was held by his countrymen and the manner in which they appreciated his sacrifice in prison, he must have been a proud man.

About this time I secured the position of foreman with the firm of Ammermann & Reid, merchant tailors, Suffolk street, where I remained until the dissolution of the firm, and then went with Mr. Ammermann, who had suffered financially in the deal that took place. I was now independent to a great extent, but it took me some time to pay the many debts I had incurred while leading a wandering life.

During this time, the latter part of '59, our work was progressing slowly. Langan's was still our headquarters. James Cantwell came back to Ireland about this time, his first appearance since he was obliged to leave in '48. He had lived in Philadelphia, and was an active member of the Fenian Brotherhood. In Dublin he renewed his love for his old sweetheart, who had married in his absence, but had buried her husband some time before. He married her and became proprietor of the Star and Garter Hotel, Westmoreland street, of which she was sole mistress.

Cantwell and Stephens did not agree very well, so he fell away from our organization and joined the Young Ireland Party. He was always, to my mind, a good, sterling man. He was one of my bondsmen when I was admitted to bail, Michael Hogan, of Baggot Street Bridge, being the other.

P. J. Smyth, the '48 leader, was a great friend of Cantwell's, and I often met him at the Star and Garter. He allied himself with the Sullivans (1), who were still doing all in their power to disrupt the I. R. B. Smyth was a counsellor at law. He called on my wife after my arrest and offered his services to straighten up my business and attend to my legal requirements, but Stephens would not hear of his being retained.

The St. Patrick's Brotherhood came into existence at this time. Its organization was first publicly announced at a Patrick's Day banquet held on Monday, March 18, 1861, Mr. Thomas Neilson Underwood in the chair. After the viands and other good things had been freely partaken of, Mr. Underwood rose and started the oratory of the evening. At the close of his speech he pulled a paper out of his pocket and read to the assembly the programme and constitution of a new National organization which would be carried on within legal and constitutional lines. He put it for adoption on the spot by a show of hands. No time was given to discuss the new idea, to suggest amendments or anything of that sort.*

His friends and men who had been informed in advance, located in different parts of the room, led off the applause which greeted his announcement and the resolutions were declared carried.

Whatever object they had in the project was not apparent on the surface, but it served us as a recruiting ground, and as it was an open institution to everyone who wished to join, we all became members and maintained a controlling influence in order to prevent anything detrimental to us being brought forward.

We were now working among the commercial young men of all the big drygoods houses, Cannock & White, McSweeny & Delany, and others. James O'Callaghan,

---

(1) A. M. and T. D. Sullivan, brothers, were then editors and proprietors of the Dublin Nation. They believed in parliamentary agitation and fought bitterly the formation of the I. R. B. Their bitterness was returned with interest, and the Sullivans got worsted in the conflict which ensued. They afterwards became members of Parliament and took a prominent part in the Parnell movement. A. M. Sullivan was admitted to the bar and practiced in London, where he died. T. D. Sullivan is the author of the National Anthem, "God Save Ireland," and a poet of distinction, and is still living.

* See Appendix IV, Page 164.

a young County Cork man, Maurice O'Donohue and Frank Dunne, all did fine work and soon had their quotas filled up. The last mentioned was a valuable aid, as he was liked by all his acquaintances. Whenever we had anything of importance to do, we would call an informal meeting and discuss it.

EDWARD DUFFY.
(From An Old Daguerotype.)

It was at one of these meetings I first met Edward Duffy. I happened to occupy the chair. James O'Callaghan at this time was a good talker; in fact, had an aptitude for such an accomplishment, if I may use that term. In holding forth, he forgot himself, and said something which was very uncomplimentary to Connaught.

I called him to order and told him he couldn't mean what he said; that if we wanted a pure and unadulterated Celt we would have to go to that province to find him. He made the necessary acknowledgement of his love for good men wherever they came from, and so qualified his remarks that they were acceptable to all.

When the meeting adjourned, Edward Duffy called me aside, and said that he was willing to join us and would devote his life to the cause, and he kept his promise. After that night he and I were the staunchest friends. After an interview with the "Captain," he gave his whole being to the movement, and was the medium through which Connaught was organized.

About this time I started in business on my own account in South Ann street, aided by a friend who was totally outside the organization. I had for my clients some of Her Majesty's most devoted servants. My connection with that most conservative house, Ammermann & Reids, served to throw suspicion entirely away from me. I got married about this time, and Duffy, who made my place a second home, was happy, as he knew all the disadvantages of a life of change. Stephens considered it a safe place to meet any particular person, and availed himself of it on all occasions.

Kingstown being in the near vicinity of Dublin, was practically considered a suburb and was thoroughly organized, mainly through the efforts of John Hickey and his three brothers. They were engaged in the building trade and were all good, true, patriotic men. John was the head of the family and a host in himself. He was very widely acquainted with men of his craft in Dublin, and was the means of bringing a great number of the best class of young men into our organization.

Hugh Brophy was another prosperous young man in the same line of business. He was a large employer wielding considerable influence among men engaged in the building trades. Denis Cromien, a foreman and assistant architect, was also influential among his fellow workers. All were exceptionally good men, working night and day for their country's cause, never tiring, never sparing their time or means when called on. The work went on gloriously and although the greatest care was exercised in making selections, membership increased rapidly and soon general confidence in the Movement began to assert itself. Thus matters went on until the close of 1859. every effort being made to extend and solidify the organization, while frequent communication was held with America where a serious split had taken place in the organization.

HUGH F. BROPHY.

CHAPTER VIII.

In the early part of 1860, John O'Mahony arrived from New York and stopped with his friend James Cantwell at the Star and Garter. His coming had been announced in advance, and he met the captain (James Stephens) by appointment at Langan's. That meeting of the leaders is historic, and I was present and shall never forget it. I was requested to escort O'Mahony to Langan's, as he did not know the way, neither was he prepared for the reception which he received from Stephens when he got there.

Stephens, after the formal greetings were over, asked a number of questions; wanted to know why the organization in America had not been kept together, a unit; he wanted to know why O'Mahony and his colleagues had not kept their promise to the men in Ireland and had not furnished the funds necessary to defray the cost of spreading the organization, etc. To all of those questions O'Mahony failed to give satisfactory answers, whereupon Stephens reproached him in words of the most cutting sarcasm, telling him of his shortcomings, feebleness and insincerity and wound up by reminding him how he, Stephens, had dragged him out of obscurity and put him in a position he never dreamed of.

O'Mahony did not answer this terrible arraignment and remained sitting while Stephens paced, restlessly, up and down the floor.

Langan and I were the only witnesses present at this terrible scene, and it impressed us very much indeed. O'Mahony's conduct toward the organization some time before this was really undefensible, and it was plain to see he felt deeply humiliated. The interview terminated there and I accompanied him back to his hotel. On our way back to the Star and Garter he sought my sympathy and asked me if I would stay by him.

COLONEL JOHN O MAHONEY
President of the Fenian Brotherhood

"No," said I, "the man who serves Ireland best will be the one I will stay by. I am no partisan and these personal jealousies and quarrels must cease. Confidence must be restored or the conflicting elements must resign and withdraw from the movement." I left him at the hotel anything but a happy man.

He and Stephens met again next day and evidently came to some kind of understanding. No one was present at the meeting but themselves. I do not know how they fixed up the matter or on what basis the agreement was arranged, but I felt such serious breaches as I had witnessed are seldom or never made up, and, unfortunately for Ireland, that breach was never wholly made up

Shortly after this O'Mahony went to Tipperary and from there returned to New York.

Stephens and Luby went South on a business mission after he had left, and remained away some time. This was the most successful trip they ever made. It was on this trip they met Considine, of Clare, known for his exertions in the O'Connell movement. All his patriotism and influence in the country was fully utilized in this undertaking in 1861. During their absence Arthur O'Leary called on me on his way to Tipperary. It was one of the Orange festival days, I think, the 12th of July. He and I were standing in the Glendenning Hotel, Wicklow street, on our way out after taking lunch. An Orangeman with the regalia of his order pinned on his breast, pretty well under the influence, came in. A young man who afterward turned out to be R——, came up to him and kept looking at the badge, and after making some inquiries, told him such ornaments might do very well in the North, but in Dublin they were insulting to most of its citizens. He tore off the insignia and threw it out of the door.

A scuffle ensued, R—— had some friends with him and Arthur interfered, not knowing the cause of the quarrel. The Orangeman pulled off his watch and fired it at R——'s head, but missed and struck the wall close to the mirror and it fell in pieces on the floor. Arthur thought R—— was imposing on the Orangeman and wanted fair play. A few passes were exchanged between Arthur and R——. I got between them and an understanding took place, when the Orangeman was put out. All who remained became friends. This was Arthur's first experience after arriving from peaceful Paris. He left for home next day, and I never saw him again, as he died a short time after, regretted by all who knew him. He was the soul of honor, generous, frank and true. We lost a most devoted and sincere brother in him. His early death was a great blow to his brother John.

Edward Ryan, College street, Dublin, was a prominent member of the St. Patrick's Brotherhood, so was Denis Dowling, also Geo. Hopper. Charley and John Hopper, the latter's brothers, were also members of it, and belonged to the I. R. B. It was about this time I first met Hugh Brophy. He played a most important part in the movement up to the time of his arrest.

Edward O'Donovan (afterward the famous war correspondent), his brothers John and Willie, Nicholas Walsh, artist; Henry Crowley, also an artist, both members of the Art Institute, Wm. Horan and Martin—a civil engineer, joined the organization about this time and formed a class or an athletic club, whose meetings were held in Great Britain street. J. J. Kelly was also a member of this club. We kept it running for some time until suspicion rested on it and then we retired temporarily.

CHAPTER IX.

It was about this time we first heard of the intention of the men in California to send the remains of Terence Bellew McManus to Ireland for interment.* Stephens did not appear to like it, as it was mooted around that it would be made the occasion for an uprising when the re-

TERENCE BELLEW McMANUS.

mains would arrive in Dublin. However, after all the large cities in America had taken it up and finally decided in carrying it out, he had no other course open but to acquiesce and see what we could do in Ireland. Plans were made and committees formed, to take charge of the

* See Appendix VI, Pages 167-179.

undertaking and to receive the accompanying delegates when they arrived. Our committee was formed of the best men we had available, and the result will tell how they did their work.

The St. Patrick's Brotherhood rooms were secured for the occasion. The Pope's Brigade was after being disbanded, and we had some members of that body in our organization. Among them was Red Jim McDermott, who made himself very conspicuous, and was, in fact, one of the most prominent of the military staff. The remains left San Francisco Aug. 21, and New York in November, 1861. Nothing happened to mar the proceedings until the week before the arrival of the remains. Then the Young Ireland party thought they would take a hand in, although none of them up to this had desired to be on the committee. They now determined to make a stand; in fact, they aimed to take charge of the funeral.

Everything was working in harmony with us. We had control of the committee, delegates were appointed to go to Cork to receive the remains from the Cork men, when they had duly honored it. The delegates were Hugh Brophy, Andrew Nolan, Edward Ryan and myself, Joseph Deneiffe. The delegates found everything in the best form when they arrived in Cork—all under discipline, every man at his post; in fact, the arrangements were so complete that they surpassed anything they had seen before.

When the procession began to move the enthusiasm was immense, swelling at every step, and awfully profound, which could be seen in the eyes of every one you met. The women, as usual, outdid the men. They could not control their feelings, and consequently, were more ostentatious in displaying what was in them. God bless them. Marching along the quays the sight was very imposing. Among the shipping was one vessel with the Union Jack floating, the only one in sight; presently could be seen a boy climbing up the rigging and in a moment he had hauled it down. The grim silence that pervaded the multitude up to this moment was broken with a tremendous cheer all along the line.

After all had done their duty on that memorable day,

the remains were put on the train that waited at the depot, and after the Cork men had given it in charge to the Dublin committee, we departed among the cheers and prayers of the truly faithful people.

There was nothing occurred along the line of railroad of any moment until we reached Tipperary Junction, where a solemn scene presented itself. A great many were kneeling with their heads uncovered. They remained in silence until the train was about to move, when they all arose to their feet and waved a farewell.

On the arrival at Kingsbridge Station, a great assemblage was waiting, and an escort from the St. Patrick's Brotherhood took the remains to the Mechanic's Institute, as there was no church in the city that would give it shelter for the night. Cardinal Cullen's orders to that effect were carried out to the letter. In vain we looked around for the Saggarth Aroon, but he was nowhere to be seen. (1)

---

(1) It is now a recognized historical fact that during the years of the Fenian movement England came nearer to lessening the influence of Rome in Ireland than during any other period of our history since the Norman Pope Adrian sat in the chair of St. Peter and issued a Bull authorizing the English to conquer Ireland.

Once the attention of the British Government was attracted to the movement, it did not take long to discover that it was widespread and numerically very strong. Its members were almost entirely of the intelligent, law-abiding class and correspondingly difficult to coerce. While proceeding against individuals, through their legal machinery, with the aid of informers, false witnesses, packed juries, etc., they brought all possible political influence to bear on Rome, with the result that the Vatican instructed the bishops in Ireland and the United States to discourage and denounce the Fenian movement, and ncidentally, in order to be consistent, all other secret societies -social, political, or otherwise. Soon after Fenianism was being publicly and vigorously denounced from nearly every altar in Ireland and the United States, and its members informed they would be refused the sacrament of the Church and the rights of Christian burial unless they renounced and abandoned the organization.

Bishops Moriarity, of Kerry, and Duggan, of Chicago, in their denunciations of the Fenians, were the two most conspicuous representatives of England in the English-speaking church.

Bishop Moriarity's notorious anathema, closing with the sentence, "Hell is not hot enough nor eternity long enough to pun-

The American delegates were taken to the Shelbourne Hotel, where Miss McManus, sister of the deceased, was waiting to receive them and offer her thanks to them and their American brothers for the great interest taken in her brother.

Soon she was approached by the Young Ireland men, who considered themselves the only ones entitled to the honor of laying him in his grave, and did all in their power to get her to consent to that new, but unreasonable demand. After hearing them, she promptly told them that the men that disinterred her brother in San Francisco and brought the remains such a great distance with much labor and expense, were the only ones entitled to the honor of the patriotic undertaking. This rebuff did not deter the politicians from pushing their claims further.

The last night he was to remain above the earth was the most eventful of any since he was taken out of his grave in San Francisco. The coffin was placed on a catafalque in the center of the hall in the Institute, and the solemnities witnessed by an eager crowd, the American delegates standing around the bier with Miss McManus close by it during the ceremony. The sight was most imposing. Many comments were made on the course the

---

ish the miscreants (the Fenians)," will sufficiently explain to the present generation what Irish patriots had to contend with and endure in Ireland and in the United States in those days.

Writing on this subject in the Irish World of Jan. 6, 1905, Mr. Michael Scanlan, an old-time Chicago Fenian, says:

"Bishop Moriarity represented, more or less, every bishop in Ireland, save the 'Lion of the fold of Judah,' the great MacHale, who, when I sent him something over $300 from the Fenians of Chicago to help his starving people—money which Bishop Duggan refused to transmit, even to save a Catholic people, because it was Fenian money—sent his blessing to our 'great organization' for its timely succor. I cannot call to mind a single bishop in the United States who did not re-echo Bishop Duggan's denunciations. In fact, with some rare exceptions—and these exceptions were mum—the entire Irish hierarchy and priesthood in the United States and in Ireland followed the example of Chicago and Kerry.

"In Chicago, where I then lived, there was one glorious exception, the Jesuit Church, presided over by a noble Belgian, Father Damien, who welcomed us all to the rights of the Church, for which, as he said 'our fathers had suffered so much,'

clergy took on this occasion, Father Lavelle was the only priest present, and he appeared to be as much confounded as others at this state of affairs, for all saw plainly nothing good could come out of so cold and heartless a proceedure on the part of those who professed to be on the side of the disconsolate. It would take a great many sermons to restore the reverence and respect lost to the dignitaries who failed in their duty on that occasion.

Stephens and Luby kept away all this time, but on hearing there was a surprise to be sprung that evening on the committee, Luby was on hand and became a member of it, as did also all of the American delegation. After waiting some time in expectation, a knock was heard on the door, and the usual response "Come in" was given. Father John Kenyon, "The O'Donohoe," John Martin and James Cantwell entered. After stating the purpose which brought them there, the committee, not being formally organized, some one proposed "The O'Donohoe" for chairman. I think it was Father Kenyon. James O'Callaghan proposed Maurice O'Donohue, who was elected by a large majority.

---

and out of which British clerical agents were seeking to drive us, as we had been driven from homes and country.

"I need scarcely say that the power of England is great, even in Rome, nor that that power, through all its insidious ramifications, is ever at work to get between Ireland and Rome, hoping by some interposition to break down the political faith of Ireland, for she knows by this time that she cannot weaken or change the spiritual faith of the Irish people.

"With the very happy results flowing from a united priesthood and people, and the very evil results which flowed from the union of England and the so-called Irish priesthood—the latter the sleuths of the former, as they ever must be when they owe their existence and advancement to her—if ever again the priest and people of Ireland permit the 'Devil's Advocate,' England, to represent them at the Court of Rome, they will deserve, without pity and with the contempt of all freemen, to become the tools of England for ever."

This political, but unpatriotic attitude of the bishops, explains why the remains of Terence Bellew McManus, when brought from America to Ireland for interment in Glasnevin, were not permitted to rest over night in any Catholic Church in Dublin. They were taken to the Mechanics' Institute, where they laid in state under a special guard.

Father Kenyon asked "Who is this Maurice O'Donohue?" He was duly informed, and Maurice took the chair. Then commenced the memorable debate, they claiming the right of taking possession of the remains and performing the obsequies. This was objected to by our side. In opposing it, Luby stood up, radiant with noble impulse, and took them to task for their conduct and denounced their motives for such actions. They stood like statues, while he launched his invectives and condemnation on their heads. It was a complete refutation of all their pretensions and worthier of a nobler occasion. Luby was grand in his denunciation, his little frame swung gracefully to his utterance, he spoke energetically and animated with fervor. All stood spellbound during his speech. It was Luby's best effort and worthy of a better cause.

"The O'Donohoe" manfully asked to be forgiven for the part he had taken. He said he had been misinformed and was now convinced that the remains were in safe keeping, and the people in charge fully competent to discharge the duty with honor. They all left except Father Kenyon, who put his back against the door and talking very excitedly and incoherently said we would not have the body in the morning. James O'Callaghan told him the days of miracles were passed, and if the remains should be taken away, it would be over the dead bodies of those who were prepared to guard it. After a little while he followed his companions.

Captain Smith, chairman of the American delegation, commended Luby and the committee for the able and manly manner in which they had defeated these disappointed men.

Colonel Kavanagh, of the San Francisco delegation, followed him. He said if he ever had any doubt of Irishmen being able to take care of their native land, that doubt was dispelled forever. What he had seen that evening assured him we were competent to accomplish the end we had in view. Oh, what a glorious evening that was; what a victory for the despised and lowly people!

No further trouble presented itself. All flocked next day to honor the dead. There were guards appointed to watch all night, and, let it be noted Red Jim McDermott, Knight of St. Sylvester, late of the Pope's Brigade, was captain of the watch!

The night passed off quietly up to nine o'clock the following morning, November 10th; every minute after that time brought fresh delegations, and about 10 o'clock there was a goodly number present, which kept swelling by accessions from all quarters. At the time of starting all were drawn up in military array, John Clohissy in command and John Healy chief aid. Platoons were formed as wide as the streets would permit. The cortege at last began to move, and was augmented at every street corner until it became about seven miles in length. The sidewalks were jammed and the windows all along the route were occupied. Mourning was displayed in many places.

The point that commanded the fullest view was at Kingsbridge Station, as the full length of the Quays were in view before turning into Thomas street.

Arriving here and passing the spot where Robert Emmet was murdered, the sight was very imposing and impressive—sadly so. All was as silent as the grave he sleeps in. As a mark of respect all heads were uncovered while passing that consecrated spot.

Standing on the corner of Parliament street and Cork Hill, a spectator remarked at this point that the military precision and deportment of the men in line was most pronounced; turning round the angle at the Castle Gate, it was noticed the movement was as perfect as any of Her Majesty's regulars could execute. This was taken notice of by the authorities, and gave them to understand that such marching could not be accomplished without considerable practice.

It was night when the hearse entered Glasnevin Cemetery. The day was a trying one on all who participated, but none gave way under the rain and slush. At the grave torches were used, which added to the solemnity of the scene.

Father Lavelle performed the religious rites of the church, and made a few remarks appropriate to the occasion. Captain Smith, the orator of the day, delivered an effective and impressive oration. Thus ended a most auspicious day seldom, if ever, equalled for solemnity and devotion.

At the close of the funeral obsequies Stephens was the most jubilant man in the city. This great, patriotic demonstration was admittedly an emphatic ratification of the work done by the organization and a proof of its strength and vigor. It had alarmed and confounded its opponents. It showed what men could do when determined and united, clinging together, respecting each other, all having but one object in view and with all abominable prejudices swept away. The odious slang "Fardown," "Corkonian," "Connaughtman" and "Leinsterman" were heard no more as reproaches—all were simply Irishmen and brothers. Surely that ought to be commended, as a fact accomplished which the united efforts of all gone before, both lay and clerical, had failed to do. The American delegates were astonished on beholding the change which had taken place within the last decade in Ireland. After a short stay in the metropolis, they left for the provinces, and, with one or two exceptions, soon after returned to America. The demonstration proclaimed the I. R. B. supreme over all the land. The Sullivans, the Grays and the prelatists were hors-de-combat. The people at last had arisen to the occasion and saved the honor of the country.

CHAPTER X.

On the 9th of November, 1861, Captain Wilkes in command of the San Jacinto, a Federal War steamer intercepted the English mail steamer Trent on the high seas, and sent Lieutenant Fairfax on board with an armed guard which seized and removed Messrs. Slidell and Mason, two Confederate envoys on their way to Europe, also their secretaries. They were taken on board the San Jacinto and conveyed to Boston where they were imprisoned.

This arrest, on the deck of a British steamer on the high seas, caused a great commotion in England, and for weeks the newspapers were filled with fierce denunciations of the "outrage" as they called it. Lord Palmerston introduced a bill in Parliament giving belligerent rights to the Confederates, and an immediate demand was made on the United States Government for the surrender of the Confederate envoys.

The excitement extended to Ireland, and as a result placards were posted all over Dublin and vicinity announcing a public meeting at the Rotunda where leading men from all parts of Ireland would express their sympathy with the Federals. It was rumored and intimated that a new organization would result from this meeting, one that would embrace all shades of Irish politics and extend a welcome hand and offer an open door to all.

This rumor reached us and caused some anxiety, but, eventually, we came to look upon it as a covert attack on the I. R. B.

The St. Patrick's Brotherhood, with Thomas Neilson Underwood at its head, offered all these advantages to its members, then why start another organization? We looked upon the scheme as a challenge, secret or otherwise, to our organization, in fact, we considered the challenge obvious, and decided to meet it As a result of our conferences we appointed a working committee, of which Thomas Clarke Luby was a very active member, to quietly take charge and control the meeting.

The evening of the 5th of December, 1861, arrived, and the doors of the Rotunda were thrown open in due time. There was a large number of persons waiting for admission and the hall filled rapidly. There were about seven or eight hundred of our men on the floor and quite a few on the platform. Amongst them was Jeremiah Kavanagh, one of the California delegates, who had remained behind and was there under instructions. "The O'Donohoe" was in the chair, and made the opening address which was well spoken and manly and was applauded several times. Daniel O'Donohoe, better known as "The Donohoe," Chieftain of The Glens, was a nephew of Daniel O'Connell, and a man of some property. Outside of the Fenian Brotherhood he was very popular with the public. Luby was sitting close to him, and when he resumed his seat entered into conversation with him.

The first resolution offered was one of sympathy with the Federals, and was carried unanimously. This was according to arrangement, as we knew what was coming.

The second resolution was to the effect that a new patriotic organization be formed which should be open and above board, and embrace all classes. Before a vote could be taken on this, Jeremiah Kavanagh offered an amendment to the effect that a committee be first appointed to report on the business aspect of the question, whether the crisis demanded it.

This amendment was carried unanimously because our people dominated the meeting. P. J. Smyth spoke to the resolution in a very nice speech, followed by Thomas Neilson Underwood, T. D. Sullivan, and I think, Martin A. O'Brennan. Each did his best,and there were no slurs thrown at any one. T. D. Sullivan appealed to the audience to be guided by the counsels of harmony and peace invoked by the memory of Emmet's bleeding body in Thomas Street, etc.

That was really a very remarkable meeting to say the least of it. The masses knew nothing of what was going on under the surface, and were simply carried away by the enthusiasm evoked by the first resolution and the speeches made in favor of it. The whole affair was very cleverly handled, and demonstrated clearly what could be accomplished by a well disciplined organization properly and intelligently directed.

During the meeting in the Rotunda, Luby found opportunity to make an appointment for "The O'Donohoe" to meet the Captain (Stephens). This meeting took place soon after, but nothing came of it. He had told some of our friends that he would like to join us, but after his interview with Stephens he abandoned the idea altogether. It was thought Smith O'Brien had influenced him against joining, but, in any case, Stephens did not think much about them and refrained from making advances. The O'Donohoe soon perceived that the control of the committee had passed from him, therefore he refrained from attending meetings and eventually withdrew from the organization. Stephens and Luby started out on an important mission in the southeast, and after a short time got stranded in Clonmel, where a remittance was sent which brought them back to Dublin.

The attitude of the Irish press, with the exception of Dennis Holland's "Irishman," was at this time most annoying. For some unknown reason it was pronouncedly antagonistic, and undoubtedly retarded and delayed our work.

After the return of the American delegates they attended meetings in various cities where they told of their experiences. In Philadelphia a monster meeting was held at which Col. Michael Doheny discussed the Trent affair, and took occasion to show up the obstructionists at the McManus funeral and how they got their desserts. A printed report of the meeting was sent us in pamphlet form. The Dublin papers also printed reports of the affair. The Sullivans, naturally, were disappointed at the failure of their party to control the McManus funeral, and considered their prestige had been injured and their pride hurt. Taking advantage of the discussion which ensued in the newspapers, they issued a pamphlet in which they attacked Luby and were again guilty of "felon-setting." "The Irishman" was the only paper which had a good word to say for us. Dan McCartie published a letter in it addressed to Smith O'Brien. Rossa and Charles Kickham also published letters reflecting severely on Sullivan. Kickham's letter was very severe and irritated Sullivan so that he entered suit for libel against Denis Holland, publisher of "The Irishman," and received a verdict awarding him damages. This was the condition of affairs in Dublin in the winter of 61-'62. Our position between the Government on one side, and hostile political opponents on the other side, required, patience fortitude and perseverance all the time.

CHAPTER XI.

About this time John Devoy (1), appeared on the scene in Athy. He had served some short time in the

JOHN DEVOY.

(1) John Devoy returned to Ireland in 1862 from Algeria, where he had served a brief term in the French foreign legion. He settled in Athy, where he secured employment and became connected with the local Circle of the I. R. B. He wrote some letters to the "Irish People," but his real service to the organization began after the arrests in 1865, when he succeeded Roantree (who had succeeded Pagan O'Leary) in the work of organizing the British soldiery.

French Foreign Legion, and had returned to Kildare. He and James J. O'Kelly had joined the French service in order to become expert in military matters. O'Kelly, while in the French army, was sent to Mexico at the time Napoleon tried to establish Maxamillian as emperor of that country. Bazaine was then commander-in-chief of the French forces. After being taken prisoner by the Mexicans, O'Kelly made his escape at the risk of his life and, after a perilous journey through an unknown and untravelled country, got into Texas and afterwards to New York. Later he secured a position on the New York Herald. His exploits in Cuba as special correspondent for that paper were full of adventure. He is now a member of Parliment.

During the year 1862 Stephens remained in Dublin, receiving visits from our country friends and directing them in their work. In this year we lost a staunch and true friend, Col. Michael Doheny. He was the first man in America I spoke to about joining the Emmet Monument Association. I had many opportunities of seeing and knowing him intimately. While on my second mission to America I lived in his home for over a month, where John O'Mahony visited nightly. It was with O'Mahony, on one of these occasions, I first met P. J. Meehan, editor of the "Irish American." During this time I had good opportunity of knowing the Colonel, and can truthfully say that, among all the men I have met before or since, I never knew one more constant and true to Ireland. It was Col. Doheny who kept the fire aglow from '48 until he saw it in full blast in '61.

It was at this time, owing to British influences exercised at Rome, that the altar denunciations commenced. Our organization was banned and its members refused the rites of the Church. This mingling of politics and religion was intolerable to a great many good Catholics, and I knew a great many who felt grieved that such a misunderstanding should exist, still there were many patriotic priests who stood by us.

The year 1863 opened very gloomy. Want of money

almost caused suspension of all work. There was a great strain on a few in Dublin at this particular time. It was deemed necessary for Luby to go to New York with instructions to stir up John O'Mahony, and, if he found it necessary, to suspend him; Luby was too mild a man for the mission, and, as his power was discretionary, he did not utilize it, but left O'Mahony to pursue his ambitious policy.

At this time I was located in St. Anne Street in business for myself. Over my shop, or store as we call it in America, I had fitted up an apartment for myself—a sort of bachelor's hall. It was here Stephens kept his appointments with his Provincial friends, in fact, it was his headquarters. It was a very handy place for many purposes, and was a special rendezvous for my own particular friends: Hugh Brophy, Andrew Nolan, Edward Duffy, Wm. Horan, Edward O'Donovan and his brother John, Henry Crowley, Nicholas Walsh, Bernard O'Connor (who occupied the top floor), and Pagan O'Leary.

My tailoring business threw off suspicion, and my former employment with one of the most conservative business houses in the city left no chance of a doubt regarding my being a loyal citizen. Up to the day of my arrest there was not a whisper of suspicion, notwithstanding the fact that it was here almost all the American officers and men were sent by John O'Mahony to report with their certificates and commissions, which were invariably torn up and burned to the chagrin of a great many.

We had, at this time, an engineering school on Stephen's Green, with all the necessaries and appliances for such an institution, links, chains, theodolite, etc., etc. This school was attended by the above mentioned persons. Martin was the instructor; none were admitted but the most conservative and capable men. Martin took us out frequently to the suburbs to teach us the rudiments of civil engineering. We objected to carrying the theodolite which used to embarrass us, but he insisted on its use, and at night we worked out the problems given to us. This useful school continued and was never disturbed until my arrest. Then Nicholas Walsh, as soon as he heard of it, had everything removed and concealed that had any value.

Luby returned in July after visiting Colonel Corcoran and others in the United States. He brought back about one hundred pounds, some of which was a personal gift to the Captain. He did not seem to be in great spirits, on the contrary he had the blues and a very severe attack of bronchitis. The Captain was not satisfied with the small sum sent him. His inactivity while Luby was away, together with the report of serious dissensions in America brought by the latter, put all the Dublin centres in doubt with regard to the management of our officers. Stephens went south, and during his absence this dissatisfaction increased and became outspoken, so much so that Luby informed him and was ordered to call a meeting and find out the cause. If they wanted him to return he would do so, but that would interfere with an important newspaper project which he then had in contemplation. This Luby told us at the meeting which followed and at which he read Stephens' letters. The meeting did not amount to anything.

Luby, when in America, visited Father O'Flaherty, a patriotic pastor at Crawfordsville, Indiana. After leaving Father O'Flaherty, Luby visited Chicago, where he met Michael Scanlan, the Centre, who afterward became one of the most prominent members of the Roberts or Secessionist party. There Luby also met Henry Clarence McCarthy, who was afterward sent to Ireland to take charge of the goods donated for the great Fenian Fair at Chicago.

Father O'Flaherty came to Ireland in 1863 on a visit, when I had the great pleasure of meeting him and spending a few days in his company. He was a man of fine personal appearance, dignified and courteous and of a most amiable disposition, but his love of Ireland far exceeded all his other characteristics. After spending a day in the County Wicklow with him, I learned how intensely he was imbued with this feeling. I remember we visited the Glen of the Downs and that he was enraptured with its beautiful scenery. We stopped at the "Half Way House" and had some refreshments, while he enjoyed the beautiful prospect, than which there is none fairer.

We visited Powerscourt Waterfall, where a party of tourists were making merry and enjoying themselves amid the beautiful scenery. They were accompanied by a local musician who knew how to cater to the lovers of nature. The "Coulin" was evidently a favorite air with him, for he rendered it with a pathos and feeling which, mingled with the cadence of the falling water, sounded like an enchanted lullaby to a weary traveler.

On leaving the Waterfall, a few steps brought us to a turn in the road from which point the famous Sugarloaf Mountain was in plain sight, its stately form apparently blocking up the passage formed by the green wooded slopes at either side of us. It was mid-day, bright and warm, with the sun in the South while we were walking in a westerly direction so that we saw the graceful mountain clearly outlined in its entirety against the clear sky. The beauty, magnificence, and impressiveness of this scene evoked from him a burst of praise for its great designer. After gazing at it for some time, he said, slowly, "Let us go, we have had enough enchantment for one day; I shall carry this scene in my memory forever."

We returned to the city, and that evening he was introduced to the Dublin Centres, whom he addressed in the most fervid manner, encouraging them in the good work in which they were engaged, and calling down a blessing on their efforts. Among those present was Pagan O'Leary, whose better feelings were thoroughly aroused, and, when leaving, no one among them shook the good man's hand more warmly than he.

Because of his outspoken advocacy of the Cause in Ireland and in Indiana, Father O'Flaherty, on his return, was severely censured by his bishop, which may have had some effect upon him, although it did not lessen his zeal. We were all deeply shocked and grieved on hearing of his death in his own parish at

Crawfordsville, about three months after. His loss was deeply regretted, as Indiana at that time was considered the Banner State of Fenianism.

Stephens returned early in September and called a special meeting of the Centres. He regretted there was any dissatisfaction, and wished to know the cause. Hugh Brophy told him plainly there was an apparent lack of activity on the part of the Executive, and that progress had practically come to a stand-still. He was proceeding when Stephens interrupted him and said we should go into the business in a regular way. He placed a sheet of paper before each one and told them to write down their grievances. They could express their feelings better than they could write them, therefore this plan succeeded in stopping any further talk on the matter. Bernard O'Connor got on his feet in a hasty manner and objected, telling Stephens he was arrogant and set too high an estimate on himself and was becoming intolerant. He then took up his hat and left the room.

It was considered by a majority of the Centres that they had gained their point, as they showed the Captain they were dissatisfied with the passive way he took matters, and that was all they wanted to do at that time. I happened to know that they also desired to have some provision made for the direction of the organization in case anything might happen to Stephens. He seemed to be aware of that, and announced his intention to make Luby Lieutenant of Ireland. This was in itself the cause of a friendly smile from all in the direction where Luby sat, as we all liked him and knew him well. Why the Captain sprung this on the meeting no one could understand, except the motive was to please and compliment Luby. After considering the matter, next day Luby refused to accept the honor.

CHAPTER XII.

The idea of publishing a weekly newspaper in Dublin, through the medium of which he could reach the great mass of our people, was one that appealed to Stephens' fancy in the strongest manner. He saw in it a quick method of communicating with the organization, together with a prospect of its becoming a powerful medium for propaganda work with results which could not be secured so effectively, so directly or cheaply in any other way.*

While the Captain was most enthusiastic regarding this scheme, yet there were few of the Dublin Centres who fully approved of it. They somehow felt it would ultimately bring us into trouble, in fact, that was the sentiment which generally prevailed in the minds of the most influential and most far-seeing of our men. Our objections, however, were overruled and set aside by the overwhelming support given the project by the men in the south and southeast.

Stephens, as I have said, was enthusiastic regarding the enterprise, and finally succeeded in launching "The Irish People" on the 28th of November, 1863, our misgivings being somewhat allayed by the confidence we had in the men in whose hands it was placed.

John O'Leary was brought from London to take charge of the editorial department, with Chas. J. Kickham, Denis Dowling Mulcahy and Thomas C. Luby on the staff. John Haltigan was the printer and Rossa and James O'Connor had charge of the business office. All of these were tried men, and were all active workers in the organization with one exception, John O'Leary, who never formally joined, but who, nevertheless, was honored by all who knew him, and those who knew him intimately were well pleased to see him in control. He attended exclusively to his edito-

* See Appendix VII, Pages 179-181.

rial duties and let the other departments take care of themselves. (1)

All the precautions taken before this to mystify the Government and throw spies off the scent were now ignored. Rossa was now in charge of the business office, but among the very many good qualities which he possessed lacked the keen business tact necessary for such a position. His geniality and big heartedness overcame his love for order and carefulness. From the start the office became a lounging place for anyone

CHARLES J. KICKHAM.

(1) O'Donovan Rossa was the business manager, and James O'Connor his assistant. The latter was arrested and sentenced to seven years' penal servitude. After his release from prison he became sub-editor of the Dublin Irishman and is still connected with the Irish National press. He is at present a member of Parliament and prominent in the United Irish League.

who wished to take advantage of it. At first none but the curious, inquisitive, and those who had otherwise good intentions were continually around, but soon we saw detectives hovering around like birds of prey. The Castle birds were known to all.

The year of 1863 was a memorable one in our organization. It embraced Luby's first visit to the United States, in February, Langan's death, Stephens' marriage, the birth of "The Irish People" newspaper, and Luby's return on July 6th.

The death of Peter Langan was felt and lamented all through the organization in America and Ireland, but it was only those in close contact with him who felt the real loss of such a good, sterling, patriotic man. Those who visited him in the early days of the organization, from '55 to '57, when his home was the only place to meet, went away rejoicing that they knew such a man. He was one of the links that connected the '49 movement with the I. R. B.

The marriage of Stephens to Miss Hopper in the summer of 1863, was an event that pleased very few of his real friends and those who knew his ideas on that important subject, or at least his expressed opinion on the marriage state, looked upon it as a selfish, foolish proceeding.

After a while he decided that he required a house in one of the suburbs, and after a search fixed on Fairfield House, Sandymount. I had to see about his getting possession of it, and rented the place in the name of "Mr. Herbert." It was just the place for a man with Stephens' tastes, as it was enclosed with a wall all round, had a greenhouse, and all the appointments necessary for a gentleman of moderate income.

Hugh Brophy and myself were the only ones who knew of this retreat except his wife's family, the Hoppers. I will have to speak more of this retirement further on, but I must remark here that Stephens was an ardent horticulturist and had a place then to please his fancy and spared no means to gratify that whim. He tilled it, lived very quietly, and never went abroad except on some matter of very great importance.

George Hopper, his brother-in-law, and, in fact, all the Hoppers were reliable people. The most important meetings were held in George's house in Dame Street.

Denis Cromien was an active member of the building trade. He was superintendent of John's Lane

DANIEL H. GLEASON. (1)

Church, which was in course of building at this time. He had a fine lot of men under him, all of whom had been made members of the I. R. B. Among them was

(1) Daniel Gleason emigrated to America after the failure of the Movement in '67. He at first settled in New York, but in 1872 removed to Chicago, where he became a power in politics. He was the candidate of the Democratic party for several important positions, and on one occasion came within a few votes of being elected to Congress. On another occasion he was tendered the Democratic nomination for Mayor of Chicago, but declined. He was always an ardent worker in the Irish cause and a man of the most genial and kindly nature. He died in Chicago a few months ago.

a young Tipperary man named Dan Gleason, and Michael Malone, a cousin of the Captain, and a young man from Kilkenny, James Lawless. They had a drill room where drilling went on every night. The risk becoming too great, on the suggestion of Dan Gleason, they all joined the Dublin militia, where they could drill without fear. Dan, under Capt. John Kirwan, became their instructor, for which a former experience in the Tipperary militia thoroughly qualified him. They became very proficient in the manual of arms and such other requirements as the service demanded. Dan appeared later on in the seizure of "The Irish People."

"The Irish People" was being issued regularly, but up to this was not bringing in enough to pay expenses, although it had a fine circulation. Most of its subscribers had already advanced money to put it on its feet, and the returns were slim. These facts were patent to a few of us in Dublin—to Hugh Brophy, Andrew Nolan and some others. (3)

(3) Hugh Brophy was among the Irish prisoners who, with John Boyle O'Reilly, D. B. Cashman and others, were sent to Australia. After his pardon Brophy settled in Melbourne, where he is now a prominent builder. Andrew Nolan and his brother John are long since dead. John Nolan took Stephens' place while he was in prison. He emigrated to America and died in Kansas City, where a monument has been erected to his memory.

CHAPTER XIII.

In order to extend the Fenian organization in America special organizers were sent out who made it their business to visit all cities and towns containing an Irish population, where they held meetings and organized Circles from which, in course of time, other Circles started. Sometimes military companies were formed and equipped, which in time became proficient in military tactics, ready to take the field for Ireland when opportunity should offer. The enthusiasm and energy displayed in Chicago was something remarkable, and early in 1864 they decided to hold a grand Fair or Bazaar in that city, the proceeds of which were to be handed over to the Fenian Brotherhood.

In furtherance of their design circulars were sent everywhere at home and abroad asking for donations of merchandise and goods of any and every description which could be disposed of at the Fair.

"The Irish People" printed the appeal, and offered to receive and ship to Chicago any articles that might be donated to the Fair by people in Ireland.

A young Chicago man, named Henry Clarence McCarthy was sent to Dublin to the office of "The Irish People" to receive and ship the goods donated to the Fair. This young man impressed in the most favorable manner all the Centres and others with whom he came in contact.

They all liked him, as he was of mild disposition, genial deportment and possessed a very pleasing manner. His father and himself were born in the United States, his grandfather was born in Ireland. He possessed more of the American traits than any we had met up to this. There was no spread eagleism about him; on the contrary, he was modest, unselfish, practical, and business-like in everything, but a pronounced and determined revolutionist all the time. He expressed himself disgusted with the way business was being done in the office of "The Irish People," and asked me to help him pack the contributions to the fair. I listed them while he put them away in boxes, and before we got through I shared his feelings with regard to the condition of the office.

Edward Duffy was absent much of the time, mostly in the West, where he was doing good work as an organizer. John Nolan was equally successful in the North. These two men were fine propagandists, and had both given up lucrative positions to spread the light. Andrew Nolan, John's brother, whom I have before mentioned, was also a successful organizer. He was a traveller for a large hardware house in Thomas street, Dublin which gave him a splendid opportunity of spreading the organization through Carlow, Kildare, and the adjoining counties.

John Morris, for whom a large reward was offered in 1865, was a native of Myshal, County Carlow. He was, I think, a relative, or if not, a close personal friend of Andrew Nolan and of John his brother. He was a surveyor and was employed as such in his neighborhood, and usually called on me in Dublin whenever his business brought him there, consequently I saw a good deal of him and was delighted with him. He joined the movement through Andrew Nolan, and was one of his best men. He had his section of Carlow well in hand, his profession and wide acquaintanceship giving him a large scope, and bringing him in contact with the most prominent people of the district. Carlow at this time was like one of the northern counties, very conservative and, in a sense, was considered the special dominion of Colonel Bruin (O'Connell's great adversary), and Squire Cavanagh of fox-hunting fame. These two landlords had their estates well garrisoned with police, and had their tenantry pretty well terrorized and subdued. Colonel Bruin cleared his estate after the election in which O'Connell opposed him as member for the county. His tenants having all voted for O'Connell, he dispossessed every man of them. I remember the occasion very well, as all the poor fellows and their families were lodged in Smithwick's Brewery, Kilkenny, until means were found to send them to America. This event took place in the Repeal of the Union times, but the people never forgot the useless sacrifice that was made, and the heartless wholesale eviction and exodus remains to this day without a parallel in the history of the county. Such was the vineyard that John Morris worked in until he was obliged to fly. He is now in Chicago, father of a large family, all doing well, and, as I can vouch, the same sterling fellow he was in his younger days.

Patrick O'Leary, who professed to be a pagan and was known as"Pagan"O'Leary, had charge of the men engaged in winning over and organizing soldiers in Her Majesty's service who were flocking into the organization daily. He did wonderful work up to the time of his arrest. He was a unique character, and had no compeer and, although he professed himself a pagan, did not altogether forget Christian customs. He was a pronounced temperance man, and would share his last shilling with any poor person who might excite his pity in the streets. I knew him to take a poor barefoot woman he met in Grafton street into a shoe shop and buy her a pair of shoes, and after that bought her a couple of pairs of stockings. The same evening he had to borrow some money until he got his pay at the end of the week. Take him all in all he was a most worthy man.

He was arrested in "The Irish People" office at the time of the seizure, and when brought before Magistrate Strong insisted on keeping his hat on. When ordered to take it off he told the magistrate he would not. The justice remonstrated with him, and told him it was a custom and a compulsory one in courts of justice.

"No matter," said he, "General Juarez, in Mexico, told me at one time never to take off my hat to any one until I met the Lord of Heaven, and I have not met him yet."

A policeman removed his hat.

William Roantree of Leixlip, late of the United States Navy, was very active in the movement. He was a daring, dashing fellow with a splendid physique, full of ardor and a favorite with all the boys. He was a constant caller at my place and I a frequent visitor at Leixlip. His father was a victualer, and was respected by all throughout the country round. William, full of energy and hope, threw himself actively into the work and became one of the best organizers. His re-appearance and presence in the village was not at all pleasing to the parish priest, although his family and himself were regular attendants at his church, and were all of them exemplary subscribers to the Catholic faith. Bill wore his beard full and long with a mustache to match, but for some unknown reason his reverence did not like the cut of his jib. One Sunday this priest surprised his congregation by some remarks in the course of his sermon which Bill thought were directed towards himself. His Reverence alluded to returned Americans, wearing a badge of impudence under their noses and an independent swagger in their gait, etc. As Bill was the only one in the village who had been to America, no one could be mistaken regarding the person who was meant. His sister was with him in the pew, and was greatly mortified with these remarks. The priest had, on former occasions, touched on the subject, but this time he was pointed—almost personal.

The priest was a young man, robust and domineering, and Bill called on him, determined to have an explanation, as he was wrathy at the insult. His reverence said he did not have him in his mind when he made use of the expressions, and was sorry that Bill had imagined they were intended for him. In other words, he backed down. He lost some of his parishioners who, I heard afterwards, went elsewhere to attend their devotions.

General Millen arrived from New York about this time, sent by John O'Mahony. He claimed to have earned his spurs under Juarez in Mexico. Also at that time Col. Denis F. Burke,* Colonel Kirwin, Colonel Byron, and several other American offi-

* See Appendix LXXXVI, Page 284.

cers reported. They had no special duties to perform that I was aware of. General Halpin was in the batch. He had been assigned to the duty of inspecting the enemy's forts, barracks, etc. I remember going with him on one of those occasions to Mullingar, where we spent one entire day, taking notes, etc.

Finally Col. Thomas Kelly (1) came at a time when

---

(1) Colonel Thomas J. Kelly, the Chief of the Military Department in 1865, was born in Mount Bellew, County Galway, in 1833. His father belonged to the farmer class and brought up his son for the priesthood. On that account he received a better education than usually falls to the lot of farmers' sons.

After a time the young man found he did not have a vocation for the church, so he was apprenticed to the printing trade in Loughrea. Finding his prospects in a country town somewhat circumscribed, he came to New York when he was eighteen years old, where he joined the Printers' Union and soon secured employment. He took an active part in the proceedings of the Emmet Monument Association. On the recommendation of some friends he went to Nashville, Tenn., in 1857, where he founded a paper, which he had to abandon at the breaking out of the Civil War.

On his way North to join the 69th Regiment he heard of the enrollment of the 10th Ohio, an Irish regiment, which he joined as a private. He rose to the rank of captain and was for a time Chief Signal Officer with General Thomas. Having been severely wounded and his health impaired, he was invalidated, but became identified with the Fenian Brotherhood and was sent to Ireland as the first military envoy. His interview with Stephens in Ireland was satisfactory to both parties and Stephens soon learned to place implicit confidence in Captain Kelly. He was deputed to make an inspection of the condition of the I. R. B. in the Provinces and to report on them to Stephens on his return. His report was fully satisfactory. He expressed himself as amazed at the ramifications of the Brotherhood in Ireland and could not believe it had he not seen it for himself.

He was employed in various offices, sometimes in visiting circles in various parts of the country, at other times assisting Stephens in the executive management of affairs at home.

On the arrest of James Stephens, Captain Kelly took temporary charge of affairs and managed all the plans for Stephens' escape. He met Stephens on the outside of the prison, and later accompanied him to Paris, where both arrived safely. Stephens left his home in Dublin on an open car undisguised and went on board a boat in the Liffey. They spent three days beating about in the channel, and owing to adverse winds were at one time driven into Carrickfergus Bay. They ulti-

the Captain and Luby were out of town.* His mission was to closely examine the strength of our forces and resources, and report to O'Mahony; thus the dilly-dallying was kept up while there was no actual revolution

COLONEL THOMAS J. KELLY.
Reproduced From "The Irish People."

mately reached a port in Scotland, spent a night in Kilmarnock, rode in the mail train to London next day, slept that night in the Palace Hotel, not far from Buckingham Palace, and started next morning by train from Victoria Station for Dover, whence they crossed to Calais in safety.

In 1865 after the War of the Rebellion many Irish-American officers went to Ireland prepared to participate in the uprising which they had been led to expect was about to take place.

* See Appendix XI and XII, Pages 186-188.

in sight. Kelly expressed himself satisfied with what he saw, and reported everything O. K.

Everyone was now at fever heat, and the reports from the disaffected military were becoming exciting, as they were becoming discontented with delay, and wanted to revolt. An undercurrent of insubordination had been apparent for some time, for they did not know the moment they would get orders to leave Ireland. One regiment wanted to revolt and take to the Dublin mountains sooner than leave, but Stephens told them to obey orders and go, we were not ready yet.

At this time the Pigeon House Fort, near the mouth of the Liffey, was held by a friendly garrison, and would be placed in our hands when we desired. This was the best opportunity which ever presented itself

---

The uprising was planned to take place in 1866, but the movement proved a failure. Nothing daunted, the leaders planned another for March 5 the following year. To obtain arms and ammunition for this contemplated rising an expedition was projected by the Irish Republican Brotherhood against Chester Castle, Chester, Wales, where some 25,000 stands of arms were known to be kept in storage guarded by a small body of English soldiers.

The plan was well laid and would have been successfully carried out were it not for the treachery of John J. Corydon, an informer, who notified the authorities and warned them in advance, so that when the Irish soldiers reached Chester they found the town filled with troops.

The projected rising was therefore a failure and many of the Irish-American officers fell into the hands of the Government. Others escaped and scattered through the larger cities in England and Scotland.

Colonel Thomas J. Kelly was in chief command at that time with Colonel Rick Burke in London, and Captain Timothy Deasy in Manchester and Liverpool. Colonel Kelly as commander-in-chief found occasion to visit Manchester to attend a meeting of the organization and later, while in company of Captain Deasy, both were arrested. They were taken before a magistrate and remanded.

Some days later while being driven through the streets in a prison van the vehicle was attacked and the prisoners rescued. In breaking open the van a policeman on guard inside was accidentally killed for which three men were afterwards hanged. Kelly and Deasy escaped in safety to America. Colonel Kelly is still living. He holds a position in the New York Custom House and resides uptown.

for a successful outbreak, but it was allowed to slip. The three disaffected regiments stationed in Dublin were shortly after sent off, one to Malta, one to Gibraltar, and the other to India, disheartened and disgusted.

At this particular time the Captain, Luby, and O'Leary frequently met and consulted with Generals Kerwin,* Halpin, Millen, Colonel Burke and others, in my place. A feeling of dissatisfaction with Stephens' management of affairs had sprung up and found expression and there were rumors to the effect that an effort would be made to remove him.† No matter what may be said nowadays in regard to any one being appointed in Stephens' place, Luby and O'Leary urged him not to yield his position to any one. I heard this repeated more than once. (1)

---

(1) The members of the I. R. B. who had been led to believe that a rising would take place about this time became impatient at the prolonged and, to them, inexplicable delay, and a feeling, or belief, found expression, inside the organization that Stephens and O'Mahony had not performed their full duty in making the necessary preparations for the uprising, with perhaps a faint suspicion that they did not mean to fight. This opinion regarding Stephens in Ireland was somewhat strengthened and apparently corroborated by statements made by American officers who came to Ireland and reported that O'Mahony in New York was also being blamed for the delay. As a result of this dissatisfaction it was vaguely rumored an attempt would be made to remove Stephens and replace him with a more active and aggressive successor. That this feeling found expression and gave serious cause for alarm to the leaders is proven by the fact that they deemed it necessary to call a meeting and pass a vote of confidence in Stephens and O'Mahony.

At that meeting the following paper was drawn up and signed by the four persons whose names appear first on the list. The other signatures were added later as opportunity offered.

"We the undersigned local representatives in Ireland, of the Irish firm, over the American branch of which John O'Mahony has been appointed Supreme Director,—hereby express our unlimited confidence in the ability and integrity with which that gentleman has conducted our affairs in America; and also our admiration of the noble constancy which has enabled him to sustain our interests, unflinchingly, amid the severest trials and in the face of the most shameful and unmerited calumny.

"We also hereby testify, in the strongest manner, our approval of the conduct and devotion of James Stephens, in the general

* See Appendix LXXXV, Page 281. † See Appendix III, Pages 163-164.

On July 3, 1865, Captain Patrick Magrath, of Chicago, arrived in Dublin. With him, and under his charge, were Captain P. Tolen, Major Martin Wallace, Sergeant Matthew Higgins and Private Owen Cunningham, all of the Twenty-third Illinois Regiment, and Sergt. John Dunne of the Regular Army. Immediately after landing he reported to me and I introduced him to Stephens. He was assigned to An-

---

management of the firm, under similar trying circumstances; and, finally, we confirm both those gentlemen in the authority, originally conferred upon them; and express our unalterable determination to stand by them, while they represent us, against all their enemies, whether open or disguised—their enemies being ours also!"

1. Peter Langan, Dublin.
2. Thomas Clarke Luby, Dublin.
3. Joseph Denieff, Dublin.
4. Charles Beggs, Dublin.
5. James W. Dillon, Wicklow.
6. Thomas Purcell, Bray.
7. William Butler, Waterford City.
8. John Haltigan, Kilkenny.
9. John O'Cavanagh, Carrick on Suir.
10. Edmund Coyne, Callan.
11. Thos. Hickey, Coolnamick, County Waterford.
12. Denis D. Mulcahy, Jr., Redmondstown, Co. Tipperary.
13. Brian Dillon, Cork City.
14. William O'Carroll, Cork City.
15. Jer. O'Donovan Rossa, Skibbereen, Cork.
16. Daniel McCartie.
17. James O'Mahony, Bandon, Co. Cork.
18. Thomas P. O'Connor, Laffana, Co. Cork.
19. James O'Connell, Clonmel.
20. William O'Connor, Grange, Clonmel.
21. Michael Commerford, Newtown, Carrick on Suir.
22. Mortimer Moynahan, Skibbereen, Co. Cork.
23. Eugene McSwiney, Tomes, Macroom.
24. Denis O'Shea, Kenmare.
25. Martin Hawe, Kilkenny.

Accompanying some of the above signatures are marginal notes stating they were obtained or attached at various times. Thus the names of James O'Connell of Clonmel and William O'Conner, Grange, Clonmel, are accompanied by a side-note written by Luby stating they were obtained by Denis Dowling Mulcahy. The signature of Michael Commerford, Newton, Carrick on Suir, is written on a separate note sheet and pasted on. He said: "Dear Mr. Luby, I authorize you to sign my name to the paper expressing confidence in the devotion and wisdom

trim, but found that section in a very poor state of preparation, Belfast being the only place possessing arms in any considerable quantity. Captain Magrath was afterwards sent to Kilkenny, where he reported to John Kavanagh, then centre of the city, and a warm friendship sprung up between the two. Captain Magrath remained in Ireland until all hope was temporarily abandoned, when he returned to America, and is now a worthy resident of the City of Chicago.

---

of our leaders James and John." The date is given as August 8, 1864, which fixes the time.

The signatures of Mortimer Moynahan, Skibbereen, and Eugene McSwiney, Tomes, Macroom, were obtained by Dan McCartie.

The original with all the signatures attached is at present in possession of the Editor of THE GAEL, together with a large number of other original documents, papers, letters, etc., written by Stephens, O'Mahony, Luby, O'Leary, Kickham, John Mitchel , Colonel Kelly and others.

Towards the end of 1865 John Mitchel was sent by O'Mahony to Paris to act as Financial Agent for the Fenian Brotherhood which position he filled in a most satisfactory manner.* Some years later he changed his opinion regarding the *advisability* of attempting the freedom of Ireland by physical force *while England is at piece.* †

* See Appendix XXII, XXXV, XXXVIII, XXXIX and XL.

† See Appendix LXXXII, LXVIII, Pages 276-277.

CHAPTER XIV.

Matters were in this state when P. J. Meehan of the "Irish-American" arrived. As this is a most important episode in this narrative, I shall give verbatim the conversations and the circumstances as they occurred.

PATRICK J. MEEHAN,
Editor "Irish American."

I was surprised to hear that Meehan had been sent, as I had met him in New York, and knew the antagonistic attitude he had taken towards our organization during my time there.

One morning, after I had my shop opened up, a gentleman and a boy came in, and asked to see the proprietor.

"I am the proprietor," said I.

"Well," said he, "I am P. W. Dunne, from the United States, and wish to speak privately with you."

My salesman and bookkeeper was standing a little distance off from us, so I showed Mr. Dunne some goods, as if he were about to make a purchase or leave an order, and then took an early opportunity to send out my man with some bills to collect, so that we had the place to ourselves.

"Now," said I. "you can speak freely."

"Mr. P. J. Meehan, of New York, is in town, sent by John O'Mahony to see James Stephens. I want to see Stephens before he does. I want to post him on some matters on which he should be well informed. That is why I want to see him."

Mr. Dunne was the leading Fenian in Peoria, Illinois, and was very influential in Irish affairs in that State. I had never met him before, but had heard Stephens speak of him as one of the best friends he had met while in the United States. Mr. Dunne informed me that he had been sent to Ireland for the purpose of making a personal investigation into the condition and strength of the home organization, and if he found it as well established and as vigorous as it was represented to be, and made a report on his return to that effect, then his colleagues would be satisfied and more funds would be promptly forthcoming.

Mr. Meehan came from New York on a similar errand, but Mr. Dunne believed the Captain should be made acquainted with existing conditions in New York before he saw Mr. Meehan. I arranged to have the Captain meet Mr. Dunne at eleven o'clock, and Mr. Meehan at noontime. Mr. Dunne requested me not to let Meehan know that I had seen him previously, and asked me to receive Meehan in a kindly and cordial manner, which I agreed to do, and he then went away.

Shortly after, to my great surprise, he returned accompanied by Mr. Meehan. I, of course, knew Mr. Meehan, and greeted him cordially, but acted towards Mr. Dunne as if I had then met him for the first time. After the usual salutations were over, Mr. Meehan stated his mission, and further said he had some important documents to deliver. I asked where they were, and he said they were in his trunk at the hotel, hidden in the back of a brush. I told him he ought to have them with him, somewhere about his person, especially if they were at all important.

They both left, and after some time returned again. It has been said that Meehan had the papers when he first called, and offered them to me. I have no recollection of ever having seen them. They both went away again, and I went and brought Stephens to meet them according to appointment. Stephens and I were waiting for Mr. Dunne to call at eleven o'clock, when to our surprise both Meehan and he came in. Meehan came right up to us and exclaimed, "What shall I do? I have lost the documents which I brought from America?"

"Lost them?" said the Captain. "Where?"

"I don't know."

At this juncture, James O'Connor came in on some business for "The Irish People." Meehan asked the Captain to allow O'Connor to go with him to search for the papers.

"No," said Mr. Stephens, "Mr. Denieffe will go with you."

"Now," said I to him," where did you come from to my place?"

"From Westland Row Station. I came in from Kingston."

"How did you come from the station? In a conveyance?"

"In a covered car."

"Will you know the man that drove you?"

"Yes, I think so."

We went to Westland Row Station, and saw the old man that drove him. I opened his cab and searched

P. W. DUNNE.

the cushions, and asked the old man if he had found any papers.

"No sir, there were none found."

We went to the superintendent's office, and inquired if there were any papers found on the trains. He went to a pigeonhole desk and looked over it. No, there were none found.

I then decided I would go to Kingstown, and search there. As we were going to take the train for Kingstown, to continue our search, Edward Duffy was met, coming from a train that had just arrived. He saw us. I took him aside and told him who the person was that was with me, and that we were in search of important papers that he had lost. I asked him to follow us and keep us in sight. Arriving in Kingstown, I saw William Roantree going to board a train for Dublin. I went to him and told him to see Edward Duffy, and he would tell him what to do.

When we got opposite the Anglesea Arms Hotel I noticed Meehan kicking every bit of paper and straw that came in his way. I told him if the papers were lost here there was a good chance of finding them, as there were a great many friends in the place, and that we had detectives of our own always on the lookout.

Soon he noticed Roantree and Duffy following us, and inquired who they were. I told him they were two of our men. We went up the little street, a cul du sac, next to the Hotel, to a house on the end, where he knocked. A middle-aged lady opened the door, and asked, "Patrick, did you find them?"

He told her they had not yet been found.

"I wouldn't bother with them," she said, "come in and make yourself easy."

"No," said he, "I must go with this gentleman."

"Must go!" she said. We then came away. The lady was Mrs. Nicholas Kelly, his cousin, formerly of Limerick, whom he had previously visited and from whose house he had come that morning.

This was all the search that was made. My two trusty friends were at the end of the street when Meehan came out, and turned in the direction of the railroad. I signalled them to stop, and when we came up to them introduced Meehan. (1)

---

(1) P. J. Meehan of New York and P. W. Dunne of Peoria, Ill., were two of the most trusted men in the Fenian Brotherhood. Mr. Meehan was a young man of brilliant parts and was editor of the "Irish American," then the leading Irish paper in New York City. Mr. Dunne was associated with a Mr. Fuller in business in the West and was a prominent merchant. Messrs. Meehan and Dunne were sent to Ireland to personally investigate the condition of affairs there. It is true that many others had been sent on a similar errand before, but those men were instructed to particularly and critically examine into the standing of the organization, the number of men enrolled in the provinces, their efficiency, quantity of arms on hand, etc., and, if on their return their report should be favorable, then the entire organization in America, which for some time previous had not been entirely harmonious, would unite in sending ample financial means sufficient to complete the organization and make ready for the rising. In addition to this an elaborate financial scheme i volving an issue of bonds of the Irish Republic had been arranged for and the issue of those bonds depended on the report to be made by Messrs. Meehan and Dunne on their return to America

Meehan brought with him certain documents consisting of an official letter of introduction from John O'Mahony addressed to James Stephens, Chief Executive of the Irish Republican Brotherhood, also a draft for £500 ($2,500), which was to be handed to Stephens and a letter from O'Mahony requesting that O'Donovan Rossa be permanently assigned to the New York headquarters. Rossa was returning to Ireland on board the vessel on which Meehan and Dunne sailed from New York and accompanied them across.

Mr. Meehan was several days in Ireland before he appeared in Dublin, and through some mischance lost the documents at Kingstown on the day of his arrival. He said he had brought them across concealed in the hollow back of a clothes brush. When he got ready to present them he took them out and at first concealed them in one of his socks, but not believing them safe there removed them and pinned them in his underwear, from which they became detached and fell in the street unobserved by him.

The documents were found near the railway station in Kingstown by a messenger boy who turned them over to a Miss Charlotte Mitchell, a young woman employed in the Telegraph Department, who at the trial testified they were placed in the hands of a police inspector who took them to Dublin Castle.

The loss of those papers, together with the seizure of the Irish People newspaper and the arrest and conviction of its editors and other employes caused an immense sensation. It was undoubtedly a most unfortunate occurrence, but now after

Duffy and he walked on together, and Roantree walked with me. Roantree had known Meehan in New York, too. The first words he said to me were that he believed Meehan never lost the papers, and to tell the Captain so, and not to let him out of my custody.

"No," said I, "don't fear that. I shall take charge of him until the papers are found."

Stephens was awaiting our return. I told him of the fruitless search we had made. After a short parley, Meehan said he would go, and was in the act of doing so when I stopped him and told him he could not leave until the papers were found.

I could see Stephens smile as he walked away. He came back after a few minutes and took me aside and said:

"I think it is better to let him go. He has promised me to do what is in his power for us."

From what I could gather from both Meehan and Dunne it appeared that all depended on the report

---

an interval of forty years it is universally conceded that Meehan lost the papers through an excess of care in trying to conceal them.*

James Stephens, at one time, was inclined to severely blame Meehan, but he afterwards exhonorated him as far as anything like a suspicion of unfaithfulness to Ireland was concerned. Leaving out this episode of the lost documents, P. J. Meehan was one of the most unselfish and devoted men that ever labored for Ireland. He may have been mistaken in his views regarding the invasion of Canada, but his honesty and sincerity can never be questioned. Possessing ample means in those days, he devoted the bulk of his fortune to the prosecution of the cause he believed in and died a comparatively poor man on that account. He died at his residence in Jersey City in 1906. Mr. P. W. Dunne, now an honored citizen of Chicago, whose son is Mayor of that city can look back with pride on his patriotic career. He has always been faithful to Ireland, and though he has been engaged many times in his life in business of vast dimensions he was never so busy as to forget his native land or to find time to work in its behalf. Faithful to the end he is still as ardent and enthusiastic as ever in his devotion to Ireland.

* See Appendix XCI, Pages 292-293.

which Meehan would make. If favorable the united forces of the two sections of the Fenian Brotherhood in the United States would join, and give us all we desired. The lost documents consisted of a bank draft for a large sum and letters of credentials.

I then asked Meehan not to blame me for the action I took in the matter. That up to the present I understood we were a military organization, and although not in the field, we had observed the rules in such matters, but I found I was mistaken. What would a British general do to an aide who came up to him and told him he had lost important dispatches given to him by Wellington? He would send him to the guardhouse to await court martial.

Next day P. W. Dunne introduced me to a friend and business partner of his. They had some bills of exchange to get cashed, and I took them to the Dublin branch of the London bank, where I used to do business and get accommodation.

Stephens arranged a meeting for the next evening to hear Meehan's statement of his case. General Halpin, Meehan and P. W. Dunne, Luby, John O'Leary, and the Captain himself were present. The first three represented the American wing, and the last three the home wing. Edward Duffy, Rossa, and myself were present, sitting by.

Meehan stated he had been sent to learn if everything was according to representation—men, arms, organization, etc., and it depended on the report he would make on his return, what action the American directory would take. If his report was favorable we could have all we desired. The meeting broke up early next morning. Meehan declared he was fully satisfied, and said he would report accordingly. After spending a couple of days in Dublin, Meehan and party left for the west, Connemara, etc., via Limerick, where they stopped for a week or so.

In a few days "The Irish People" was seized, and all persons in the office arrested. We learned afterwards Meehan's papers were found in Kingstown telegraph office by a young lady, the daughter of the manager, who handed them over to the castle authorities.*

All the moneys coming from America were now sent to John O'Leary, and the officers and men reported to General Halpin. Up to a short time before this they were all sent to me. Stephens sent a bill of

JOHN O'LEARY.

exchange to me by Edward Duffy and asked me to have it cashed. I did not look at the bill, but went immediately to the bank, and deposited it. These bills of exchange had to be sent to London before they could be cashed. Two days after I was sent for by the cashier of the bank. He asked me if I did not know that this was the duplicate bill of exchange, that I had already got the first cashed. This cashier was not the one I had done business with before,

* See Appendix XVI, Page 193.

whose name was Manley, and who was in London on his vacation.

I was asked to step into the office. There were three gentlemen sitting there. One of them had the bill in his hand, and asked me did not I receive payment on the first bill of exchange, and why I presented the duplicate; the sum being large, how could I make the mistake? I told him the money did not belong to me, that it belonged to gentlemen I had introduced to Mr. Manley, and who had deposited some bills of exchange and got some cash. Before they left town they requested me to deposit any bills that might come to me. I told them if Mr. Manley was present he could account for the mistake. They talked together in an undertone, and handed back the bill.

"I wish," said I, "you would make some inquiry about me. I am well known in the neighborhood," and referred them to houses I did business with.

"We have done so already," said the one who handed me back the bill, "and we're glad to find your reputation good."

I came back to my shop. Ed was waiting for me. I told him the circumstances and the dilemma in which I was placed. He was dumbfounded for a moment. "How," said he, "could Stephens make such a mistake? It is monstrous and stupid. If it were not for your reputation and presence of mind you would be held for swindling, and you could not say a word for yourself in defense."

I wrote to Meehan at the hotel in Limerick, where he, Dunne, and Fuller were stopping, asking him to write me a letter that might clear me if there was anything more about the matter, but I never received an answer nor my own letter back.

CHAPTER XV.

On September 15th, 1865, "The Irish People" newspaper was seized by the Government, its type destroyed, and the editors and printers, and many prominent men were thrown into prison.

There was a great lull in matters at this time. Extra precautions were taken. Every suspicious or incriminating paper was put away, and everything made ready for the worst that might follow.

One day I was out making collections, and was late in coming back to my place. Ed Duffy had called, and left word that the Captain wanted to see me as soon as possible. I went to Fairfield House. The Captain asked me where I had been, which nettled me a little. He handed me a package and some money.

"Find Captain Jim Murphy," said he, "and give him this. Ed was looking for him, but could not find him. He must leave to-night for New York. Don't let this be found on you, as it is a hanging matter; tell the same to Jim."

He then gave me his revolver in case I was held up. I knew what to do. Ed Duffy came with me. It was past eleven o'clock P. M. We went to Phibsborough, where Murphy's lodgings were, changing cars and dismissing our last one at the viaduct. I had Ed to wait here for me while I looked for Jim. It was a very quiet neighborhood, and all appeared to be asleep. There was no one to be seen. I got to the house and knocked on the door, but received no response. Across the street there were a few shade trees. A man came from under one of these, and I saw another who stayed in the shade. The first man came over to me and asked:

"Did anyone answer?"

"No," said I, "they must be all asleep, Mr. —— may not have got home yet," naming the proprietor, who was a good loyal citizen.

I went back to Ed, and the other joined his friend under the trees. We went up the steps at the viaduct to the canal, and turned in the direction of Phibsboro bridge. Prepared for trouble, I carried the parcel in one hand and my pistol in the other, and told Ed to be ready for any emergency. The poor fellow was tired, and had not been feeling good for some time, and we walked slowly on that account. Soon we heard footsteps behind us, and, as the bridge was some distance, we thought it best to stand and wait. There were no houses along here, but there were back entrances to the houses on the street running parallel to the canal. Immediately we heard the shrill blast of a dog-whistle and thought we were to have a tussle, but that was all. It was sounded by someone getting in the back way of his house. We felt relieved, and walked to the bridge. A poor old fellow with a covered car happened to be passing as we got on the bridge. He was going home, and at first refused to take us up, but he changed his mind on being offered double fare. He took us into his cab; poor Ed was used up after climbing the stairs and taking the long walk on the canal, and thought the cab was a godsend.

We got at last to Carey's hotel in Lower Bridge street, and found our man, Captain Jim, talking to Miss Kelly, the young lady who attended there. She was a trusty friend of ours, and was Jim's fiancee. I delivered my message. Jim said it was hard to go on such short notice, but it must be attended to. He left that night, and arrived safe in New York with his message to John O'Mahony, later he returned to his post, as I heard some time after, and married Miss Kelly. On that trip from Dublin to New York and back Captain Murphy made the quickest time on record for that period. Murphy was a brave man, and remained faithful to the last. He died a few years ago in New York. (1)

We returned to Stephens and reported, and after seeing Ed Duffy in safety I went to my home. It was then past two o'clock in the morning. My wife was waiting up for me somewhat excited. She told me there were two detectives looking for me, and that Mr. Marshall, who kept the hotel next door, wished to see me as soon as I got back. This man was a conservative and a staunch loyalist. I did not call on him. My wife asked me if there was anything that would compromise me about the house, I thought not. I never kept anything that could do so.

Captain James Murphy had a most brilliant record in the United States Army. He was made a captain in the 20th Massachusetts Regiment by merit alone in July, 1861. He drilled Colonel W. Raymond Lee, Lieutenant-Colonel J. Winthrop Palfrey, Major Paul J. Revere, the Crownshields, Oliver Wendell Holmes, Jr., afterwards judge of the Supreme Court of Massachusetts, and now judge of the United States Supreme Court; Mayor H. L. Abbott, and the Putnams and Lowells of that State. He acquired the warm esteem of all his comrades and during his long period of service received several wounds, an especially severe one at Mary's Heights, on May 3, 1863. He was discharged for disability in consequence of his wounds and received a pension on that account. Captain Murphy was a sergeant in the 4th United States Artillery at the age of 18, was stationed at Fort Independence, Boston, from 1854 to 1856, served in the Seminole campaign in Florida under Gen. W. S. Harney and was on duty in Kansas during the troubled period of "Border Ruffianism." He crossed the plains from Fort Leavenworth to Fort Bridges in 1858, subsequently served again in Florida in 1858, served again in Florida and was one of the forty-five men who held Fort Pickens from January 10 to May, 1861, under the gallant General Adam T. Slemmer, afterwards killed at Chickamauga. When reinforcements arrived the brave little band, completely worn out, was sent North, and those who composed it were presented with medals as a reward of their valor by the New York Chamber of Commerce. Capt. Murphy fought at Yorktown, Fairoaks, Westpoint, Peach Orchard, Savage Station, Glendale, Malvern Hill and Fredericksburg. After the war he was appointed superintendent of national cemeteries, and in 1890 was made deputy collector of internal revenue for the first district of New York. All through his life he was devoted to the cause of Ireland. He died in New York on Nov. 2, 1891.

"What are these?" said she, pulling out a bale of pamphlets—a lot of Chas. Beggs' "Military Resources of Ireland." "Let us destroy them, they are no good now."

We hauled them down to the kitchen, and burned them. This was a tedious job, as there were about four or five hundred of them, but we succeeded and put the ashes into the vault. My wife had discharged our domestic a few days before. So there was no one in the house but ourselves. We were ready now if the enemy came.

It was then about six o'clock. We set about getting breakfast ready. My wife asked could I not fly and save myself.

"No," said I, "the order of the day is that no one shall leave."

We were going to sit down to our meal when Detective Clifford, accompanied by two men, entered.

"Does James Deneiffe stop here?" he asked.

"No," I answered.

"What's your name?"

"Joseph," said I.

"You are the man we want. I arrest you in the Queen's name, for high treason."

"Are you not making a mistake?" said I.

"Oh no, but I am sorry to see a respectable man like you connected with such people."

"If you came to arrest me I wish you would do so, and cease your lecturing me."

"I must search your house."

"All right, I shall give you all the assistance in my power."

During this colloquy, one of his fellows rushed into the room, holding out his hand and exclaiming, "No use searching, they have done away with everything, the kitchen grate is red hot, look at my hands."

I could not help laughing at his blistered hands. He was the meanest piece of humanity I had ever seen. He saw an escritoire, belonging to my wife, and asked me to open it. He took out some letters. In looking over them, he exclaimed, "They speak

French, here are a lot of letters in that language."

I told him if he knew anything about French he would be less gleeful over the discovery.

My wife was standing by my side when he approached her. I seized the carving knife and went between them, resolved to attack anyone who laid hands on her.

Clifford, seeing this, called them off, and said he had nothing to do with Mrs. Deneiffe. I must say Clifford acted as gentlemanly as I could expect, but the other two, and particularly the imp who burned his hand, were low ruffians. I vowed if ever I came across him elsewhere I would remember his brutal conduct. Such were the servants in the pay of Her Majesty. England may boast of her humane laws, but they are only a sham.

When they brought me into the street it was crowded. I was immediately taken to College street station, where Clifford went through some legal formalities, and handed the inspector three revolvers and a bowie knife, which he said he found in my place. I knew of one only, the others belonged to two American friends named Hyland and O'Brien, who were stopping with me, and who had left a few days before. They had left the revolvers concealed in the bottoms of two chairs in their room, I knew nothing about them.

While standing there waiting for something or other, the officers present amused themselves at my expense, commenting on the quality of the latest improved arms they found. "Oh! nothing but the best, the most improved!"

I remarked I wished there could be some improvement made in the unmanly and unfeeling conduct of Stalworths like them, taunting a prisoner with cowardly insult before the charge was proven.

I was soon committed and placed in a cell, which was a water closet. Soon I heard footsteps pacing up and down outside. I would have given anything for a smoke. There was a hole through the top part of the door, through which I could see a policeman. I asked could he get me some tobacco.

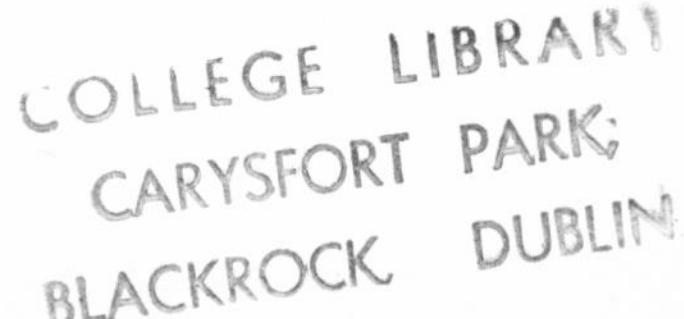

"Keep quiet," said he, "and wait a minute." He come to me in a short time, and handed me a pipe and a match.

"Stand up on the closet, and let the smoke out at the top," he said, and vanished. That simple act comforted and cheered me. Evidently all was not rotten and perverted.

After some delay, I was removed to Richmond Bridewell. My mind was made up for the worst, and so I became contented. I had nothing to accuse myself of and felt cheerful. The cause was not given up, and hope was bright as ever.

When I entered my cell it did not take long to see the layout; an iron bedstead and a block of wood to sit on. When night came I would receive my bed and covering. The aperture that furnished light was about eight feet from the floor, being out of reach, it could only be opened by a rod. Everything was secure.

The warder in charge, whose name was Lennon, soon came back, and handed me something to read. I found it was a series of evangelistic tracts. This man appeared to me to have some kindness in him, as he had a good face. Whatever his duties were he performed them in a quiet, inoffensive manner. The touch of kindness I had experienced from the policeman gave me hope that all were not heartless in the service of the Crown. I made up my mind to live up to the prison rules, and take my punishment without a murmur. I concluded there was no use kicking, and philosophically accepted the situation; thus the first evening closed. My bed was thrown in with the covering nicely folded.

"You will have to fold these in the same way you see them now, and have them ready to be taken away in the morning when the gong sounds the second time," said the warder, leaving me to study my task.

I fixed up as quickly as I could, for I was very tired after the day's exploit.

After getting fixed for the night, "Where are the others, and will I see any of them," were the thoughts that occupied my mind, after a longing wish and a prayer that I might see my wife, and hear how matters were shaping themselves.

When the gong sounded next morning, I had my bed and bedding ready. After it was taken away breakfast was served; coffee and bread. I inquired of the warder if any food would be allowed from the outside.

"Yes," said he, "if you are married, your wife can bring you anything you desire."

"Well," said I, "I'm all right, I will have a good dinner then."

I saw my cheerfulness was making a good impression on the warder, and I asked him could I get any books in, and he told me to ask the governor when I went down to see my wife. Matters began to brighten up a little and I felt good.

At one o'clock the cell doors were thrown open, and all the prisoners ordered out for exercise. We had to stand opposite our doors until the word march was given. To my great surprise, I found my friend, James O'Connor, was my next door neighbor. We had a recognition. The smile that came up on both of our faces could not be interpreted by anyone but ourselves, for it spoke volumes. We were soon in the yard, formed into a circle about three or four feet apart; no conversation was allowed. The warder and a policeman standing by to enforce discipline.

Notwithstanding all this, there was a great deal passed from one to another in a mute language only known to ourselves, and there was not a sad face in all the circle, on the contrary, all looked jolly and dignified.

Patrick J. Hayburn, whom I knew well was one of the circle. His laugh was contagious. He was on the opposite side of the circle from me and O'Connor. His eyes were set on both of us, and when he saw the warder's attention taken from us, he was sure to display some antics which caused a titter all around. After an hour had passed we were brought back to our cells

Shortly after I was called down to the governor's room to see my wife, who had a nice roast chicken for me, and in our greeting passed me a plug of tobacco. We were allowed a few minutes together, the governor sitting close to us. She had a message from P. J. Smith, who volunteered his services to me as attorney to look after my business outside. I told her to see Ed Duffy and be guided by him.

When told our interview was at an end, I asked the governor could I get some books. "Yes," he said, "any book the chaplain approves of will be admitted.

"Can I have Shakespeare, Byron, Moore, and Campbell?"

"Yes, you can have any of those." Next day I got all of them and enjoyed reading selections from them. This was how my first day and night were spent in jail, all the others were passed in about the same way, excepting one or two which I will notice and also how we spent the Sabbath Day.

On Sunday we were allowed to go to our respective places of worship, according to our faith or religious beliefs. We were brought to the gallery of the chapel, which was so arranged that the row in front could not see those behind, nor the prisoners behind those in front.

When we got seated I found Denis Dowling Mulcahy next, on my right, and James O'Connor on my left. Our devotions took the shape of a conversation in undertone, between the solemn parts of the mass. This was an hour well enjoyed, and lasted without change during my stay in the institution.

The lower part or ground floor contained all the petty malefactors such as thieves and all that class. Amongst these Martin A. O'Brennan chose to be placed We were surprised to see him there. We found afterwards he was afraid he would compromise himself if he came amongst us.

I think it was the third Sunday we were treated to a pastoral circular, or whatever it was by Cardinal Cullen. Before Father Bently, the chaplain, read it for us, he said he read it over and over, and left out some remarks which he thought would not be pleasing to some of his hearers. He was quite nervous. We could notice the paper shaking in his hand. He was obliged to read it for us, he said, as it was to be read in all the churches in the city on that day. From beginning to end it was a denunciation of us, which was all very well, until he came to the passage that said there was not one in the whole business that could make a living for himself. We agreed in an undertone that it was cowardly and a lie. Mulcahy was going to leave. I asked him to hear it all out. His leaving would do no good, and be considered insubordination. James O'Connor laughed, and said that settled it. After talking the matter over, whether to attend any more, we concluded that an hour of undisturbed chat together, all things considered, was not to be thrown away.

Some time after this, Lennon asked me if I would like to read the ecclesiastical history of Ireland. I said yes, and he brought it to me. I looked it over and saw the margins and spaces through the pages all written over. The notes were half Irish, and pointed to Lennon as their author. The book belonged to the chaplain, and had been lent to O'Brennan. After a short time the chaplain himself called with Lennon, who introduced his Reverence to me.

"I am sorry I cannot ask you to sit down," said I, "but you see it would be a very ungracious compliment. I cannot help it. This book," I went on, "is in a mutilated condition and was so when I received it from the warder.

"That is that old fool, O'Brennan," said he.

"Father, why don't you come around oftener and see your flock," said I to him.

"I thought," said he, "ye were all a lot of ragamuffins."

"Even so," said I, "were we such, did not the Saviour die for all men, but I tell you if the Saviour had not put his mark deeply on the hearts of the Irish people they would all leave the church that is now dominated by politicians."

"Oh, don't say that," said he, and left. This gentleman was a brother of Bently, the auctioneer, one of the castle gentry, but was a convert and was disowned by his family, as I heard afterwards.

Another item I wish to give, we were all at exercise one day when Charles Underwood O'Connell was brought in. It happened I was on the far-off side of the circle when he entered the prison yard. He had been arrested in Cork, on his arrival from New York, and letters for Stephens were found in his possession. He walked across the circle to me, and held out his hand and asked me how I was. That was very injudicious on his part, and likely to be harmful to both of us.

"You might reserve your compliments," said I, "for a better opportunity."

The warder noticed this incident, and said it was his duty to report the fact that we were acquainted and recognized each other, but, being a good man, he only commented on the danger men placed themselves in by such associations. Judas came to mind, but I knew him to be a sycophant and full of vanity, and let the matter rest.

John J. Breslin was connected with the prison, but I was not acquainted with him until after I was arrested and imprisoned. He was the hospital warder and always accompanied the physician and surgeon on their rounds. He also acted as apothecary, prepared the prescriptions and treated any patients needing his care.

He was treating James O'Connor for his eyes, the glare from the white-washed walls having affected them. John would come round after the physician had gone, and while washing O'Connor's eyes would deliver all the news from the outside, together with scraps and cuttings of newspapers. These clippings were passed around surreptitiously, and thus we were kept posted on the news of the day. We found out a way for transmitting these scraps from one to another, without letting it be known where they came from, so Breslin's visits to James O'Connor were known only to him and me. He called regularly every morning, and was always pleasant and kind.

Lennon, the warder, spoke to me again about Charley Underwood O'Connell. (1) It appeared to me he was uneasy in his mind about not doing his duty, and wanted to know how I got acquainted with him.

JOHN J. BRESLIN.

"You know," I said, "I am in the merchant tailoring business. A friend brought him in one day, and I made him a suit of clothes."

"That will do," said he, smiling. He appeared to be satisfied with my explanation, and never spoke of him again.

(1) Charles Underwood O'Connell was one of three Cork Centres, the two others being James O'Connor and Bryan Dillon, all three of whom, subsequently, were arrested and convicted. They were imprisoned in Pentonville and Portland.

CHAPTER XVI.

A few days later Warder Lennon came into my cell, and told me that Stephens had been arrested during the night, and had just been brought in. He said this with some feeling. I was very much disturbed, but kept cool and asked where they had found him.

"In Fairfield House, with three or four others."

I knew then he was correct in what he said, but the news shook my hopes somewhat, which up to this had been very strong. "Who was the wretch this time?" was the first thought that struck my mind.

Next day we had all the particulars. Pierce Nagle, an employe in the mailing room of "The Irish People" office, and clerk of St. Laurence O'Toole's church, was the informer, and had for some time been giving information to the government. The day following there were six of us brought before Justice Strong, in the castle yard, to be identified by Nagle. We were arraigned on a long bench with three others, outsiders or new arrivals whom we did not know.

After waiting a short time a curtain was drawn aside close by where the magistrate sat, and Pierce Nagle confronted us. Strong asked him,

"Do you know any of these men?"

Nagle looked along the line, glancing at each, and after a pause said,

"Yes, I know the three on the extreme right."

"Look again, and see if you can identify the others."

He looked again up and down, "No," said he.

He stepped back, the curtain was drawn to again, concealing him. The three men whom he had recognized were unknown to us.

"Mrs. Nagle saved me," said I to myself, for the wretch knew me well.

About a week or so before my arrest Mrs. Nagle and

young James Haltigan, whose father, before his arrest, lived with the Nagles, called on me at my home. It was Sunday, my wife and I were sitting together just after dinner when they arrived. Mrs. Nagle said all the Prisoners' Fund was exhausted, and they had no money with which to buy provisions for them. I gave her a sovereign, and told her I would see some of the men that evening about the matter. I presume she

JAMES HALTIGAN.
(From a Recent Photograph)

told her husband, and to this circumstance I attributed her husband's reticence in my regard.

There had been no pointed suspicion of Nagle previous to that, but a few days before, as Mrs. Nagle and Mrs. Hannigan were going to the prison with a basket of food for the destitute prisoners, Dawson and two other detectives met them. Mrs. Hannigan was one of the Women's Committee who attended to this matter. Her husband was a sculptor, one of Denis Cromien's men.

Detective Dawson accosted Mrs. Nagle and said he wanted to speak to her. "If you have anything to say to me," said she, "say it, this woman is an intimate friend of mine," pointing to Mrs. Hannigan.

"What I have to say is strictly private, it is a message from your husband."

She flew to him, and, after a moment, turned round and told Mrs. Hannigan she would see her later, and went with Dawson. After Mrs. Hannigan had delivered her basket at the prison, she came directly to me, told me all I have stated, and said she feared Nagle was not right. This was the first indirect intimation of his treachery that I received. I went directly to Cronin, head of the cloth department at Pim Brothers, who was then the head Centre for Dublin. This was on a Friday. When he heard the story he said,

"Who can we depend on now? What do you advise?"

I suggested that he should secure or secrete any papers he might have and get away for a day until we would see what would happen. He got leave of absence for a few days, and went to Liverpool. The day after he left his residence was searched, and his department in Pim's overhauled. I have never since heard what became of him.

Mrs. Hannigan was one of the great souls of that time. She went around amongst the men she knew, warning and encouraging them, and saved some of the arms that were hidden, nearly all the time being escorted by the young man named above, James Haltigan, whose father, the printer of "The Irish People," was then a prisoner, and who was afterwards sentenced to seven years penal servitude.

Lawless, the attorney for the political prisoners, came to me one day on his rounds through the cells, and told me my wife and her sister, Mrs. Kavanagh, were constantly calling on him. Mrs. Kavanagh, by the way, was an old friend of his wife.

"They want me," he said, "to try and get you out on bail. You know," he said, "there is no use in trying."

"No, I am too sure of that," said I, "but the only way you can convince them is to try, and then they won't disturb you any more."

"Well," said he, "among the next batch of applicants for bail I shall send in, I will put your name among them."

In a day or two after, Denis Dowling Mulcahy and he came into my cell. Denis, being a law student, was allowed to help Lawless take the depositions of the prisoners.

He handed me a paper, and asked me could I subscribe to it. It read, among other things,—

"I am not a Fenian and never was. None of the arms found on my premises were mine. If admitted to bail I will not abscond."

I studied it for a minute or so, and said, "I can swear to the first and third conditions, but not to the second."

"Why not?" said Denis. "I would if I were in your place."

"Because I feel I cannot conscientiously do so."

"Then," said Lawless, "that ends it," and was about to leave.

"Can't you change the second condition?" said I.

"How?" said he.

"Make it general, and not particular. If you put it 'Those arms are not mine,' I shall swear it."

He took the amendment to Isaac Butt, chief counsel for the defense, who said, "that man ought to be in my position or in yours."

Lawless told me this when he brought me the amended form to sign.

We in Ireland were not Fenians, as we were in existence long before this romantic name was given to the American wing, by John O'Mahony, we were members of the I. R. B., so it was one of the Colonel's whims that saved me.

While taking dinner a couple of days after, Lennon the warder, rushed in, and congratulated me that I was to be admitted to bail.

"Don't fool me," I said to him.

"It is even so," he said, "come and see Lawless yourself—he is attending to some business in the second cell south."

When Lawless saw me he laughed, and shook my hand, saying "I want two sureties to go on your bonds." I gave him the names of James Cantwell, of the Star and Garter, and Michael Hogan, of Baggott Street Bridge. Two days after I was released on bail. Among others, I remember Patrick Hayburn was one of the lucky ones who left prison with me.

My wife was waiting at the gate of the jail to welcome me, and I can truly say I never felt more happiness than in seeing her on that occasion, and I know she felt equally happy. We drove to the residence of her sister, Miss Doyle, in Molesworth street, where I was heartily welcomed, and my release made a matter of rejoicing.

As soon as I found opportunity, I visited my shop, which I found closed and empty, and my business utterly ruined.

CHAPTER XVII.

I made an appointment with John J. Breslin before leaving the jail, to meet him that evening at eight o'clock in Leeson street. We met, and he told me of the efforts they were making to get Stephens out. Next day I saw Colonel Kelly and John Devoy who gave me the particulars. False keys were being made with which to unlock the prison doors, and arrangements were under way looking to the safe concealment of Stephens until he could be got out of the country. My friend, Patrick Durkin, a County Mayo man, whom I have not before mentioned up to this time, was very active in the movement. It was in his place the impression of the prison keys were taken from which the false keys were made. He was a grocer, and did a good business for Mr. Hogan at Baggott Street Bridge, and afterwards, on his own account, in Brunswick street. He was best man at my marriage, and a great friend of Edward Duffy. John Flood was another who was assigned to the work of rescuing Stephens. He was in disguise when I met him in Grafton street, dressed in a midshipman's uniform. I don't think his brother would have known him. He saluted me, and told me to follow him to the Star and Garter. He was jubilant about the project on hand, as all arrangements were nearly ready, and success seemed assured.

The key was made by Michael Lambert, a working optician and an active member of the organization. Mr. Lambert still resides in Dublin and was recently (June 3, 1905) the recipient of a handsome testimonial presented by his friends and admirers.

The night of November 24, 1865, was the date assigned for the rescue which was carried out successfully and with great secrecy.

Colonel Kelly originated the plan of escape, which could not, however, have been carried out were it not for the active co-operation of two members of the I. R. B. who held positions within the walls of the Bridewell.

These men were John J. Breslin, who held the post of hospital warder, and Terence Byrne, an ordinary warder in the prison. To these Colonel Kelly unfolded his plan; and although its carrying out entailed enormous risk on the part of Breslin, he did not for a moment hesitate when the liberty of his chief was concerned.

The principal difficulty was to procure a duplicate of the key which opened Stephens' cell, which was kept with others in the Governor's office. Breslin, with great daring, succeeded in taking an impression of the important key. This impression, on instructions from Colonel Kelly, he handed over to Michael Lambert, who lost no time in fashioning a duplicate, which he at once sent back to his friend Breslin.

On the night arranged for the rescue a picked party of armed men from the ranks of the I. R. B. assembled outside the walls of Richmond Bridewell somewhere about midnight. Colonel Kelly was in command, and the night was a magnificent one for his purpose. The rain came down in torrents, the wind blew great guns. Heaven's artillery boomed and reverberated through the deeps of the dark, impenetrable sky, and the daring Fenians only saw each other's faces in momentary glances by the lightning flashes. There was not a soul abroad but themselves that dreadful night.

Such was the scene outside the prison. A dozen daring men braving the fury of the elements, and the risk of transportation, through the fidelity to a cause. Inside in the ghastly, dark silence of the prison, broken ominously by the crashing and rolling of the thunder, John Breslin watched the minutes creep slowly toward the hour appointed by him with Colonel Kelly to open the door of Stephens' cell and deliver him safely into the charge of him and his companions.

The appointed hour, one o'clock, at last arrived, and Breslin introduced the key made for him by Michael Lambert into the lock of the Chief Organizer's prison cell. It did its work just as well as if it were the original key, and James Stephens, led by Breslin, lost no time in stealing rapidly, but cautiously, along the gloomy corridors. In the prison yard they were met by faithful Terry Byrne, who had two tables placed on top of each other against the

JOHN FLOOD.

wall, by the aid of which, and a rope thrown from the other side, which Breslin and Byrne held while he descended, James Stephens was delivered out of the hands of his enemies and into those of his good and faithful friends.

The names of the men who took active part in the memorable rescue were: Colonel Thomas J. Kelly, John

Devoy, Matt. Neill, Denis Duggan, William Brophy, John Harrison, John Mullon, John Lawlor, John Ryan, Patrick Kearney, Michael Cody, John Flood and the two prison warders, John Breslin and Daniel Byrne.

Next day all Dublin was agape. The Government was astounded. James Stephens had secretly and successfully made his escape from his closely guarded cell in Richmond Bridewell. Consternation, or rejoicing, as the case might be, was on every face as they read the news bulletins. Immediately a reward of one thousand pounds was offered for his capture or for information leading to his arrest, and three hundred pounds for the arrest of any person harboring, aiding, or assisting him.*

The second day after his escape, Stephens held the largest meeting of Centers and American officers he ever held in Dublin. He met provincial Centers from all quarters during the day, and the night session was for the Dublin Centers. This meeting was called for the purpose of bringing before the organization the great question, "Shall we strike now or wait?" Each one was asked in his turn what he thought best to be done.

I was more than surprised when Stephens selected me to give my opinion first. I told him I had only left prison two days before he did, and had not seen many friends, but would cast my vote with the American officers, who had closely investigated the situation, and were well posted on the true condition of affairs. All the Americans and all the Dublin Centers expressed themselves in favor of immediate action until he came to Denis Cromien, who was the only one at the meeting that argued and voted for delay. Stephens evidently was glad that our opinion was not unanimous and, to our surprise, endorsed Cromien's views.

Notwithstanding the majority were in favor of immediate action, and our discussion took up considerable time, it was eventually decided, mainly through Stephens' influence, that we would postpone the rising and wait. This resolution, to me, seemed simply a hocus pocus. Stephens plainly did not want to fight,

* See Appendix XXIII, Page 203 also Appendix XXVII, Page 208.

and I made up my mind that he did not want to proceed any further; in fact, I concluded then and there that Stephens' work was done, and his usefulness ended on that night of November 26, 1865.

With the aid of informers and perjurers, assisted by prejudiced or packed juries, and with civil laws suspended, our men were being arrested, tried and found guilty, and sentenced to life imprisonment or for long

JAMES STEPHENS.

terms. Few escaped. Edward Duffy, at this time in an advanced stage of consumption, was let out on account of the precarious condition of his health. I met him daily, either at my place or at the Star and Garter. John Flood I also met frequently. He always looked like a sailor or petty officer who had just stepped off one of Her Majesty's ironclads. He was invariably in great spirits and the picture of health, and was a man of resources, courage, and aptitude for any emergency that might arise.

On one occasion we talked over Stephens' escape, and how it was discovered. He told me that one of our friends, an Irish-American visitor, a good man, too, who knew the hour that it was to take place, left Dublin that evening for Cork. At the bar in the hotel where he stopped on his arrival in Cork he got into a chat with a gentleman, as he thought. In the course of conversation he spoke of Stephens' capture, and the apparently complete suppression of the revolutionary party. This was said, no doubt, with a view to bringing out the opinions of his chance acquaintance, and see what he thought on Irish affairs. Seeing this fellow rejoicing, as he went along, he became so enraged that he took out his watch and said: "I will bet you ten pounds that you have not got Stephens now." This, of course, was very unwise, but it is given as a fact. The fellow ran out and telegraphed to the chief secretary in Dublin, Sir Robert Peel, who in a short time was thundering at the gates of Richmond Bridewell. He did not have patience to send for information. He went himself. He asked the governor had he all his prisoners in safe keeping.

"Yes, Your Excellency, the keys are all here as usual, and all prison cells are secure."

"Let us see," said Sir Robert, "have you Stephens secure?"

They went to his cell and found it wide open, and the bird flown!

We could never find out the name of the individual who gave this information that came so near spoiling this great exploit. Any delay, any false steps, any miscalculation or accident would have resulted in failure.

The 24th of November, 1865, which was the date of Stephens' romantic escape, was a red letter day for Ireland because of its moral effect on the people. Stephens remained in Dublin until March, 1866, when he left for Paris in disguise. After a perilous voyage across the Channel to Scotland, he made his way to London, where he stopped at the Buckingham hotel, remained a short time, and then left for Paris, where he arrived in safety.

The evening he left Dublin Edward Duffy called on me in great glee.

"I have great news for you," said he. "The Captain is on his way to France."

"Well," said I, "Ed, I firmly believe you will never see him again."

"Don't say that," said he, "'tis treason."

"Nonsense," said I, "I saw him exhibit the white feather at the meeting of the Centers, held on the night after he got out of jail, and I felt then he would never fight."

I did not attempt to shake Duffy's faith in him, but he afterwards came to share my views, and when in the dock denounced him.

CHAPTER XVIII

Stephens, before leaving for France, had appointed Duffy in his place, as head of the organization in Ireland, and promised to send him money when he arrived in Paris. Poor Ed was stopping quietly at the European hotel, and had not a pound in his possession.

Miss Ellen O'Leary was there also, meeting all demands and attending to everything connected with the organization. She filled up with her counsel and advice the gaps caused by the arrest of the various leaders, and so matters went for some time.

No financial assistance came from Stephens, although he sent for his wife and her sister, and according to Eddy O'Leary, John's youngest brother who was in Paris at the time, it required two cabs to take their baggage to the hotel, and afterwards had his sister-in-law put into an aristocratic seminary. It required considerable means to do this, but not a shilling for poor Duffy and the cause. I knew the condition Duffy had been left in. Were it not for the kindness of Mrs. Moloney, the lady of the hotel, he could not have existed. No wonder he denounced Stephens in the dock.

Stephens' arrival in Paris caused consternation in Dublin Castle, while the accounts given in the newspapers of the particulars of his escape made them the laughing-stock of the world.

The large rewards offered for his capture or information regarding his whereabouts had been offered in vain, the vigilance of the secret police had been baffled and set at naught, and in consequence the authorities were paralyzed.

But after all it would have been better for Stephens and for Ireland that it had never been done. If he had been left in prison his fame would have remained untarnished. If he had kept faith with those who had given him his first commission, and when it was demanded of him, had handed over the organization to a military council at the proper time he might have

MISS ELLEN O'LEARY.

saved it. Our American friends did not preserve those papers, and when they made the demand had nothing to go on. (1)

---

(1) While affairs were progressing slowly in Ireland, a serious division occurred in the governing ranks of the Fenian Brotherhood in America.

When the organization became numerically powerful and influential throughout the States, it became necessary to adopt a representative form of control and management for the

Duffy went to the West, to his home, but still continued as tireless and persistent as ever in the good work, until he was arrested on the 11th of March, 1866.

Colonel Kelly went to America, rallying the men there, and took charge of the Central office on the 18th of June, 1866. From that date to the close of the year all was excitement and although the arrests continued (a large number being amongst the military) the feeling of resistance remained as intense as ever.

---

whole body, and to that end an annual congress was inaugurated and at which plans were formed and policies promulgated looking towards the advancement of the Cause and the early preparations for a revolution on the soil of Ireland.

For various and, as we know now, good and sufficient reasons the invasion of Ireland was repeatedly postponed, a course of action which caused much openly expressed dissatisfaction, mixed with blame for O'Mahony and Stephens, as the delay was attributed to them.

In this connection it may be well to say a few words about the relations existing between Stephens and O'Mahony. After the collapse of the '48 Movement, when in Paris together their relations were those of fast and close friends. In the Fenian Movement their relations continued as of old up to the time of Stephens' visit to America, and perhaps a year after, when things began to change. It would seem as if a mutual dissatisfaction in a mild form sprang up. Each felt his personal responsibility keenly and no doubt considered he was not receiving that support from the other which he had been led to expect or which the condition of affairs demanded. In addition to this, a strong outside pressure was continually being exercised demanding immediate action in Ireland.

Stephens on several occasions expressed dissatisfaction with what he considered an inquisitorial tendency on the part of O'Mahony, who continually kept sending over on special missions men who wanted to "investigate" and then return to America to "report." Nothing came of those reports, and it is a fact there were instances where men came over ostensibly to investigate, but in reality they came on their own business.

John O'Mahony was Head Centre and Chief Executive Officer of the Fenian Brotherhood in America. The executive power of the organization was vested in him, and among other duties he was authorized and empowered to sign all bonds of the Irish Republic. The Central Council consisted of five members, with the Head Centre as presiding officer, and constituted a military board. This board had power to appoint a military and naval director or one for each department, and had full authority to adjudicate all questions pertaining to the organi-

After all was considered, the chances, we thought, were in our favor. Col. Tom Kelly returned from America, took Ed. Duffy's place, and gave new vigor to the movement. His late visit to New York confirmed our faith in the promises made at that side.*

General Halpin was again active, as was also Captain O'Rourk (Beecher), an indefatigable man who managed everything he undertook with tact and address. His movements baffled all the vigilance of the detectives who were continually on his track.

John Flood, the man of resources, and Ryan, of Liverpool, were unknown to the police, they could go where they pleased.

So matters went on. Every man stood to his post. We were gaining in prestige and influence.

---

zation. They were supposed to be constantly in session. District Centres were elected to represent District organizations at the Annual Congress, and when elected received a commission from the Head Centre. Their duty was to supervise the organization in their respective districts, to establish Circles and make regular monthly reports to the Central organization.

To assist O'Mahony in governing the organization, a body called the Senate was called into existence, which body in a short time attempted to take control and dictate the policy to be pursued by the Fenian Brotherhood. Two parties developed in the Senate—one in favor of invading Ireland, the other Canada. See Appendix XLIII, Page 239.

O'Mahony wrote to Stephens complaining of the attitude of the men advocating the invasion of Canada. They argued that it was inopportune at that time to invade Ireland. England possessed then, as now, a powerful navy, with her base of unlimited supplies only a few hours' sail from Ireland; consequently, they said, it would be madness to raise the banner of revolution then. As a substitute they suggested that the power of the Fenian Brotherhood be turned towards Canada as an objective and that an army could be quickly thrown across the border and a blow struck at the power of England without crossing the ocean.

In reply to O'Mahony's letter Stephens denounced the dissenting Senators as "rotten branches" and said he would soon come to America and lash them into line. The receipt of this unwise and indiscreet letter resulted in still further widening the breach. The Canadian party in the Senate seceded from the parent body and elected Colonel William R. Roberts President.

* See Appendix LXXXIV, Page 278.

CHAPTER XIX.

The Special Commission for the trial of political prisoners opened in Green street, Dublin, the 27th of November, 1865, and the trials commenced. It took a long time to get a jury, and all out on bail were obliged to attend from day to day.

The third day, when my wife and I were going into court, the policeman on guard at the door stopped me, and asked if I had a sheriff's order. I said I had none.

"I can't admit you," said he.

I told him I was one of the prisoners out on bail, and was obliged to attend.

"I don't care who you are, I can't admit you."

Pat Roantree was with us, and he was told the same.

A big burly sergeant who was walking up and down said, in passing, "Damn fools, go tell your friends on your bail bonds you would not be admitted, and get out."

Pat and I took the hint. We went to Kingstown and put in a very pleasant day. In the evening I went to see Lawless, after court adjourned, and told him the circumstances. "I am glad," said he, "as you won't save yourself as I told you to do. Don't come to me until I send for you."

The same evening I was at my friend's Patrick Durkin's, which was a place we frequented for news. To my great surprise the policeman that refused to let me in the court room was there. I did not know he was a friend of ours, but he was, and proved afterwards to be a staunch one.

Towards the close of the commission, my name was called. In explanation of my absence, Lawless got up and explained to the court that I attended until I was refused admission. Lawson, the attorney-general, asked for a warrant, to have me brought to court, but Judge Fitzgerald said, "Mr. Attorney, serve him with a short order." Another case was called in my place, the last for that commission, and was found guilty. The court adjourned to Cork, and left me still at large.

It was in Cork where Counsellor Dowse gave Nagle the worrying that vexed him, when he asked the Counsellor: "Do you think I'm a dog, that you speak to me in this manner?"

"Oh no," said Dowse, "God forbid I should compare you to such a faithful animal."

"Well," retorted Nagle, "there are some decent men I have not identified, but now I won't spare one of them."

That remark made several of us uneasy, and we were sure he would carry out his threat when the court would come back to Dublin.

The uprising was now the question of the hour. All began to prepare and make ready. No lack of ardor could be seen; on the contrary, all were at the highest pitch under the circumstances.

The failure of the attack on Chester castle by the treachery of Corydon did not deter the rising of the 4th of March, because Corydon's treachery was not known then.

CHAPTER XX.

The 4th of March, 1867, the night of the rising arrived, I was at supper with my wife and her sister when John Ryan called. General Halpin had sent him for me. He was waiting at the Bleeding Horse in Camden street. I took leave of my wife and went with him, and found General Halpin. As there was a report given out at the time that the General was drunk on that occasion, I take this opportunity of again pronouncing that it was a calumny—without a shred of truth to support it. I never saw him more cool, calm, and rational than he was on that night. He gave me my orders, but told me to await hearing from him before putting them into execution.

I called on my friend Durkin, and found that acting on instructions all the men had gone to Tallaght. As soon as Durkin shut up his place we remained together and prepared to execute the expected orders when received. While waiting in his back parlor, he brought in a young man who had come some distance, and who wanted to see the man in charge.

I satisfied myself that he was all right. He handed me a paper signed by the parish priest of that place. asking for orders to blow up the bridges and stating that all was ready.

We told him that action in that quarter would depend on certain contingencies, which had not yet arisen and advised him to return and hold himself in readiness to execute their purpose, but to take no action until he received positive instructions which we guaranteed would be surely forwarded to him should occasion require it.

On further inquiry we found he had come post haste and had no money to take him back. We furnished him with sufficient funds and sent him away full of hope that the men of his town would be given a chance to strike a blow for Ireland.

Of all the nights that have ever passed over my head that memorable night of the 4th of March which had been scheduled as the night of the "rising" was the most furious that I remember. The wind blew a hurricane, accompanied by sleet and rain. The streets were deserted, save by an occasional car passing now and then, and the only sounds heard were those of wind and rain falling in torrents.

We waited impatiently and anxiously during the long hours of the night, and coming towards morning the strain became, if possible, more intense from the continued anxiety. At length news came, but not direct to us. One or two returned friends in passing reported that the attempt was a complete failure and that the rendezvous had been betrayed. Sir Hugh Rose and staff, with a strong military force, had anticipated their assembling at Tallaght, and on the morning of the 5th had captured the most daring of our men. The only casualty reported was the death of Stephen O'Donohue, who was shot and killed.

A few hours later we witnessed the saddest sight I had ever beheld. Marching down Grafton street, manacled and disarmed, were some of our bravest and best men, surrounded by a strong force of military, who were escorting them to the Castle Yard for examination, to be followed by punishment and degradation.

During the day General Halpin came into Dublin in a discouraged and disheartened state of mind and body. As the rising had collapsed and nothing more could be done just then, he was conducted to a place of safety. Soon stragglers began to arrive from Stepaside, each with his own story of what might have been done. Poor Stephen O'Donoghue was the only one who did not return.

To explain this fiasco, for such it was, I must go back to Stephens' return to Paris in '66. After he had failed in uniting the O'Mahony and Roberts parties, the

Fenian Military Council besought him to fulfill his oft-repeated promise to start a revolution in Ireland, as they considered the time had arrived for a rising, but he emphatically declined. Notwithstanding his refusal, the Military Council felt that the time had come when an attempt to fulfill the many pledges made by the organization should be undertaken, and they decided that, come what may, the flag of insurrection

WM. R. ROBERTS.
President of the Fenian Brotherhood.

should be raised in Ireland without further delay. They commenced active preparations at once. Early in January, 1867, the following Irish-American officers arrived in Ireland quietly, unobtrusively, and entirely unobserved by the Government: General Thomas F. Burke, General Halpin, Colonel Kelly, Captain John McCafferty, Captain William Mackay and many others. They were assigned each to a special locality, and without delay set to work energetically to organize the insurrection. They found the difficulties in the way almost insurmountable. The people were badly armed or not armed at all. Many of the local leaders were opposed to a rising at that time, and the clergy almost to a man antagonistic. Still they persevered and accomplished wonders in the brief time given them.

February 11th, 1867, was fixed on as the date of the rising, and officers and men were sent to their respective posts with instructions to take the field on that date. The veteran Irish-American officers of distinction who came to lend the aid of their military experience gained in the Civil War, were quetly assigned to important and strategic points, and every arrangement possible under adverse conditions were made in advance, it being distinctly understood that the rising was to take place as far as possible simultaneously at all points. Chester Castle, in England, in which was stored a vast amount of war material, was also to be surprised and attacked on that date. (1.)

Before the 11th of February arrived the leaders

---

(1) William Randall Roberts was born in County Cork, Ireland, on February 6, 1830. He received an academic education and came to the United States in 1849. He secured employment with A. T. Stewart, the great dry goods merchant, New York, and eventually started in the dry goods business himself at No. 252 Bowery, when that thoroughfare was the great shopping district. His store was called the "Crystal Palace," and was as well known as is the most typical establishment of that kind in New York to-day.

Roberts did an immense business and retired in 1869 with a fortune that passed the million dollar mark. His real estate holdings were extensive, as may be judged from the fact that he went on Richard F. Connolly's bond for $250,000, qualifying in $500,000, when that noted politician of Tweed times took office as Comptroller of New York.

After retiring from business Roberts went into politics, and to this is ascribed the loss of the greater part of his fortune. He was elected in 1869 a Representative to the Forty-second and Forty-third Congresses. In 1877 he was elected Alderman-at-Large, and was President of the New York Board of Aldermen that year and the next.

To the scheme for the invasion of Canada was due in a great measure the disastrous split which took place in 1866 in the

learned that the Government was in possession of their plans. An informer, named Corydon, who was present at Chester, had been supplying information to the Government since September, '66. On finding their plans betrayed, urgent dispatches (in cipher), were sent by messengers and otherwise, to all the leaders at the various places, to postpone the revolt for the time being.

In Kerry, where Colonel John J. O'Connor was in command, the dispatch failed to reach him and, promptly on time, he led a revolt which extended to Cork and Limerick, scaring the "loyal" and "law-abiding" people around Killarney and Cahirciveen in a most unseemly manner.

When, later on, O'Connor received the belated dispatch and learned that the rising was not general, he retreated to the mountains and disbanded his force. Colonel O'Connor's rising, it is true, was premature and isolated, but it demonstrated the fact that he and his

---

Fenian Brotherhood. John O'Mahony was opposed to the scheme, and his opposition cost him much of his popularity. A convention was held in New York, when a Senate, a War Department, a State Department and a Financial Department were provided for, chiefly as a means of robbing O'Mahony of his power. Later he was deposed by the Senate and Roberts chosen as President. Two factions then came into being, and between them they brought disaster upon the cause.

"Envy, hatred and all uncharitableness" took possession of the hearts of men on both sides, and day by day the breach was widened.

Roberts persevered in his plans and the battle of Ridgeway was the beginning and the end of his invasion, although it is claimed that but for the interference of the United States Government the victory won by General John O'Neil would have been followed up by the veterans from the Union armies until the green flag waved over every city in the Dominion.

O'Mahony, urged by B. Doran Killian, sought to foil Roberts and snatch whatever glory might come to him by sending a force to Campo Bello. It was failure, however, everywhere. The fight went on bitterly between the two parties, and even James Stephens, who came across the ocean specially to try and put an end to the dispute, found his mission practically without results.

William R. Roberts died in New York City on Monday, August 9, 1897, aged sixty-seven years.

men were ready to do and to dare, and there were a hundred thousand others equally ready, waiting an opportunity to emulate his example.

Colonel Horsford, in command of the British forces in that section, was sent in pursuit, but he prudently decided it was unnecessary and perhaps unhealthy, to follow the "rebels" into the mountains, and telegraphed to Dublin Castle that the insurrection was squelched.

The rising was originally intended to have taken place on the 11th of February, but for various important reasons it was postponed to a later date. In the last week of February word was sent out that Shrove Tuesday, March 5th, was to inaugurate the beginning of a supreme effort for the liberation of Ireland, and they were to assemble at their various posts on the night of the 4th. It happened that the date selected was extremely cold and tempestuous, which caused much suffering to the men who went out.

The principal place of rendezvous for the Dublin men were the Palmerston fields, Rathmines, and the village of Tallaght. At the former place some 500 men assembled at 11 p. m., while at Tallaght the number was about 800. The arrangements for arming them were of the most unsatisfactory character, and many had to content themselves with an indifferent pike, which is rather a poor weapon with which to meet a man armed with a rifle. There were many skirmishes between the police and the insurgents on that eventful night, the Fenians capturing several of the police, whom they disarmed and took along as prisoners of war. At Tallaght there was a brisk encounter in which Stephen O'Donoghue was shot dead. A party of Fenians, under Patrick Lennon, attacked Stepaside and Glencullen police barracks, both of which he captured, seizing and carrying off the arms.

In Drogheda the people assembled in the market square to the number of one thousand, and placed themselves under the command of Colonel Patrick Leonard, an American officer of ability and bravery. He made a bold stand for a little while, but had to succumb to the superior forces of the enemy.

The Tipperary Fenians assembled in force at Bansha, under the command of Colonel Thomas Francis Bourke. They marched to Ballyhurst, where, being armed only with pikes, they met defeat at the hands of the Thirty-first Regiment of Infantry. Colonel

PATRICK LENNON.
Who led the Fenians at Stepaside and Glencullen.

Bourke was captured while rallying his men, and was afterwards sentenced to be hung, drawn and quartered. The speech he delivered in the dock is second only to Emmet's immortal utterance. His sentence was commuted to imprisonment for life and he was finally pardoned.

In Limerick, Cork and Clare attempts to arouse the people were also made, but were attended with little or no success. Peter O'Neill Crowley, aided by Captain John McClure and Edward Kelly, made a noble stand in southeastern Cork. They held their forces together for nearly a month, but were finally captured in Kilclooney Wood, after a gallant stand, in which the brave Crowley was killed. Captain McClure and Edward Kelly spent many years in prison, but were finally pardoned. Kelly died some years ago in Boston, but John McClure is still living—a prominent lawyer in New York.

In the City of Cork over two thousand men turned out in response to the call to arms.* They were under the command of Colonel O'Brien and Captain Mackey, but were soon defeated by the forces sent against them. Captain Mackey carried on a desultory warfare for almost a year after the rising, appearing here and there and capturing many police barracks and coast guard stations and then disappearing just as rapidly. He kept the authorities in a ferment until he was finally captured on February 7, 1868.

No attempt at a rising was made in the West of Ireland, as they had been promised the services of experienced military officers who were not sent them, consequently they declined to turn out without competent leaders.

The rising was attended by many acts of bravery and self-sacrifice, and stands out as an evidence of Irish patriotism under the most hopeless circumstances. The people were virtually unarmed, had to face one of the best equipped armies in Europe, and were crushed by overwhelming numbers. In addition to this, the movement took place during one of the most terrific storms which ever visited Ireland, and this fact alone would have been sufficient to scatter the thousands of brave and devoted men who risked their lives in defence of their country.

Soon after the collapse of the rising, the leaders, in

* See Appendix LXXXVI, Page 282.

explanation and extenuation of their failure, issued an address or proclamation simultaneously in Ireland and America, setting forth the grievances of the Irish people and appealing to lovers of liberty the world over, particularly to the brave, fair-minded men of England, showing them the cause of Freedom was theirs as well as ours. The Government in turn took occasion to issue another proclamation, declaring the country was tranquil and peaceful, while every vessel entering an Irish port was boarded by police, armed with rifles and cutlasses, who arrested all suspicious persons without the formality of a warrant, and took them to jail.

Public attention was now directed to the military courts martial, which revealed conditions in the ranks that surprised every one, but none more than the Government itself. It finally became alarmed, as the investigation progressed, at the great number of men accused and eventually the publicity given to the honeycombed and dove-tailed conspiracy which had grown up within the army, compelled them to suspend military tribunals, as the deeper they probed the more disaffection they found. Even soldiers in Scotch regiments were found to be connected with the movement.

The men who were mainly responsible for the demoralization of the British army were John Boyle O'Reilly, Pagan O'Leary, John P. O'Brien, Charles McCarthy, Thomas Chambers and James Montague. As a result of their work, it was found that some 13,000 Irish men in the English army had taken an oath to bring about the independence of their native country.

The last sitting of the Special Commission was in session in Dublin, and a great many of us were in suspense regarding Nagle's forthcoming evidence and the nature of the disclosures which he had threatened to make when in Cork. He evidently reconsidered the matter, as he did not implicate any others during the session. But informer Corydon did. He testified, among other things, that he attended meetings in my house and at James Cantwell's, but his evidence on this occasion was broken down. This terminated the work of the Commission in Dublin, and Cantwell called on me and advised me to leave the city, saying that as the Commission had closed its work, my bondsmen were no longer responsible for my appearance; in fact, he suggested that I would act wisely in getting out of the country as soon as possible.

I made hurried arrangements and left that night for Liverpool, where I met William Horan, an old friend, who took me to his lodging in the suburbs. I learned that all hope was not yet abandoned in England, and that Colonel Tom Kelly was expecting aid from America, but after a few weeks' time word was passed around that all was over for the present.

CHAPTER XXI.

I took passage in one of the Anchor Line packets via Quebec, for New York, by the northern passage. Through the instrumentality of a friend I secured an introduction to one of the officers of the vessel, who favored me in many ways during the voyage. He gave me the key of his room, with permission to use it at any time. Fortune also gave me a congenial traveling companion in the person of a young Cockney, not long married, and employed by a London stock broking firm, who was on his way to Canada to see after some investments for his company. Our first day out brought us together, and we became fast friends. I got talking with him about the loneliness I felt after parting with my wife and child, and he, happening to be in the same mood, confessed that he felt equally lonesome and blubbered through his tears that this was the hour they expected him home every evening. "I was just thinking of them when you spoke," said he. "How singular that our cases are so remarkably alike. Let us go down to the cabin and have a bottle of Guinness." We went down and consoled each other, and every day after that we put in an appearance in that hospitable quarter.

The Anchor Line boats had to call at Moville for the Irish mails. Our steamer entered the mouth of the River Foyle and came to anchor awaiting the mails and passengers, which were brought alongside in a lighter. We had on board a few emigrants from Liverpool, who climbed on the rail and looked towards the town while awaiting the approach of the mail boat. Soon we noticed two long boats approaching: one filled with red-coated soldiers and the other with police, which gave rise to alarm in my breast. As soon as they came near I decided I had better keep out of the way for the time being and quietly made my way to the officer's room, where I locked myself in. This room was on the port side of the vessel and they came on board from the starboard side, consequently I did not see them arrive or depart, but waited with the best patience I could until I thought they must have gone away, when I came out from my place of concealment.

When I came on deck I accosted a shrewd looking fellow, one of the emigrants, and asked him what the police wanted and what the military were doing on board. "I don't know," said he smiling knowingly. "They said they were looking for a couple of absconders, but I think they are in search of some political suspects who are expected to make an attempt to reach America by this route. The police have not gone yet, perhaps they may find the men they are in search of before they leave."

A little later, while going down the companion way, I met a sergeant of police coming up. I went to the bar and found my friend waiting for me, who commenced to talk in his pleasant, good natured way with his Cockney accent, and I noticed that the sergeant had followed me down and was lingering around, listening to what was being said, but after a while went away. My friend asked what was the object of this visit of the authorities.

"I cannot say," said I, "but I understand it is a common occurrence in this country to search boats and scrutinize passengers entering or leaving port."

"I don't wonder," said he, "at the Irish being disaffected, and I am sure we would not tolerate this thing in England."

We slowly finished our bottles, while I remained as quiet and inconspicuous as possible until I heard the anchor weighed, when I knew the police had departed.

I found my Cockney friend a genial, pleasant and cheerful companion and we became quite good friends during the voyage. I also cultivated the acquaintance of the shrewd looking chap who told me the police were looking for political suspects. He informed me that he was leaving his home in Ireland because he was suspected of being a Fenian, and if he remained his father, who was steward to some landlord in Donegal, would undoubtedly lose his position, while he would be sent to prison for an indefinite period on mere suspicion. It was his first trip away from home and naturally he was anxious and nervous about his future in a strange land. When I told him I was acquainted in New York and could possibly help him on his arrival there he became a changed man.

We had a tedious but pleasant voyage across the Atlantic, made agreeable by the fact that the officers and crew were genial and obliging. In due time we arrived in British territory, steaming up the St. Lawrence, a noble and majestic stream. Very few craft hove in sight until we reached Quebec, which contains a fine fortress on a well-selected spot commanding all the approaches from the river. The splendid view of this fortress and the beautiful river scenery engaged our attention until we reached port.

We remained in the city but a couple of hours and, of course, had little opportunity of closely observing the people. From casual observation they seemed to be careless, easy going and without the "go" and "get up" about them that distinguishes Americans. They were living under an accursed flag, which perhaps accounted for the ear-marks of slavery that I imagined were visible to me.

We took a train on the Grand Trunk R. R. for Montreal, which we found a beautiful city, delightfully located on the St. Lawrence and where we remained some hours before proceeding to Rouse's Point, which is on the boundary line separating Canada from the United States. When I crossed the dividing line I distinctly felt a great and perceptible change come over my whole being, as if an oppressive weight was lifted from me. I immediately declared myself to my friends and gave them my real name, as up to that I had been traveling under my wife's name.

In a few hours we were transferred to one of those nice little steamers plying on Lake Champlain and which are only to be found on American waters, and felt so much at home that after supper I went to bed and slept undisturbed all the way down until the boat was moored. When awakened by one of the deck hands I was surprised to find that my friends had got off at Burlington. The captain, after hearing my story and enjoying my discomfiture, told me it was all right, I would meet my friends at Albany by taking the train which was about starting. He was right and I found no difficulty in locating them in Albany. They did not know what had become of me and were puzzled regarding what to do with my baggage. We proceeded to New York by the Albany boat, enjoying a delightful sail on the grandest and most picturesque river in America.

Coming down the Hudson that evening I found myself alone, gazing at the ever changing panorama visible from where I sat, and all the events of the past few years came floating around me. Was all lost? What had been accomplished? Had anything been gained? Those questions I asked myself over and over again, but could not find a satisfactory answer. In summing up I found one certainty: Ireland was united. She had been taught to stand up and assert her rights. She was no longer a corpse on the dissecting table. A great many abuses had been set aside, a great many changes had taken place for the better, and there had been a general awakening to the emergencies and necessities of the hour. For those blessings I thanked God with my whole heart and finally concluded that our efforts had not been wasted and that a great deal had been accomplished.

In analysing causes and results, I decided that Stephens and O'Mahony, who never worked in harmony, were both of them unfit for the great responsibility they had undertaken. In my opinion, it was mainly O'Mahony's fault. He always kept around him a lot of flatterers, an imbecile pack, who were no use whatever to the movement, who could not get the confidence of anyone but that one good natured soul who loved to listen to flattering stories of himself and of the chieftains of old, without taking a single lesson from their misfortunes and ultimate extinction.

Among these worthies was Red Jim McDermott,

the informer, a wretch who was ostracized in Dublin by all his associates after his return from Italy. His conduct was said to be of the most immoral kind, so that the Dublin men refused to have anything to do with him. This was reported to Stephens, who said they were merely eccentricities which might be attributed to the life he led in the Papal Brigade!

When leaving Dublin for America he asked for a letter of introduction to John O'Mahony, which was not given him, but a letter signed by six Dublin Centres was sent to O'Mahony, advising him not to place any confidence in him as he was a bad man. O'Mahony provided him with a position, I think that of assistant secretary, because he abused Stephens. Red McDermott was the illegitimate son of a Dublin police magistrate named O'Brien. His mother's name was McDermott. Before joining the Papal Brigade he had been an altar boy in a chapel at Haddington Road. When in Italy he had succeeded in imposing on his Holiness the Pope, who invested him with the Order of St. Sylvester, which regalia he took care to display on every possible occasion.

I must say before closing that throughout the whole organization a strong moral and religious feeling prevailed and a great respect for Christian Doctrine when it was untrammeled by political influence or personal animosities. Our love and respect for the Soggarth aroon was never questioned.

Some of our best men were devout Catholics, among them, General Thomas Burke, Charles J. Kickam, Hugh Brophy, John Haltigan, Mulcahy, Duffy, and thousands of others. It is true, there were a few fire-eaters, but they did not amount to much. Some of them, afterwards, became members of Parliament and some others informers.

My impression, gained by experience and observation, is that the better the Christian the better the soldier he makes when fighting for liberty, truth and justice. A reliable, faithful friend and stanch lover of his country never despairs, but continues to trust in Providence that the end will make amends for his devotion.

CHAPTER XXII.

In the preceding chapters the names of many brave men who did noble duty in distant places, and with whom I did not often come into personal contact, do not appear, for the simple reason that my narrative is a personal one and deals only with the matters with which I was identified or closely connected, and the facts of which I can vouch for as being absolutely true.

But as these men were part and parcel of the movement and deserve the most honorable mention that could be given them, I will endeavor, in this chapter, to do justice to the memory of all whose names I can now recall.

Among the brave and faithful men whose names I have not yet mentioned, or perhaps barely mentioned, and the noble, heroic women who took up the cause when their husbands or relatives were arrested and imprisoned were: Miss Ellen O'Leary, Miss Catherine Mulcahy, Miss Maria Shaw, Miss Butler, John O'Connor, James Haltigan, John Hallowed, Michael Lambert, William Brophy, Matthew O'Neill, Jeremiah O'Farrell, Edward Martin, John Neville, Daniel Downing, James Cook, Samuel Cavanagh, James O'Callaghan, Patrick Lennon, Michael Monks (1) and Mercer McDermott.

In speaking of the work performed by individuals I cannot refrain from mentioning the following: John O'Connor, brother of James O'Connor, a boy at the time, who was of incalculable value to the organization—trustworthy, discreet and business-like—to him

---

(1) Patrick Lennon died in Florida in 1901. He owned an orange plantation there. Michael Monks died in New York about 1894, and is buried in the Irish Patriot's Plot in Calvary Cemetery, Brooklyn. A monument to the memory of all the veterans of the I. R. B. buried in Calvary is now being gotten up.

was intrusted most important secret messages, which couldn't be intrusted to the mails. He had many narrow escapes, but through his dexterity and perseverance succeeded in every project he undertook.

Another boy deserving of special mention is James Haltigan, who stood beside his father in the dock and

JAMES AND JOHN O'CONNOR.

endeavored, as far as a mere youth could, to make amends for his loss after he was sentenced. He, too, was discreet and unassuming, and frequently carried safely and successfully many important despatches which were matters of life and death to individuals and to the movement, not only in Kilkenny and the surrounding counties, but in Dublin itself.

After the escape of Stephens, when Edward Duffy, then in poor health, took charge of the organization on the request of the fugitive chief, Miss Ellen O'Leary volunteered her services to the organization. She possessed great executive ability, while her social position gave her many advantages which few in the movement possessed at the time. She was respected by all who knew her, not only for being the sister of the condemned editor, but for her own accomplishments and charmingways, which made her like a ministering angel among the families of the prisoners, imparting hope and confidence to all by her firm belief in our ultimate success. Duffy being at the time in a most pitiable condition on acount of lung trouble, most of the executive work devolved on Miss O'Leary. At this crisis John O'Connor was always on hand, and his invaluable services were fully appreciated.

When Col. Thomas J. Kelly became Chief of the Organization, after Duffy's second arrest, he imparted new vigor to the movement. Among other things, he organized a Signal Corps and selected the members himself. One of his first selections was John Hallowel, a young man who worked in Fitzpatrick's, corner of Dame and George streets, Dublin, a friend of John Devoy, both coming from the same place. Young Hallowed was an expert in the corps, was appointed lieutenant and had a great deal to do with Stephens' rescue. although not one of the actual rescuers. He gave his overcoat and revolver to one of the parties, which by some chance or accident he never saw afterwards. He was also a friend of Michael Lambert, the artist, who made the false keys used in the escape of Stephens, also of Wm. Brophy and Matthew O'Neill, two of the rescuers. He was a trusted messenger of Colonel O'Kelly between Stephens and himself, and is now a successful business man in Chicago.

Another lady who deserves a niche in the temple of honor is Miss Butler, a fashionable Dublin dressmaker and a true Nationalist, who was above suspicion, having for a clientele the loyal elite of the city. No one would ever dream her home could be a retreat for a famous outlaw and rebel, but it was in her cosy, comfortable home that Stephens found safety. It was from this asylum, months later, he departed with Flood to risk his fate in a coal schooner. After his safe arrival in France it began to be mooted around where Stephens had been so carefully concealed, notwithstanding the great rewards for his capture and threats of ruin for anyone who would harbor him. No one knew for

MICHAEL BRESLIN.

sure but a few, and Dublin was lost in bewilderment. After some time suspicion fell on the good Samaritan, but it was only suspicion, still it was sufficient to cause her to lose all the patronage of the flunkeys, including the respectable "loyal" shoneens, who considered themselves superior to the mere Irish.

Miss Mulcahy, sister of Denis Dowling Mulcahy, leaving her nice, quiet home by the Anner, came to the city on hearing of his arrest. Miss O'Leary soon found occupation for her talents, which up to this time had been confined to the care of her aged father, who was as hopeful to the last as the youngest among us. She threw herself into the cause as earnestly and unsparingly as might be expected of her. It was wonderful to see what these good young women were capable of doing and the fatigues and anxieties they underwent, when once they became interested. She loved her brother Denis and, if necessary, was willing to take his place in the ranks or in the prison cell.

In this connection Miss Shaw well deserves to be remembered. She was in charge of the Ladies' Committee Rooms and devoted herself unsparingly to the task of attending to the wants of the families of the prisoners.

Neil Breslin, a modest, unassuming young man, rendered good service. He was a brother of John and Michael Breslin, but much younger. He was a stripling at this time but took a man's part—the work done and the services rendered by this class of youths can never be fully known. They worked with a will, they received no pay, no emolument of any kind, all their young energies were concentrated in the movement that took possession of their every faculty and they never wearied and never failed in the good work.

Jeremiah O'Farrell, of Kilkenny, was one of the most active young men in his native city. When Haltigan was leaving there to take charge of the Irish People newspaper he brought O'Farrell with him to Dublin and appointed him caretaker of the office building, No. 12 Parliament Street. He also brought two printers with him, who were devoted to the movement—Edward Martin and John Neville. These men continued their activity in the metropolis and soon had a Circle of their own, of which Haltigan was the centre.

Daniel Downing, of Skibbereen, brother of Colonel Patrick and Major Denis Downing of the American army, was another of these young men who distinguished themselves, as was also the good and earnest Cornelius O'Mahony, of Skibbereen, an unsophisticated but gifted school teacher who was one of the first convicted. He was acquitted by the first jury, but Barry, the prosecutor (called Judas Barry for his recreancy to the Irish cause), immediately put him on trial again with a packed jury and, of course, found him guilty. He was sentenced to five years' penal servitude.

NIAL J. BRESLIN.
(From a Recent Photograph.)

James Cook, Samuel Cavanagh, James Callaghan, Patrick Lennon and Mercer McDermott, all of the city of Dublin, were among the most active workers in the cause—all faithful men who nobly did their duty. They have all, with the exception of Samuel Cavanagh and James Cook, passed to their reward. May they and all who have suffered in Ireland's cause rest in peace.

FINIS.

APPENDIX

TO

DENIEFFE'S RECOLLECTIONS.

FOREWORD.

The following Fenian letters, papers, reports, etc., collected from many sources, have been arranged in chronological order and printed verbatim from the originals.

O'Donovan Rossa placed at my disposal not only his own papers, but also the papers and correspondence of John O'Mahony which were given him after the death of the latter. The papers of General Sweeny were made accessible through the courtesy of his son, Mr. William M. Sweeny. Autograph letters by James Stephens, John Mitchell, and others were supplied by Mr. John Quinn, Secretary of the Irish Literary Society. The papers of Dr. Denis Dowling Mulcahy are in the possession of the writer of this brief instroduction—in fact, there is so much material, I have been unable to find space for all and have therefore made a selection which I think sufficient for the purpose.

Photographs and portraits for the Recollections and Appendix were supplied by Mr. P. J. Meehan, Mr. James Haltigan, Mr. P. W. Dunne and others.

It is to be regretted that all these historic letters, papers, photographs, etc., have not been collected and deposited in some public library, where they would be accessible for all time to future writers and students of history. They are added to this work, in the form of an Appendix, because they have a direct bearing on Mr. Denieffe's Recollections and are supplementary to and corroborative of his Narrative. In addition they give an interesting *inside* history of the movement and throw a strong light on the personality of the principal characters and the motives which governed them. Apart from this, because of their historical value, they deserve to be preserved by publication in permanent form for use, perhaps, by some future historian who shall do justice to the earnest and sincere Fenian men of '61-65, who cheerfully and ungrudgingly gave up all that life holds dear—family, friends, fortune, even life itself, for the Cause.

STEPHEN J. RICHARDSON.

APPENDIX TO DENIEFFE'S RECOLLECTIONS.

I

This letter, in the handwriting of James Stephens, was written from Paris on New Year's Day, 1858, (in the early days of the movement), to Michael Doheny, and tells what could be done in the way of organizing an armed revolutionary force in Ireland if only the necessary money could be provided. The letter is incomplete, and, of course, unsigned.

Paris, January 1, 1858.

My Dear Doheny:—As this is strictly a business letter you will excuse the absence of all explanations of a personal nature. I reserve everything of the kind for some future occasion—perhaps the hour I shall grasp your hand in mine with all the truth and fervor of our hunted days.

To the point.

Presuming the information given by Mr. C. to be correct, I proceed to state the conditions on which I can accept the proposed co-operation of our transatlantic brothers, and the great personal responsibility devolving on myself. Lest you should have over-rated my capability and influence, it may be well to inform you what I am convinced I can do in a given time, always provided you are prepared to comply with my conditions, which I believe essential. Bearer of this letter leaves by to-night's mail, and I undertake to organize in three months from the date of his return here at least 10,000, of whom about 1,500 shall have firearms and the remainder pikes. These men, moreover, shall be so organized as to be available (all of them) at any one point in twenty-four hours' notice at most. It must be needless to say that such an organization as this represents the whole body of Irish Nationalists—even the indifferent would be inevitably drawn after us, the start once given. Nor do I hesitate to assert that, with the aid of the 500 brave fellows you promise, we shall have such a prospect of success as has not offered since—I cannot name the epoch of our history.

Now for the conditions. The first is money. There is a slight reproach in my words when I say: you ought to have foreseen this, knowing as you do that the men of property are not with us (of course I speak but of the national men of property), and that we are without means, you would have shown a wise foresight by sending us the nerves of organization as of war. I shall be able to borrow enough to go on with the work till I hear from you; that is, on a limited scale, and at great inconvenience to myself and friends, but anything like delay on your part will not only retard its progress, but otherwise injure the Cause and should you be unable to come into my terms, the business must be given up altogether. You must then be able to furnish from £80 to £100 a month, dating from the departure of bearer from New York. Had I a casting voice in your council, I should, moreover, suggest you sending 500 men unarmed to England, there to meet an agent who should furnish each of them with an Enfield rifle. This, of course, would involve considerable expense; but were it possible it would so stave off suspicion that we might fall on them altogether by surprise. Of course, too, this money should come from you, and I beg of you, if possible, to raise it and act on my suggestion.

A few words as to my position. I believe it essential to success that the centre of this or any similar organization should be perfectly unshackled; in other words, a provisional dictator. On this point I can conscientiously concede nothing. That I should not be worried or hampered by the wavering or imbecile it will be well to make out this in proper form, with the signature of every influential Irishman of our union.

* * * * * * * * *

N. B.—Bearer may be trusted unto the death.

II

This letter was written by James Stephens in Paris on March 5, 1860, and was brought to John O'Mahony by Patrick Downing (afterward Colonel Patrick Downing, Tammany, or 42d Regiment in the Civil War).

Paris, March 5, 1860.

John O'Mahony,

Brother:—This will be given you by Patrick Downing, one of the "State prisoners." He is a townsman and particular friend—a blood relation, too—of Donahy, who, should I forget to bespeak bearer a cordially, honorable reception, would not fail to secure it for him. Indeed, bearer is of the stuff that recommends itself, and should give you a high opinion of the manhood of his district; for what but a high opinion can you form of a district, the sub-centres of which are at all like my friend Mr. Downing. He has been by my side for the last fortnight, and every day has raised him more and more in my estimation. I answer for it, circumstances shall not swerve him from what he believes a high and holy duty. Receive him, then, in all earnest brotherhood—be a real brother and a friend to him.

To be able to say conscientiously that we have lost nothing at home since you last heard from me is, in my opinion, more than our transatlantic brothers can possibly expect. This is a simple statement, and must not be construed into a complaint of the men at your side. No complaint shall ever be written by me—no murmur of any kind, however skilfully hidden in a mental reservation. My words are to be taken for what they bear on the surface—I nothing extenuate, nor set down aught in malice. I can affirm, then, that we are as strong as when Donahy left home. That is so far as I know; for, unfortunately, I have not been able to effect communication with all our centres as yet. Though I have written this last sentence, it appears to me next to superfluous. You understand organization and must consequently know that, with the means at my disposal, I could not possibly have got our widely scattered forces into complete order.

All our friends, however, are not equally acquainted with the nature of the machinery I have to work, and to these it may be necessary—at all events I deem it my duty—to say, that a great difference between our position and that of men of large resources is that we must pay more for an inferior article than rich folk pay for a superior one. I leave it to you to complete my ideas. Some dozen centres, then, are working in the dark, or with such light only as comes to them by what I may call refraction. Thirty-two centres are at their post; five or six of whom, however, require a very effective curb, and two others a touch of the spur.

One of the latter has written to me lately to the effect that his circumstances will not admit of his remaining longer in the country. I do not believe him; but should he go we shall not, probably, lose another man—B., C. or D.—but himself; it is even likely we shall gain by his loss. To make up for the persons in question, a centre reported lost or doubtful in my list turns out all we could wish with terrible reasons for working himself into our van. No additional centres have been made; and, in our present circumstances, I am by no means desirous they should unless in some very exceptional case. Thus, the details carry out the affirmation that we have lost nothing since you last heard from me.

And here I may as well state once for all that you need apprehend no very essential loss. Were what I did at home the work of a petulant schoolboy, blustering agitator or "Young Ireland" ramschackle, you would have just cause for apprehension. Rely on it, brother, it is the work of a man. I am so sure of this myself that should you be unable to send me a dollar I would still undertake to maintain an organization of at least 15,000 men, not only for a year longer, but for seven years if needful.

And what I am able to do you may rely on being done, come what may; for it would be as impossible to swerve me from my fixed resolve as for might of man to wrest a star from its orbit. With such a basis of operations at home I should be satisfied to suffer as the zealot suffered at the stake, and should not cease to toil while soul and body held together. Brother, I ask you to do no more than I myself have been doing and shall do to the end. Fear nothing, then, but double, over and over again, your efforts. You and I at least have gone into this cause resolved to succeed or die. Can I not answer for your resolve as for my own? I should say "yea," though the contrary were written in fire in the heavens above my head. Say as much for me, believing it in the depths of your soul. Do not think, though writing thus, that I am insensible to the hardships of your position. I feel them all to the quick as keenly as if every base and coward blow were aimed at my heart. But no great aim like ours has ever yet been attained without suffering as well as toil. Toil and suffer on.

By the way, it has become a trueism among men of our stamp that suffering, so far from being a misfortune, is a positive blessing: it purifies and ennobles. No small nature, I am convinced, can bear suffering without loss; but the soul of a man comes out of it a thing of great worth. Suffer and toil on I say. I would not for my own self be spared the one as I am sure never to relax in the other. Nor think for an instant that the M's and this set, with all their various wretched tales can materially check, much less, foil you. They have already done well-nigh their worst, and I heed them no more than the passing breeze. Verily! you altogether over-rate their influence. With us they could do much good, especially a year ago; against us they are nothing, openly against us, their heels would be soon on the nether millstone.

It seems to me also that you altogether exaggerate what the returned could do were they mischief-bent. It is a very serious loss certainly the return of these men. But the simple fact of our not having been able to keep up our relations with all the centres at home fully accounts for our not having been able to do so with these men, some of whom went to districts to which the organization had never extended. You say that three are doing good business. Had I received anything like the support I was entitled to expect, every effective man who went home would have the same tale to tell. The time, however, is not far distant when we can prove to the entire satisfaction of our disappointed friends how much the reality exceeds even the picture which guided them to their native homes.

I have received all your money orders, including the four last, the first January 13th for 1055.75 frs.; the second, January 23d, for 1158 frs. 75 cent.; the third, February 6th, for 515 frs., and the last February 16th for 513 frs. About one month ago I had to send O'L., to whose address the three last orders came, to Ireland. He was to return to London immediately and there settle down for some months, sending me his address the day of his arrival. The circumstances, inseparable from men of small means, obliged him to remain longer than he expected at home, so that I did not get his address in London till Friday last (March 2d). I at once posted the third last money order for his signature. Received it signed by him yesterday (Sunday), so that I could not get it cashed till to-day. Forwarded to him the two last orders for his signature to-day. This will account for the delay my friend Mr. Downing has been forced to make here—and for other matters if they be only properly weighed. Spite of this manifest inconvenience, you must continue to send orders to O'L.'s address (here), till you hear from me again. In my next letter I expect to be able to direct you to forward your orders to the address of de la Valette; you know the significance of that, but the knowledge is for yourself alone, Doheny and Donalog.

This letter is simply a hurried jotting down of certain indispensable things. My next shall be a letter in something like form. My intention from the first had been to send out to you, one after the other, and at intervals of from a fortnight to a month, the chief if not all the prisoners. Dream you the enemy (chiefly of Celtic, not Saxon blood) could have stood out against that! My intention is still the same. You may expect another of them a fortnight, or at farthest, a month after bearer; the other shall follow, soon as I can. As most, if not all, these men are to return home you should use a certain discretion in bringing them before the public; but they, one and all, place themselves absolutely in your hands.

J. S.

III.

In 1860 an effort was made to create a feeling of dissatisfaction among the members of the I. R. B. with the work of James Stephens and John O'Mahony, looking toward their removal, with a view of filling their places with more active and energetic men.

To counteract this Thomas Clarke Luby, Denis Dowling Mulcahy and others sent out a letter in which the fullest confidence in "James and John" was expressed, and asked all the leading Centres in Ireland to sign it. The letter was fully indorsed by the Centres, although it took some time to get all their signatures.

The following letter was written by Denis Dowling Mulcahy to Thomas Clarke Luby and enclosed a slip on which he had secured a number of signatures of Centres to be attached to the letter of confidence.

The original document with all the signatures in is now in the possession of Mr. John Quinn, secretary of the Irish Literary Society of New York.

Redmondstown, Clonmel, August 6, 1860.

My Dear Luby:—I write this letter as a voucher for the names of the Centres on the enclosed slip of paper, which I have unhesitatingly obtained on representing to them the vile calumny of the base and unscrupulous men who have been endeavoring, through motives of ambition and emulation, wilfully and malevolently to asperse the characters and blast the justly earned popularity of the purest, the noblest, the most self-sacrificing—and I may add, the most trusted Irish patriots of the present day—in the persons of S. and O'M., that ever devoted their energies, consecrated their talents or sacrificed personal interest and ambition in working for so holy and so just a cause as the regeneration of their native land, and the deliverance of her children from slavery and degradation into which they have been plunged for centuries through the treachery, discord and self-interestedness of such men as those brawling, mercenary and slanderous would-be patriots, who go about vilifying and misrepresenting the pure motives of pure men, insinuating doubts as to the truth of statements made by them, sowing discord among the united, prejudicing and poisoning the minds of the credulous, who at present see neither the object nor baseness of their motives.

The confidence which the Centres of this movement shall express will, it is to be hoped, restore faith in the deserving and awaken their lethargy or distrust, and make them stand aghast at the ravening wolves in fleecy raiment, who had been doing the work of the enemy by striving to sever the bond of unity which holds together so many thousands of staunch Irishmen, both at home and in America.

The sentiments expressed in this letter are the sentiments of the Centres whose names are inscribed on the enclosed slip of paper, who would, if it were necessary go to New York to attest their confidence in S. and O'M. Now I add, my dear Luby, that these sentiments are fully indorsed by

Your friend and brother,

DENIS D. MULCAHY, JR.

Thomas Clarke Luby, Esq.

IV

The following letter, written by John Mitchell in Paris in 1861 to John O'Mahony in Ireland, was found among the latter's papers after his death, and would seem to indicate that "The O'Donohue" was in sympathy with the principles of the I. R. B.

It also anticipates the formation of a "Society" or organization for patriotic purposes, which should be conducted as far as possible within legal lines. In all probability the Brotherhood of St. Patrick was meant.

Cioisy-le-roi, 1 Rue St. Nicholas, May 8, '61.

My Dear O'Mahony:—You are still, I believe, in Ireland, so I write to you on the chance of my letter finding you. I have been expecting for a good while to hear from you and have felt a good deal more interest in your Phoenix Society since I knew that you were in Ireland taking charge of it yourself. It is not so widely spread or so efficaciously armed and prepared as you would wish, and as I would wish, but still so far as it goes, and to the extent of its organization, it is good. I write now only to tell you that I have met The O'Donoghue (by appointment) at Boulogne and spent the day in conversation with him. It appears to me that he is fully and minutely in accordance with both you and me on the hopes, chances and resources of the cause. And I wish that you were in communication with him—so far as your system authorizes you to enter into communication with an outside man.

He is to attempt in a day or two to present the national petition to the Queen (it will be refused; that is, the Home Secretary will not even allow him an audience to present it), then he will present the City of Dublin petition in the House of Commons. It will be met, as he expects, with shrieks, coughs, sneezes. Then he will quit Parliament and go home to Ireland, where it is probable he will ask the people to join in some organization for further measures. His new organization will not be illegal, but though ostensibly legal and open, it will and must naturally seek to connect itself with whatsoever secret machinations may be going on. That is to say, in other words, it will be an organization looking to revolution, foreign aid and more or less directly preparing for that, though for the moment within the forms of the law. I do seriously believe O'D. to be honest and determined and thoroughgoing. You need not apprehend the influence of G. H. Moore. I think we have so arranged matters that we shall make use of him, not he of us.

Will you ascertain the time that O'D. is to return to Ireland and give him a meeting, either in Dublin or anywhere in Tipperary you please. He wishes it, and I advised it. But of course I do not imagine or suggest that you should tell him anything more than you would tell me. All I want to impress upon you is that he is earnestly bent on turning men's minds away from Parliament and away from English parties, and fully bent on inviting and cultivating French aid.

And with such views he must be conscious, and is so, that your organization—to whatsoever extent it may exist—is a power to be counted on.

I don't exactly know your address, but hope this will find you. If you write to me address to M. Andrew Wilson at this place. But I don't ask you to write, and perhaps it is better not, as I believe all letters to me or from me will soon be in danger of hostile inspection. All I mean is to certify to you that I think we may rely upon this man and that I would expect good results from an interview between you and him.

Yours very truly,

J. M. (John Mitchel.)

V

This letter was written by James Stephens to John O'Mahony and refers to the McManus funeral, the scene at Limerick Junction, etc. This was followed by a supplementary letter dated February 25, 1862, which should be read after this.

Dublin, November 16, 1861.

Brother:—This is not the time for a full explanation, the time and circumstances being unfavorable. Nor must you think I feel at all bound to apologize for my long silence. In fact, I have not been silent. In proof of this, witness Father O'F.'s letters written at my suggestion; the Cork address, publicly recognizing you, favored by me, and, at my request indorsed by the Dublin Committee, the Clonmel and Kilkenny addresses written by me at a time I was in danger of death from over-exertion, etc., etc. Moreover, but for Father ———'s unexpected departure you should have had a long letter—such a one as I could not entrust to the post. It shall be brought you by Capt. Smith, who will leave this place in a month or six weeks.

Meantime the public press, to say nothing of the private communications you shall have received, ought to satisfy the most exigent of men. Apropos of Capt. S. He has given me and all my friends thorough satisfaction, and owing to your strong recommendation we have paid him such honor here as has rarely fallen to the lot of an Irishman. I have, however, to prepare you against one mistake of his, to which you owe this note. The report of the American delegates was drawn up by Doheny, and, Capt. S. (who with this single exception had submitted not only what the delegates had previously written but the address, etc., of the various Irish deputations) not seeing anything to object to, posted the report wihout having let me see it. Now, from the very nature of Doheny's mind, I fear that report must be faulty in more ways than one: he may have written things better omitted, and he is sure to have omitted things of importance which should have found a place in it. Even you, owing to your absence, cannot be fully sensible of the whole importance of the omissions alluded to. You are, however, in a position to judge the exceptionable matter, and I call on you to strike out anything of the kind you detect.

Astounding as the newspaper accounts of the funeral must appear to every Irishman in the States, the most favorable account is far below the reality. The funeral procession in Cork numbered from 80,000 to 100,000, about 8,000 walking in regular order. Such men as Denny Lane, John Francis Maguire, John O'Donnell, of Limerick, etc., were thunderstruck. They could not have believed such a demonstration possible without the co-operation of the clergy, at least, if not the leaders. Still, the opinion of such parties was that Dublin—rotten. Dublin—would be a blank failure! You will have heard of the sublimely touching scene at the Limerick Junction, as well as the splendid reception at the Dublin station. You will also have heard of the thousands (from ten to sixteen thousand) who daily and nightly visited the Mechanic's Institute during the week the remains lay in state there.

An infamous (I write deliberately) attempt was made on Saturday night to make the burial next day a failure. This attempt was the work of Father Kenyon (the leader) John Martin, and such carrion as Cantwell, etc., even The O'Donohoe allowed himself to be wheedled into the affair, though he has since disconnected himself from the miserable clique, who were all utterly crushed by the wise and manful action of the committee. The scene on this occasion was equal to one of the stormy ones of the French convention, and never before had the Irish people given such proof of their ability to govern themselves. Be your faith in them strong as mine is. Kenyon lost his wits all out—he insulted every member of the committee, and when leaving in a rage threatened to prevent the funeral next day, declaring: "You shall have no funeral," etc.

He and others then went to Miss McManus and by calumny, etc., endeavored to prevail on her to interfere and have the body taken from the American delegation, Dublin committee, etc. They were miserably disappointed, having succeeded in nothing but to make themselves odious in Miss McManus's eyes as well as the eyes of every true heart in Ireland. What effect had their conduct on Sunday's demonstration? In numbers, feeling and order nothing like it has ever been witnessed in Dublin. One hundred and fifty thousand took part in the general procession, 30,000 marching in regular order.

Post hour up.

Yours fraternally,

J. S.

VI

This long and exceedingly interesting letter of twelve closely written pages in the handwriting of James Stephens describes the events leading up to the McManus funeral in Dublin, and contains his personal and unflattering opinion of several men then prominent in Irish national affairs. It throws a strong light on the hidden influences behind the movement which made the McManus funeral an historic event.

Dublin, February 25, (1862).

To John O'Mahony, H. C. F. B., New York.

Brother:—It is to-day exactly a month since I began a letter to you in the following words: "You have been expecting a letter and I send you a volume. This is not to excuse my long silence, convinced as I am of your having ascribed that silence to necessity or to notions, which, while unknown to you, have to me appeared cogent and wise. It is thus that one friend should ever interpret another; and knowing you, my friend, I am at ease about your constructions of my silence."

I could not at present write anything more to the point than these words. But while deeming excuses as needless now as they then were I am more than ever pained at my inability to give you a full account of events since we parted. This inability has been chiefly owing to close confinement for more than three months. It is useless to say what the confinement itself has been owing to; but, however vulgar the cause (lack of means to move about), while this cause continues, a mental labor of any consequence will certainly be out of the question.

Now, the volume promised at the head of this letter must be rather big and well written, else it had better not be written at all. This being so, you won't be expecting it over soon; though if I had only a week's good air and exercise in the country, it would not take me very long to write my volume, embracing a full account of the McManus funeral, the "mass meeting" at the Rotunda and all the infamous action of the "trusted leaders" in connection with these events. In the present letter I can barely glance at the foregoing matter. I shall call the McManus funeral a memorable deed, the proof and test of our words and toil. No man who took part in it, either in Cork or Dublin, can forget it while he lives; and the enemy (I mean the national muck still more than the British or even West British brood) will remember it long and well. It certainly raised the national visor overmuch.

This is to give faith to our transatlantic brothers. The face-cloth is removed from the dead nation, and lo! instead of a dead face the living lines of strength and resolve are seen! It was a grand triumph. Was it a judicious one? You know what I think of it; but I will here say that had we been fairly supported even then immediately after the funeral we should have wrought great results out of the feeling awakened; whereas that feeling may now be said to have injured rather than served the cause. This and other things will not, however, be sufficiently clear to you till you shall have read the promised volume. Our words were first proved publicly true, our strength first publicly manifested beyond a doubt on the 3d of last November. This was in Cork city. I do not undertake to say what the government thought of that demonstration. Cork had nobly earned a name for disaffection to British rule and it may be the government, if a little alarmed, was not taken altogether by surprise. But were its functionaries at all prepared for what took place in Dublin on the following Sunday? Assuredly they were not, and it is scarcely too much to say that, if foreseen, they would have prevented it by royal proclamation.

Never has anything comparable to it been witnessed in this city. The National (?) newspapers have given you but a wretched notion of it, and even "honest John Mitchell" gleaning his information from these papers and their hacks, or through notions I don't profess to know, grossly understated its magnitude and misconstrued its origin and significance.

One hundred and fifty thousand men took part in the Dublin procession, 30,000 of them marching in regular order! Think of this multitude walking such a distance in such weather to honor a rebel's dust! Remember, too, that every man of all that host uncovered as he passed the spot where Robert Emmet died! It was an act of scorn and defiance of British rule almost tantamount to an act of open rebellion. Those who organized that funeral—who worked up the people of Dublin to all this feeling, spirit, power and order—could easily (and would had they but arms) have brought them to revolt—to revolution. Believe me, dear friend, that every man who saw the people on this occasion or who heard about them from reliable sources —trust me, I say, that every such man who still doubts the people is himself rotten to the heart's core. And not less a humbug—not less utterly rotten is that nationalist who, aware of our action in the McManus funeral, still doubts us. For all was done by our body.

A single fact proves this to a demonstration: those parts of Ireland, and those alone worked up by us, sent delegates to the funeral! This is a very significant fact to be brought home to the heart of every true Irishman, proving as it unquestionably proves, that outside our ranks there is no national life in Ireland. And in America, too, may we not claim the work as almost exclusively ours? Be this as it may at our side, we can allow no share at all to mere outsiders; the work was ours from beginning to end. I repeat, then, that the Irish Nationalist, who, aware of our action in the McManus funeral, still questions our power and ability is utterly rotten.

Now, the clique—the "trusted leaders" and their small tail—were thoroughly aware of the work being ours in all its bearings. It is but justice to them to say that they did not think we would have made it anything like what it turned out. But in doing them this justice de wo not stamp them with political blindness and incapacity? Oh! could they only have foreseen the great result! How promptly they would have taken action on the committee!—how gladly have got the direction of affairs into their own hands! By this means they might have staved off—not to say prevented altogether—the coming events that are now ringing in their ears like the crack o'doom! Poor purblind and bungling cravens! Oh! they were far from foreseeing what we were preparing for them. It is true they got a hint (how, it is needless to say) that the word funeral meant insurrection! It must be still more needless to say that that hint introduced them, as the fact says, "to a few of the sensations!" Yet it had been proved to them in a way to set brave men at ease that there would be no insurrection—that I, almost at the cost of my life from excessive toil, had made that next to impossible.

Whether they were at ease or not is more than I undertake to say. However this be, they used the hint not against those who wildly and criminally contemplated a rising at the time, but against me without whose efforts the quickening spirit of the land might have been layed forever; a small share of blood-letting would have done it then. But mark how baseness is the mother of inconsistency. While calling us firebrands, likely to plunge the country into bloody strife, the consequences of which were horrible to contemplate, they, in the same breath, asserted that we were only a few rash enthusiasts, who, could we get up a fight at all, would be put down by a handful of military! The government, they said, though fully aware of our doings, despised us too much to give us any attention at all! The funeral, they whiningly prophesied, would be a blank failure! Was this their reason for standing aloof from us? Or was it sheer fear that kept them away, till, on the 3d of November, the city of Cork gave the first great public proof of a nation fully awakened, if not arisen, and showed them the necessity of doing something to prevent us from proving further that not the people but they were base? For it is manifest to all who have followed the careers of these men—the "trusted leaders"—that the triumph of the people would be their infamy. The "trusted" knew this well, none better, and so they set themselves blindly and bunglingly as usual to prevent the people's triumph.

Plottings, born of many-sided baseness, began in earnest from the day the remains were borne into Dublin, where the clique had mustered in all their strength. I cannot, for the present, show up the nefarious action of the clique. They fancied it all hidden from us and hoped to steal a march on us. Their immediate object was to get the direction of the McManus committee into their own hands, taking to themselves the whole credit of the work; their ultimate object to break up our organization, and either found a legal agitation or reduce the national action to a mere aspiration after unattainable liberty.

We were prepared for them. The battle between us took place at the committee room the night before the funeral. Kenyon and John Martin, backed by the presence of The O'Donohue and the blackguardism of Cantwell and a few others, formed the opposition. We were very strong; besides the whole body of the committee (which numbered more than thirty of ours) there were present some of the American deputation and several provincial delegates. The first move of the enemy was for nothing less than the mastery of the committee! Kenyon was the chief agent in this. He was met and utterly defeated by the Doctor (Luby). On this occasion the Doctor took even our friend by surprise and raised himself to his just level in their eyes. Kenyon's second move was to prevent the delivery of the oration. You know he had been offered and declined the honor of speaking on this occasion. The offer was repeated, his refusal also, and the reasons for the refusal were pitiful.

All the "trusted" had been invited to speak and all had refused. Then it was the committee decided on appointing Capt. Smith. On hearing of Smith's appointment some days previously, Kenyon expressed great satisfaction. Why, then, this attempt to do away with the oration? Kenyon had recommended that it should be written beforehand. This had already been decided on by us. In short, every condition Kenyon had previously desired happened to chime in with our decisions. Why, then, it may again be asked, this opposition to the speech? The reason of it is plain as the way to the parish church. He came to know that the oration would be written by me. This was alarming! No man knew the action of the dead as well as I; none, therefore, could speak of him with more authority. All well and good, but what might not I say! I knew the action of the quick as well as the dead; and, in speaking of the latter, how did I mean to treat the former! They knew their action could not bear the light. What if I should show up the shortcomings of the whole clique in '48! What if the Sage of Templederry himself should be found to be anything but a hero! Could they have laid on me, who dreams they would have spared me? We judge others by ourselves, "wanting the mental range." It would, then, be hard to blame the "trusted" for trying to avoid such an exposure as was to be apprehended from so uncompromising a hand as mine! Really, he should sympathize with the poor clique in their anxiety to prevent this dreadful oration!

The Sage of Templederry did his best to procure an abortion. Again he met and was baffled and utterly defeated by the doctor. He then—nay, almost from the beginning—lost all self-control and behaved like a lunatic—to use a gentle expression. He repeatedly told the committee that he despised—he scorned them! that they were a poor—a miserable committee! etc., etc. All this was borne by my friends; because they don't forget the reverence due to the spiritual character of the priest, even when, as in the present case, he shows himself a bad man. At times, however, the bearing and language of Father Kenyon were so outrageous that the cry, "Put him out!" was fierce and general. On another occasion I shall give you all necessary details of a meeting which, viewed in all its hearings and consequences, will rank among the most memorable of our history; on this night a great principle—the sovereignty of the people—was, for the first time, really struggled for and nobly won in Ireland.

As already said, this second defeat made Kenyon frantic. Rushing to the door he turned and said: "You'll have no oration—no funeral! I'll take the body away from you!" If not certified by unimpeachable testimony, you could scarcely deem him capable of the infamy he threatened to perpetrate. He meant what he said, however, and did his best to carry it out. He rushed into the presence of Miss McManus (who was stopping with the American deputation at the Shelbourne Hotel) and tried to persuade her to take her brother's remains out of the hands of that pagan committee that he might give them Christian burial!

Now, the clique had been all the week—especially since the

appointment of Smith as speaker—tampering with Miss McManus, endeavoring to make her dissatisfied with the committee. It cost us a good deal of trouble to set her mind at ease. Therefore, when Kenyon rushed in, in this wild way, and with his unscrupulous utterances threw her into a state of bewildered excitement, it is hard to say what might have been the consequences had there been no friend there to reassure her. Fortunately Capt. Smith was present and restored her confidence in the committee. Before he had succeeded in doing so completely Jeremiah Kavanagh, who had witnessed Kenyon's pranks at the meeting, came in and speedily and utterly routed the Sage of Templederry and the Muse of Loughorm, who was with him in this vile attempt. This was their final defeat.

I have already told you what the funeral was next day; but another time I mean to give you full details of this and everything noteworthy since we parted. In this promised narrative you will clearly see what the people are as well as the "trusted leaders," and from it you can easily understand why the failure of '48 has become a byword of scorn in the world. On the heads of the "trusted leaders" alone should all this scorn fall. Never, it may be fairly said, did such little natures chance to lead a people. At no time and in no way can they give proof of anything but littleness.

No sooner were the best honors paid to the dead than the base-born plottings which had preceded the burial were renewed. The drift of them all was to put us down! Noble natures, however erring, true Nationalists, however differing in opinion or modes of operation, would have had some gratitude to the men who had made manifest to all our race that the home-clinging children of the Sacred Isle—those by whom our liberty must be mainly if not altogether achieved—were alive to their duty, powerful and healthily linked together for action big with glorious promise. In the proof of this given by us at the funeral these infinitessimally little could only see a reason for the barest hostility! We were dangerous, they said, and should be put down! More easily wished and said, however, than done. How put us down? Some tried balmy conciliation, hoping to worm themselves into our confidences, that they might betray, or that we should at least tolerate them till they were strong enough to strike. We knew, however, that these gentle conciliators had tongues and pens perpetually coining slander like a mint. Others of the clique, without any share of honey at all, secretly voided this gall on us with odious liberality. Foremost among these was Kenyon. He let slip no opportunity of slandering us in a way that accuses him of almost unleavened turpitude. A letter of his, which I may copy for you at another time, goes next to prove him irredeemably bad. On reading this most woeful production I at once stigmatized it as "a brassy, mendacious, silly and malignant epistle!" In a word, it would take many sheets to give you a fair idea of the doings of the clique between the burial and the mass meeting.

Don't for an instant forget the drift of all their efforts—chiefly to break up our work! No means were too base for them; but nothing they could devise gave promise of probable success. An organization of some kind seemed to them essential—of the driftlessly peaceable and legal kind, I should have said; none other would suit. They had all the organizing elements of driftless agitation—"trusted leaders," "patriotic" journalists, promising M. P.'s et hoc genus omne! Indeed, one element of the clique—the aspirationists—were necessarily opposed to everything but the driftless; another—the "patriotic" journalists—clamored for it as the sole means of keeping shop open; and might not a third be borne on it to that land of promise, to "National" respectable Parliament, with its vistas opening to ecstatic spots beyond!

But whatever the individual reasons of the clique for drifting on this driftless agitation one hope and aim they had in common—to put us down! To this end an organization was essential. Gods! only grant them that! It would save some of them from ruin, almost all of them from shame! How is it to be realized? They have no influence—no opportunity and rallying cry to get up an influence for the home! The active Nationalists of Dublin are with us, yet where but in Dublin should a business like theirs be started! Besides, are we not everywhere! We ring them round about and the ring is fire! They hate and fear us in their agony! Gods! will you only grant them the power to crush us! Ever so wee an organization will do it; for, have they not a many mouthed press, and should they fail in having us arrested by private canvassings of our doings—hints thrown out in a sympathetic way to friendly government officials—could they not have public recourse to the patriotic (modern) duty of Felon-setting? This duty would, at first, take the shape of friendly warnings to such over-ardent or misguided individuals as had become or thought of becoming members of secret societies! The government, of course, would be supposedly blind to those warnings! Should said warnings produce no effect on us—or the government—then were the honorable heads of the contemplated organization to come forth and point to us—set us—individually or in groups, but so as to admit of no possible mistake, as members of a dangerous "secret-society," condemned by law and religion, to be shunned by true Irishmen and hunted to death or exiled by British authority!

We have called this Felon-setting, having lacked a word to express an infamy so abominable that you may well ask yourself if even the "trusted" could have sunk to that baseness; that is, astounded and disgusted, you might have questioned my words, were they not proved beyond doubt or cavil by the organs of the clique! But I anticipate. As yet the infamy had not taken its blackest shape and was, as they supposed, unsuspected by us. We were to be thrown off our guard till they could strike with effect—as a publicly organized body. Their inability to organize any such body was fast becoming a chronic agony, and they were at their wits' end when the news came of the arrest of Mason and Slidell.

They seized on the news with the grasp of despair, meaning to make that their opportunity! They improvised a meeting composed of some of the clique—not the best or most influential—and the few weak or rotten creatures whom they had won or hoped to win over; not one of the men whose efforts had produced the McManus demonstration was invited; the really active members of the National petition and St. Patrick's Brotherhood committees were also ignored; in short, the meeting—about a score in all!—was almost exclusively confined to as worthless a brood as the "patriotism" of this country has ever brought to the surface! Yet the fellows at this hole-and-corner meeting had the brass to babble of a great national association, embracing all classes and parties, founded and welded to I know not what results by them!

I have already mentioned how they set about this union of all classes and parties by the studied exclusion of those who had reawakened the spirit and shaped into an active power the scattered and helpless fragments of our race. Let us now rapidly note their action far as it has gone. On the 29th of November those members of the clique already attended to held a preliminary meeting at the European Hotel. They called it "a large and most respectable meeting of Nationalists!" You know what it really was. "A resolution was adopted," we are informed by the Morning News of the 30th of November, "to the effect that a meeting be held at the Round Room, Rotunda, on as early a day as that plan of meeting can be had, which, it was ascertained, would be on next Thursday." Verily, on as early a day as possible! They had reasons for seizing opportunity by the forelock and stealing a march on us! To this end, they at first purposed to hold the sensation meeting on Monday; but on inquiry found the room could not be had till Thursday. We are further informed by that veracious and "patriotic" organ, the Morning News, that "the most perfect harmony and unanimity prevailed among the gentlemen present" at this preliminary meeting, and that they "trust important and beneficial results will accrue from the movement!"

The truth is that scandalous bickerings and language was the order of the day at this most important gathering! And what is to be said about the "results?" A legal agitation has always been debasing and delusive in this country. Bad, therefore, at the best, I leave you to guess the "results" of one founded and directed by such men as these! Well, the "Trent affair" gives them the anxiously longed-for opportunity and rallying-cry at last: It is only just to say that they do their best to turn them to account. But their best, alas! I am in no mode to hit off their trouble, toil and bubble—yet, of soap; only the high fantastic tricks they played—not in authority, however brief, but merely struggling for it!—must have given the angels excess of weeping! In sooth, the faith of the poor clique is sad and very sad. Saddest of all is the fact that, as the day of the sensation meeting draws nigh, it introduces them to such queer sensations that many a man of them would give the apple of his eye to avoid eating the fruit they are likely to gather from it! How has it come to this? They have been given to understand that the "silent men"—"those fellows who can do anything"—have been reading them through and through!—that their aims—proximate and ultimate—are known in all their bearings!—that we are brooding over—nay, have actually matured—a plan of action, and that said plan involves nothing less than utter exposure and defeat to the clique! It is horrible!

What do we really mean? What can we do? Long as it pleases us nobody can tell them what we do mean; but all are of opinion that we can do anything we like! Most horrible! Overtures are now made to us! Six of our friends will be allowed to take counsel with them, and may suggest changes in or then modify their programme! The rascals! how easy to set our chosen men afterwards! Without an order from me not one of my friends would now sit in council with them.

This was told them diplomatically, though our loathing of such carrion made our gorge rise at it. What, they then whined, did we mean to do?—would we violently obstruct the proceedings of the meeting and so give room to the common enemy to gloat over our dissensions? They were given clearly to know that our intent was in no way wicked or damnable: it was far from our minds to offer any obstruction to the meeting; we would give a fair hearing to any speaker who did not show himself a rascal or a blackguard; and finally, we meant to confine our action to suitable amendments to obnoxious resolutions, or perhaps, a resolution of our own. They felt our words were bitter-sweet; but it was well to know that no bones would be broken; again might not our amendment or resolution be big with discomfiture! "Sweet heavens!" shall their tribulations never end! Fain would they know the exact form our amendment or resolution would take.

On this head we are vague, but renew the assurance that our action shall be strictly in accordance with the usual rules of public assemblies. Vain assurance! Again they are turning in a ring of fire! Few would really pity them, deeming their agony the just punishment of their wilful guilt. To make them the more loathsome—to us, especially, who understand this drift—they keep up between the preliminary and "mass meeting" a constant whine about "forgetfulness of past differences," "mutual toleration," "union of all parties!" etc. Their yell, or roar, is, if possible, still more odious than their whine. Only a week ago they were whining in voice more soft than any sucking dove for "independent members"—"to make known our grievances!" etc. Hark! they are now yelling—roaring lion-like as stout bully Bottom—and the burthen is: "Imminent war with America!" "The Crisis!!!" Now, this yell and whine is a loathsome monster and elder brother to Blurt and Funk.

The family of these amorphous giants, however, is very ancient and widespread, especially in this country, and at one time possessed great influence here, only the shadow of which influence now, happily, remains. All the family were ogres and feed on the people—eating their flesh, drinking their blood and sucking their marrow. It would be useful to trace the action of the whole race, and I myself should dearly love to portray the brothers Yell and Whine and Blurt and Funk, together with their numerous offspring.

For the present, however, I can only sketch one darling child, claimed alike by both the brothers. The name of this child is "Crisis." He has been the chronic bone of Ireland—a more fatal bone than Discord, Feud, Famine, or any other begotten by the enemy to perpetuate this rule and is only equaled by the monster Home-treason, and his younger brother, Fellon-setter. A bone, I say—a disease—a devil's scourge has this Crisis proved to us. Yet is he accounted "patriotic!" Who does not know his favorite rallying cry: "England's difficulty is Ireland's opportunity!" Blind, base and deplorable motto and motive to action. Owing to it, the work that should never have stood still has been taken up in feverish fits and starts and always out of season, to fall into collapse, when each fresh "opportunity" has slipped by in the wake of all the preceding ones. Ireland's trained and marshaled manhood alone can ever make—could ever have made—Ireland's opportunity.

This opportunity the manhood of our Ireland alone, without the aid of any foreign power—without even the aid of our exile brother—could have been made any time these thirty years; and, whether England was at peace or war, with this manhood alone we could have won our own. But our countrymen, alas! giving ear to Crisis, with his imbecile or cheating or craven cry of "English difficulty," stood, mouth agape, and over and over again, waiting—"biding their time"—till "opportunity" came and left them as before. Twice, not to say thrice, this has been the case even in our own day; so that I have come to feel as if I could curse every barren lunatic, dastard or knavish clod who raises these dog-souled cries.

Now, on the first report of the "Trent affair" the monster, Crisis, who is sleeping in collapse, is stirred up by Clique, got on his legs and made to stalk through the land, making day and night hideous. Let us see what, in fear and trembling, they try to make of the stalking monster. Their "resolutions" give fair enough glimpses of what they are about. These resolutions, four in number, are to be served up, "cut and dry," at the "Mass Meeting." To the three first—expressive of sympathy with and gratitude to America, and a whine about harmony at home—we will offer no opposition, though fully aware of what they mean by "harmony;" but, with our knowledge of the men—their antecedents and present motives and aims—it is clearly our duty to take action on the fourth resolution, worded thus:

"Resolved, That the Chairman, Secretary, proposers and seconders of resolutions, be constituted a committee to invite a conference of the leading Nationalists of Ireland, for the purpose of drawing up and recommending a national organization, to be subsequently submitted for approval to a public meeting."

So, you see, the Clique are to have it all their own way; the "Chairman, Secretary (as they fancy), proposers and seconders of resolutions," are theirs, and these, the self-constituted preliminary (No. 2) committee, are to invite "leading Nationalists," theirs also—else they won't be invited—to found, etc., the grand national organization! A beautiful plan, the birth of brass and blindness! Pity it should have been marred by a nasty plan, the child of strength and foresight. Here is our amendment to the fourth resolution; or, should they withdraw it, the substantive resolution we were prepared to carry·

"Resolved, That a Chairman, 2 Secretaries and a Committee of 21 members—each having been duly and separately proposed and seconded—be chosen by a majority of voices at this 'Mass Meeting,' to take into consideration the advisability of an organization in the present state of affairs at home and abroad."

What fair objection could the Clique-Faction make to this? None that the merest political dabbler cannot easily see through. At a public meeting convened by themselves, we openly appeal to the broad principle of universal suffrage; so that if, as has been frequently and brassily asserted, they have, and we have not, public confidence, their triumph and our defeat is certain. What better opportunity for proving the truth of their words? And who that knows the men and their agonizing position can think that, did it offer the least hope of success, they would have let it slip? They, forsooth, gave way in order to prevent a row! Decorous and conscientious Felon-setters! But lying is easy to natures combined in a compact of baseness. They know there would be no disturbance, that even the branded National-approvers would be patiently listened to; but they, also, knew that, at the coming meeting, our relative strength would be more than ten to one! This is the secret of their forbearance! The Chairman, Secretaries and Committee appointed by us will show you that our whole course was marked by great moderation and forbearance as well as by practical good sense. We accepted the Chairman of their own choice. Remembering that The O'Donohoe's conduct, with regard to the National Petition, had been more than equivocal, and that he had been in very bad company the week before the Funeral, the wisdom of this acceptance may be questioned; but his letter about the McManus Committee seemed fair atonement for what appeared only a chance connection with the Clique, and he promised to explain his action in the National Petition movement; besides, a certain number of influential friends were desirous of giving him what they called "a fair trial."

We, also, accepted the Secretary chosen by the Clique, not one of whom could object to the Secretary added by us. On our Committee we admitted seven of the Clique. The remaining fourteen were ours; but let us glance at this public title to the distinction conferred on them. Every man of them were members of the McManus Committee, to say nothing of their labors on the Committee of the National Petition and St. Patrick's Brotherhood; so that, independent of their efforts and position in our movement, they were the chosen men of every public one for years. The Funeral alone proved what they were capable of and the "Mass Meeting" has given them an additional claim on the gratitude and confidence of the country at large.

When writing in full, I shall go into all the merits of the course pursued by us, merely saying, for the present, that, in my opinion, time has shown it the wisest we could have hit on. Though our plan had been matured for some days, my friends, for obvious reasons, did not receive final instructions till the night before the meeting. Some were rather anxious about the result. This was natural enough; for, spite of the victory the night before the Funeral, and the magnificent triumph next day, as yet they had not become fully confident in their own strength and ability. The "Mass Meeting," among other consequences, has taught them all unshakable self-reliance!

I can now say but a few words about the meeting itself. I suppose you have seen the Round Room, Rotunda. It can accommodate 5,000 men on foot. The night in question, this vast room was so full that several fainted during the proceedings! The O'Donohoe, on taking the chair, was long and loudly cheered; his speech, too, was often and warmly applauded; in short, any amount of popular craving sought to have him satisfied by the reception he met with. The business of the meeting then went on in a very enthusiastic way, the speakers being cheered in direct proportion to the treason involved in their words! Even T. D. Goula was applauded when he apostrophised the spirit of Robert Emmet! It was sad to hear the sacred name in such a mouth, and many a hand was clenched as the wretch dared to utter it; but they promised self-control and they steadily kept their promise to the end. Soon they were amply recompensed. The time for action had come and Jeremiah Kavanagh rose to put our "resolution." I am too unwell to give you other than a poor notion of the scene that followed, and so will not try to describe it.

Compared to Kavanagh's reception that given The O'Donohoe was pitifully tame. Seldom has any man quickened such intense enthusiasm. Before uttering a word, what we knew already was clear to the most incredulous of the Clique—that the meeting was ours. I leave you to guess their feelings! The plight of the Goulas, in particular, beggars description; in their minds, at least, our friends had realized their instructions to the letter—"to make the 'Ayes' for Kavanagh's motion ring in the Rotunda like the crack o' doom!"

Unless promptly backed by our transatlantic brothers and even now, supplied with the funds which, owing to bitter distress, cannot be had at home, agitation is at an end forever! Is our faith in you, over there, built on shifting sands! Are you awake to the duty and the position in which the McManus Demonstration has placed you and us?

The "Mass Meeting" would never have been heard of but for the Funeral! At this meting we again meet and crush the enemy! Felon-setting remains to them; and, though not so mischievous as they might have made it, had they only known how, still it may do us cruel injury. But even this work—this infamy meeting, the curse of all our race and yet so easily consummated—they cannot help but botch! They overshoot the mark! Apparently, the government has only to let us alone, and, like the notorious cats, we shall eat each other up to the very tails! This is how we interpret the forbearance of the government hitherto. If correct, the Felon-setters have probably done us involuntary service—prevented what the McManus Demonstration had made not unlikely. However this may be, we look on the conduct of our American brothers as very culpable. After the Funeral, at least, their aid should have been speedy and unstinted. Having, to give you faith, having consented to publicly show our strength, we should have had support to neutralize the risk we ran. With liberal means we should have done such work as to defy the Felon-setter and his masters. May we look for this aid from you even now?

J. S. (James Stephens.)

VII

The following letter was written by Charles J. Kickham from the office of "The Irish People" to John O'Mahony in New York, is an urgent appeal for funds with which to carry on that publication. The "Power" referred to is James Stephens. Here for the first time are given Stephens' reasons for publishing a newspaper.

Irish People Office,
12 Parliament St., Dublin, Jan. 1, 1864.

J. O'Mahony:

My Dear Friend: I wrote you a hurried note five weeks ago. I hoped to receive a line from you before this, and begin to feel a little disappointed at not hearing from you. However, I was glad to see that you had done something before you received my letter. It is more than probable if it were not for the timely aid we should have gone down before now. I am after having a long conversation with W. Power. It is his unalterable opinion that all is lost if the paper goes down. Nearly all the best men agree with him. They say the paper is a necessity as a source of revenue—which it is sure to supply if once properly established. It has been put as a test to the country and P. can have no confidence in the country if it cannot or will not support this project. Our men are doing their duty in the districts where the true state of the case has been laid before them. But this has only been done in a few places, and it cannot be done till P. is enabled to take a tour through the country. After this tour he would be sure of a circulation of 15,000 on this side of the water. He calculates that you would be able to secure one third of this, that is 5,000 in America. This once done a splendid success would be certain, and our cause would assume a position at home and abroad which would secure for it the respect of all friends of liberty in every quarter of the globe. Think seriously of this; and then think of the other side of the question. There is no use in shutting our eyes to the past; ruin is inevitable if the "Irish People" be a failure. The reason of this is because the

CHARLES J. KICKHAM.

best man in the country is determined to give up the cause as a delusion if this project cannot be successfully worked. In fact, our ship is at this moment among the breakers, and if you cannot come to our assistance we are lost. If you cannot raise £300 within one week after the receipt of this letter all is over.

Write at once to all your friends. Let them beg or borrow the money. Keep back the monthly remittance to pay it and if necessary let the proceeds of the Chicago Fair go for the same purpose. Several of our leading men were for sending some one out to you but P. would not have it lest you should feel annoyed by the step. They replied that if some immediate steps were not taken to let you know the state of our affairs that a collapse at once would be inevitable. P. then said that he thought a letter from me would have as good an effect, or perhaps better, than sending out a messenger—to say nothing of expense of the latter course. This satisfied our friends and now I have written to you. For God's sake do what is required. I am sure at all events the Chicago men will do their part. Remember me there. You will have seen by the papers that I got the letter which you sent.

On looking over this hurried scrawl I find I omitted to say that it is expected that 1,000 of the 5,000 papers which ought to be sold in America must be taken by subscribers cash in advance. These thousand subscribers you must try and send within a month after the receipt of this.

I should like to write at length to you about many things, but my mind is too disturbed for this. In fact, I feel anxious when I think how much depends upon your response to the appeal I have made to you. I have implicit trust in you. I expect a reply from you that will heal old wounds and save the good old cause from the peril which threatens its very life.

Believe me as ever,

Yours sincerely and fraternally,

CHARLES J. KICKHAM.

VIII

This letter, from James Stephens to John O'Mahony, was taken to the U. S. by Michael Joseph Egan of Tuam, a member of the F. B., who was forced to leave Ireland. Stephens recommends him strongly to O'Mahony:

Dublin, March 13, 1863.

John O'Mahony, Brother: Though more than usually desirous of writing a long letter to you, I find I can send you but a few lines. I am far from well, owing to various causes, but chiefly to confinement, and am, moreover, pressed for time. The accompanying copy of a letter just written to Father O'Flaherty contains some matter you must be anxious to know. A great deal of the letter you have, in one shape or other, already read; but you will find something new in it nevertheless. I am sorry I did not find myself in a better mood for writing, as I should very much like to please Father O'Flaherty. Another time, I hope to do my work better. I also send a copy of it to Mr. Gibbons of Philadelphia.

I have to acknowledge the receipt of the two money orders, each for £10, and to the credit of Langan and O'Shaughnessy. I have also to acknowledge receipt of several numbers of the

Boston Pilot to my friends. The meeting in Philadelphia was a good idea and I am well pleased with the speeches: Capt. Smith's is to the point, Jeremiah Kavanagh's telling as usual, and Doheny's made to cover a load of sins. Pity there should be any fault to find with a man who can speak so. Your own speech contains some thorough hard-hitting points, and has given much satisfaction to myself and friends. We have just got out the report in pamphlet form and mean to circulate it widely. It will be the starting point for a punishment which I mean to make an example to all time; for I have the will, and cannot believe I lack the ability, to make the infamy of the Felon-setters an immortal abomination to all honest Irishmen.

When I spoke of going to America about the month of April, I calculated on getting funds to accomplish a certain amount of work before I started. Owing to the great distress at home, I have not been able to raise the necessary funds, and I have received nothing worth speaking of from your side. Mr. Gibbon's sent a check for £40, but I had to refund £30 of it (money advanced for the work) in Cork, when the check was made payable. As I must give up my project of travel till my work is done here, you need not be expecting me for at least three months; nor even then, unless I can raise or receive money. The want of money has been a far greater injury than all our enemies could have done us, and the longer the want continues the greater the injury will be. It is, under the present circumstances especially, hard for us to understand our transatlantic brothers, and every man among us deems himself injured.

Bearer, Mr. Michael Joseph Egan, of Tuam, is a brother, and has done some work in his native place. Family circumstances force him to go to the States. He is a draper by profession and would gladly find employment at his business, failing in which he must enter the army. He served in the Pope's Brigade. I have to recommend him in the strongest manner; and though he did but a small amount of work, I may safely say the fault was not his; in this, as so many other instances, want of communication prevented progress. Had he been able to remain, he would have been a good workman; as it is, what he has accomplished is safe in the hands of one of his friends. Yours faithfully, J. S.

IX

The two following letters were written by James Stephens when traveling in the United States in 1864. One is dated from Chicago and the other from Louisville, Ky. In these letters he tells the measure of success received by him in various cities from the Circles visited. He signed his letters J. D. and J. Daly. In writing from Louisville he deprecates the idea of "Red Jim" McDermot being permitted to go out on a lecturing tour from New York as a representative of the Fenian Brotherhood.

Chicago, June 1, 1864.

John O'Mahony, Brother and Friend: My visit to Memphis was a successful one. I did not find so strong a Circle there as I have been led to expect, but the men are good and acted spiritedly. Mr. McCarthy was with me; and, on our return to Cairo, he saw and addressed that Circle again with good effect.

I got here last night. Fortunately the 23rd are here and I meet them to-night at Fenian Hall. To-morrow I leave for Milwaukee to meet that Circle in the evening. On leaving Milwaukee, my course will be as follows: Detroit, Friday evening; Toledo, Saturday evening; Sandusky, Sunday evening; Tiffin, Monday evening; Cleveland, Tuesday evening; Buffalo, Wednesday evening. As I believe we have no great strength at Suspension Bridge, I don't think I shall go there. If not, I shall probably go straight from Buffalo to New York; in which case, you maybe expecting me to-morrow night week. Don't, however, engage me to any meeting till I see you, as it would require very good fortune to go over the ground laid down in the time stated. Soon as I get up, you can make any arrangements you deem fit.

I am glad to find you agree with me anent that Nashville gentleman. Also, that you have had a letter from Nashville and sent a reply. Be sure to keep the folk there up to monthly communication.

You mention having written a long letter to Smith; and you add that, even if he publish it, no injury can be done. I sincerely hope so, for the man is not reliable.

You, also, mention having had a visit from a Kilkenny friend and a Callan friend, and how you don't like what they say about the spirit in their districts—how you fear a cry is being raised of their being abandoned by their chiefs in the hour of danger. For many reasons you should not have written this, though one reason alone will suffice to prove it; it cannot possibly be. So that your fears on the subject, if expressed even to me only, would hardly be worthy of a thinking man. You must have written in a hurry, or you would have recollected that there is but one chief absent. My absence is by no means calculated to raise the cry in question. It is well known why

I am away. It is, moreover, known to all who have a right to know it, that my absence had become a necessity—that I should either come out here and do what, at the risk of my life, I have been doing, or let the work of my life become a total wreck. I repeat: there was no alternative between my visit to America and utter ruin. And again, those who should know this, are aware of it. I fear nothing from the cry in question. Nor can the Clique—lay or clerical—make much of such a cry. Have faith in the People, friend, at home especially, they are not the base or stupid things this fear would make them. Provided I realize the objects I came out for, all will be well; and, hitherto, I have fully realized them. With regard to the emigration, it is appaling. Nor can it be stopped in any way but one. To prepare to take that one and only way soon as possible should be our constant labor. It has ever been my constant labor. If not the first man to see, I was certainly the first to teach Irishmen that, if we did not make ready and fight for our cause and race a few years would realize the ruin of both. The wretched men who opposed us so bitterly from the outset, are now beginning to dread what I dreaded years ago and have devoted my life to prevent. They make overtures to us now, when they can do us no harm. Be on your guard. To conciliate and gain the active co-operation of every good Irishman, should be our constant aim and labor. And, spite of what the thoughtless or dishonest may say, it has never ceased to be our aim and labor at home. But what about conciliating those who were only too eager for an opportunity to strike us behind? What about the co-operation of folk who would willingly undo our work? This Mr. Finnerty about whom you write, may be what you say. Anyhow, he is deserving of no confidence from us. He joined; but, so far from working, he, like the friends around his native place (the perjured, Gill, etc.) has prevented work. Put no confidence whatever in him; or, if any, let it be simply as a member. Be sure to give him no prominence.

Yours ever faithfully and fraternally,

J. D.

Let P. O'Keeffe be ready to sail on my arrival in New York.

X

Louisville, Ky., Monday Evening (1864).

John O'Mahony, Brother and Friend: It is not by any means an easy thing to move through these diggin's, just now. Around with a "special" and strong recommendations from Governor Morton, of Indiana, and with sundry letters of introduction to Majors, Generals and other officers in the Army of the Cumberland, I went to the Nashville station this morning. Contrary to the assurances of my friends, however, a special pass from the authorities here was needed. So I lost the morning's train. There could be no difficulty whatever, though, it was thought, in procuring this pass. Another error. It was with much difficulty that we succeeded in gaining admission to the officer to look for what I wanted, and it took a deal of persuasion to gain it. This rigor pleases me much—it looks like practical work and gives me a strong hope for speedier succor than we could have looked for even a short time since. The fighting is terrific. How our poor fellows must be falling! Is there any news from the Potomac—anything from those in whom we are so deeply interested! I don't like to dwell on the subject.

The Cincinnati Circle is being filled up so rapidly that, if nothing very untoward happen, it will soon be one of your very strong points. On Wednesday evening last 83 of the members met me and subscribed 995 dollars. I got to Madison on Thursday evening, in time to meet the Circle there. It is a very small one, only 26, of whom I met 15. They subscribed 97 dollars. Col. Mullen, however, is of opinion the Circle will furnish 500 dollars before I leave. He subscribed 25 dollars himself, and, from all I know, it is a very fair sum. The Cincinnati men will, I think, make up from two to three thousand dollars. Reached this place on Saturday morning, at 1 A. M. This Circle will, also, be a strong one, and soon—they count on 1,000 members before the "Fall." They have a fine body of men as it is, some of them wealthy and many well-to-do and intelligent. Fifty of these met me on Saturday evening and subscribed 480 dollars. This, however, is one of the places in which the total subscription is certain to exceed far the initial one. By the way, the officers here are excellent. There are two things needed, though, to make the work all it can and should be. First, the State Centre should appoint a subordinate Centre for this city; at present, he is both local and State Centre. And, secondly, there should be weekly meetings; up to this, they have met but fortnightly. The place is too important not to be looked to and an occasional letter from you would effect much good.

Should I find room, I leave for Nashville to-morrow morning. I understand the Nashville Circle is a splendid one, and the friends here expect great things from it.

I have heard, to-day, that Mr. James McDermott has announced his intention to go on a lecturing tour. This move is so highly injudicious, so calculated to do injury, now especially, that I cannot believe it has your sanction. Whatever, Mr. McD.'s zeal and activity—he has not the weight and steadiness—the ability and other essential qualifications to represent us creditably. Not having these, he injured us in his former efforts in this way, and would injure us seriously now. As to going "on his own hook," it would be still worse—it would be making a trade of his connection with us, as, without us, he could not have even entertained the notion at all. It would be disreputable for an able and accomplished man to go trading about in this way. How much more so for one who could give no value whatever—in thought or words—for the money received. You are certainly bound to look to this and give Mr. McD. to understand that you are quite opposed to it. Should he not be got to apply himself steadily to some calling for which he is fitted? It is deplorable to see men led astray in this way.

Is there any news from Ireland I am anxious to hear any you may have received. But where are you to address me? If I get to Nashville and can move to Chattanooga, I shall, of course, go there, thence, if possible, to Memphis; thence to Cairo. Beyond this last point I cannot lay down my route for the present, but I may go again to Chicago.

Yours fraternally,

J. DALY.

XI

This is a copy of a letter of instructions given by John O'Mahony, Head Centre Fenian Brotherhood, to Captain Thomas J. Kelly, who was about to visit Dublin going by way of Liverpool. The original is in the handwriting of O'Mahony on the official paper of the Fenian Brotherhood.

HEADQUARTERS FENIAN BROTHERHOOD,
22 Duane Street,
New York City, March 17, 1865.
(Box 3821, P. O.)

To Captain T. J. Kelly.

Brother: In accordance with the resolution of the C. C. F. B., of which you are herewith furnished with a copy, you will proceed at once to Liverpool and thence without any delay to Dublin.

When arrived in the latter city you will report immediately to the C. E. I. R. B. and, having delivered to him the documents which I have entrusted to your charge, you will place yourself completely under his orders for the period of three months, to commence from the date of your landing in Dublin, and you will perform faithfully such duties as he may assign you. At the end of three months, you will, as the resolution of the C. C. F. B. points out, render a full report in writing of the state of the I. R. B., specifying in the said report its constitution, mode of government, the manner of persons whereof said government is composed, its military strength, its financial resources and expenditure, and its general availability for successful action within the present year, taking in account the means at the actual disposal of its Executive aided by such assistance as can be furnished it from America within that time according to your own experience of both organizations up to the time of making your said report, and using your own military knowledge as your sole guide in forming your opinion.

In making the said report you will state nothing but what

you shall yourself have acquired an actual knowledge of. You will set down no fact from hearsay or upon reports furnished you by others, judging in all cases from such surroundings as you shall be brought in contact with while performing your duties under the C. E.

If in your unbiased judgment there should be no probability of successful action this year (1865) you will in that case return to these Head Quarters after the expiration of the three months aforesaid and present your report in person to the H. C. & C. C.

If, on the other hand, you find matters to be by that time in such a state of forwardness as to render a successful rising probable, or even possible without a foreign war, during the present year, you will continue under the orders of the C. E. and transmit your report by a special and trusty messenger. This report you shall draw up yourself without the aid or council of any person whatever, and without submitting it to the approval of any parties living in Ireland.

While in Ireland you will not attempt to influence in any way the free action of the C. E. or the P. G., neither shall you argue points with them, but shall execute literally and without demur such orders as you shall receive.

While upon this service, and until further orders, you shall receive the pay of Captain in the United States Army, which shall be paid to you by the C. E. I. R. B.

You will impress thoroughly upon your mind the vast importance of these duties which have been now entrusted to you by the H. C. & C. C. of the F. B. Upon their due and exact performance depends in a very great measure the future welfare of both the F. B. and the I. R. B. Yours is by far the most serious mission ever yet sent from America to Ireland.

May the God of our sires watch over your safety and render you equal to your high trust. I remain in Fraternity,

Your faithful servant,

(Signed) JOHN O'MAHONY,

H. C. F. B.

This document is endorsed as follows:

"No. 1—Instructions to Capt. Kelly, Military Envoy to Ireland. Left New York 25th March 1865."

XII

This is a letter of introduction carried by Captain Thomas Kelly from John O'Mahony, Head Centre, Fenian Brotherhood, New York, to James Stephens, Chief Executive, Irish Republican Brotherhood, Dublin. There is a noticeable lack of warmth and cordiality in the communication.

H. C. F. B. to the C. E. I. R. B.

17th March, '65.

To the C. E. I. R. B. (Dublin):

Brother—The bearer (Captain Kelly), whom you already know, is the first of a series of messengers voted to be sent to Ireland and placed under your orders by the late Congress of the F. B. He is, moreover, furnished with a special order from the C. E., of the nature of which the accompanying resolution will acquaint you fully. He will also show you his special orders from these headquarters.

I need not impress upon you the sound policy—nay, the absolute necessity—of enabling him to fulfill the mission to the satisfaction of the C. C. and myself, even should things be far beyond my expectations even then it is best to send him back at the time specified in his instructions. Thus you will make assurance doubly sure, and thus will you the more readily procure that which you most require for your purpose. Matters here are not now as they were when you and I were as one. An element has been brought into our councils, though by no agency of mine, that must be perfectly satisfied on the points in question. Satisfy the C. C. fully and your wishes shall be promptly attended to, otherwise they will not. This is all-important. I would also impress upon you the necessity of sending a prompt and favorable reply to the address forwarded to you by the C. C. Its anxiety will soon be looking out for it. If you do not specially want Regan it is best to send him out with it. It will be of service to have him bring good news to his comrades in this city. I understood the impolicy of the late publications all through. But by your contrivance, it would seem my opinion had got to be in light esteem by your special friends and I thought it of too much worth to be thrown away. On the whole, however, it may do good all over, but has it not made your position doubly dangerous, so much for rushing things?

You will be glad, perhaps, to learn that I have at last got a C. C. that is perfectly free from any special favoritism towards me. There is, in fact, but one upon it (Wm. Sullivan) from whom I could expect any personal regard, except on the grounds of our one common purpose in political matters. This is what I like, as I find them to be nearly all earnest, practical men in the cause. The official staff selected by the body has, also, been chosen independently of any initiative of mine. I had not much previous knowledge of any of them except Capt.

Walsh. I simply approved of them on the recommendation of the members and Chairman of the C. C. Mr. Finerty, to whom alone I objected on the grounds of his being distrustful to you, was proposed and strongly supported by your friends, Messrs. Scanlon and Dunn. I do not think him a bad man myself. My reason for having been so passive in matters of such vital importance was the fact that distrust of my capacity and intellect had been sown in our ranks, for I think Sherlock was true upon this point.

Under our revised constitution you will see that all official communication from you to the F. B. must come through the H. C. in future. I must insist upon this respect being paid to the office wherewith I am invested by my constituents. If not I shall hold myself at liberty to communicate directly with your constituents upon the matters concerning the I. R. B. You will be very sorry to learn that our friend Mr. McCarthy is very ill. His loss would be severely felt now. I trust, however, the coming of fine weather will restore him to health.

Fraternally, your obed. servt.,

THE H. C. F. B.

H. C. F. B. to C. E. I. R. B., 17th March, '65

XIII

The original of the following letter is in the handwriting of General Millen and contains an account of his arrival in Dublin and the persons whom he had met. He refers to the leaders by numbers, consequently, it is not easy to identify them. No. 9 is believed to be Col. Thomas Kelly. His suggestion that several of the Dublin editors could be subsidized for £100 is rather amusing and indicates that he considered them a cheap lot. In that he was probably mistaken, although his idea may have been a good one. The letter is signed "George Robinson," which is known to have been his nom de plume, or rather nom de guerre.

Doc. "C. 1."

Dublin, April 12, '65.

Dear Brother: In consequence of sickness aboard the steamer in which I sailed, was not permitted to anchor at Queenstown, so I was carried to Liverpool and did not reach this place until the 2d inst.

The same day of my arrival I waited upon the gentleman in Dame street, and was that evening presented to both of the other parties, to either of whom you told me to deliver the two small packages of samples numbered 1 & 2, which I immediately did. They told me that 9 was in England. Four days afterwards they sent a messenger to advise him of my presence and to-day, by return, he informs us that business of an important nature will detain him where he is until about the 22d inst.

As I have not yet seen 9 and also as the other four numbers of the firm with whom your letters brought me in contact have not volunteered me any information regarding the actual state of business affairs here, I can as yet say but little about it; if, however, I might venture an opinion after so short a stay, I would at least say that the people are all so unanimous (that is all whom I have sounded upon the matter) in their hatred of the .. that I should think it an easy enough matter to get up a respectable linen trade.

There is one thing which from this time I beg leave to urge upon the members of our firm in New York, that is, that if we wish to silence the ..s who always endeavor to keep our customers disunited, we must advertise for goods in more than one newspaper; we must make the press of this country subservient to the wants of our business; we must purchase the good will of a few Editors, so that thro' them we can place before the Irish public the nature and advantages of our business. Without withdrawing our patronage from D. (which of course the world knows is entirely ours) we ought to spend judiciously a few hundred pounds in order to procure the good opinion of some of the leading journals, as well in the large cities as in some of the cheap towns. The fact of such papers being out in favor of our house would do more to get us friends from all classes—I think—and to silence the slanderous tongue of the ..s or to nullify its effects than anything else that I can think of. I seriously recommend the foregoing suggestion to the consideration of our house in N. Y. so that if they think favorably of it, they might mention it to 9 when they write.

As you well know the great want of 5, 6, & 7, etc., experienced here just now, I feel that I need not mention to you the necessity of sending over what you can in small packages for the purpose of distribution amongst our customers here.

The Prince of Wales is in Dublin—he came over to open the Exhibition. I have seen him pass four times; thrice in the street, and yesterday at a grand military review in the Phoenix Park. In the street there was hardly a person to even lift a hat to him, and passing my hotel door once, and again yesterday in the park, I actually heard some one or more in the crowd hiss him. Besides, some wretches had the impudence to salute his Highness from across the Liffy with a fish-monger's large tin trumpet. The poor fellow thought they meant to honor him, but I didn't think so at all. What a thankless people these Irish are; did you ever know such ingratitude as they have manifested in the cold reception given to His Royal Highness? Of course when I say Irish I mean the mere people of the country and do not include our true English Place-men, who would have licked the dust before the feet of the Royal Prince.

As soon as I shall have seen 9, I will write to you again and then perhaps I shall be better enabled to form a correct idea of the condition of our affairs here. In the meantime, you may rest assured that I shall lose no opportunities of collecting all reliable data in order to enable me to remit to our house in N. Y. as true a three-monthly balance sheet as can at all be formed.

9 writes to C. C. here that within the last month 50 new C's have been entered upon the books of our concern.

I am Brother,

Yours very sincerely,

GEORGE ROBINSON.

P. S.—If you should find occasion to write, please address to the Star & Garter here. G. R.

Note.—General Millen used the assumed name "George Robinson."

XIV

This letter from Col. Thomas J. Kelly to John O'Mahony contains an account of his arrival in Ireland.

It is a good example of the exceedingly guarded manner in which important information was conveyed from one side of the water to the other. Occasionally, when matters of great importance had to be communicated, special messengers were sent to carry the papers and deliver them personally into the hands of the parties to whom they were addressed.

The letter is signed "T. J. French," which was one of several assumed names used by him at various times.

Cork, May 1, 1865.

John O'Mahony, H. C. F. B.:

My Dear Sir:—You will be pleased to know I arrived safely in old Ireland on April 6 in good health, the trip across having done me much good. My uncle was out of town, but I saw him next day and gave him the mementoes you forwarded by me. Previous to looking for active employment I spent four days home—one with mother, one with uncles and two with a sister. The state of my health, however, requiring active medical aid, I was obliged to tear myself away amid some most heart-breaking scenes. Returning to Dublin I made the acquaintance of a large number of friends, of all ranks, and on the advice of my doctor I then came to this latitude where I find the climate to be exceedingly healthy. My expectations here and in Dublin were amply realized. Among the workmen at my business, and I have been high and low, the determination seems to be unanimous that there must be a strike for wages here this year. Indeed, from what I have seen I think the union will become defunct if it does not take place, because fully one-half the best workmen I have met express a determination to emigrate if they have to live on present rates beyond next harvest. Men fitted to direct movements, as you are accustomed to have them done in America, are sadly needed, although much is being done by men versed in the English style of polishing; yet they are necessarily circumscribed in their operations by reason of the increasing vigilance of their employers. A good number of our mechanics, as far as I have seen them, are competent and skilled to undertake any kind of contract, if the plans were drawn and they only had the tools and foremen, and the remainder of those I have seen, if the proportion in other parts of the country is nearly commensurate, need but competent instructors and fitting machinery to convince the world that Irish manufactures are superior to those of England. The whole country appears to be of one mind on this point, with but few exceptions, the opposition and persecution of the Cullen police to the contrary notwithstanding. So intolerable indeed has this opposition become that the feeling of indignation it has aroused is frequently found to be the greatest stimulus to action. One fact has become plain to me, viz., that we have no one competent to hold a corresponding relation to our trade as, say, Grant holds to the American army. We have men well fitted to do anything in the way of organizing trades' unions, and who have really done and are doing all in that way that was and is possible; but the example of the lookout in the iron trade in England has convinced me that the employees should have at least one man competent to plan simultaneous action for the men in all districts. Besides the means of support of the strikers should be calculated and not left to chance, and this must be done by a person accustomed to organize committees and arrange plans for that purpose.

The gentleman who will give you this letter was formerly connected with the Seventy-fifth Regiment, N. Y. M., in the same company with myself, under poor Doheny. He joined the union here to-day, and I think would have remained at home and gone to work, but that his passage is engaged. Having been a captain in the army he could be of great assistance. As he is about to leave for the train I must close. Respects to Mac, O'K. and the boys, Yours,

(Signed) T. J. FRENCH.

XV

Letter in handwriting of Capt. Kelly, addressed on envelope to H. C. F. B., and sent by messenger. It is signed "Your sincere friend, Tom."

Dublin, May 31, 1865.

My Dear Sir:—I avail myself of the departure of a gentle man from Ballinasloe to communicate a few items.

I have been enjoying good health for some time past, and have been gaining in flesh, so that now I have attained my standard weight.

I had the pleasure of counselling with the friends the other evening, and the state of trade was represented to be in such a condition that all the available funds of the firm were deemed to be essential immediately, and that it would be too late for your house to invest after I had made full reports in July. Of course, I insisted on complying with the directions your firm gave me to the fullest extent, although I am forced to the conclusion that from the immense emigration taking place we will lose our best customers and workmen if we do not open the factory this fall. I know that the union must go to pieces after this year if work is not supplied to the hands. I talk frequently with all my hands and I find that large numbers are remaining with the promise of employment. I do not see the wisdom of having made this promise, without being certain that the resources are ample. Yet the promise is made, and I am certain, judging comparatively from what I have seen, can be realized if the machinery can be furnished. Skilled mechanics are indispensable, more especially draughtsmen and designers. Thirty or forty first-class men can do the work.

Mr. M. is here and at work. I believe he has got a job in the city. When it was made known that he, too, had a three months' job and that nothing would be determined on until after that time it had a very depressing effect, inasmuch as work is meant, and subsequent operations would run too far into the year. Yet it may be all for the best.

You have, I suppose, seen the announcement of the Palmerstown flax-cotton mills being put in operation. I do not see why we, too, cannot make a footing if the necessary capital can be raised.

I proceed to Limerick in a day or two, and will avail myself of the first opportunity to write to you. Please let John and H. O'C. see this.

My friend is not in the secret and will be treated accordingly. I remain as ever, your sincere friend, TOM.

Please give my respects to the young man in the Times office; any letters for me addressed "M. S. Kelly, Main street, Longhrea, Ireland," will come to hand safely.

XVI

This important letter in the handwriting of James Stephens, consisting of ten closely written 8vo. pages, is unfortunately incomplete. All after page 10 is missing. In it he refers to P. J. Meehan and describes the condition of the organization in Dublin after the seizure of the "Irish People" and the arrest of its editors and staff. The envelope is marked "Dispatches from the C. E. and Captain Kelly, per Lt. Corridon," and endorsed "Received Nov. 29th, '65."

I. R.

To the H. C. & C. C. F. B.

Dublin, Oct. 14th, 1865.

Brothers: The day after the memorable razzia—on this very day four weeks—I wrote you a hurried account of what had taken place, and committed my letter to the tender mercies of the British Post Office. It is reported that that letter was intercepted. But I don't believe this. Because the authorities here are stupid and blundering as they are brutal and mendacious, and because my letter was posted at such an hour that, unless they opened all letters addressed to America, it is very unlikely they should have hit on mine. But there is such a thing as chance; and on this occasion, as so often before, chance may have favored our stolid foe. A week afterwards I again wrote to you, and this time my letter was entrusted to a man esteemed by all true Irishmen who know him—Captain Murphy. The Captain has, before this, explained to you how he was detained here four or five days longer than we anticipated. I am confident that he has also explained much more important matters and fully made good the shortcomings in my letter. At the same time, I should say that I consider my own letter rather explicit and comprehensive, and that you should rely on its having given you an exact account of our actual position. This I feel so thoroughly that, even if you never received another line from me before the move, I should consider you "posted" in all great essentials. I certainly feel bound to point out to you the best part of the coast to steer to, and I make it a point of duty to send over some experienced pilots, soon as I have the means of doing so. But, even if prevented from doing these and other more or less important things, my last letter should have shown you how to act, whatever might have happened to me. This, as it has been my most constant aim, would also be my greatest glory—to make the cause altogether independent of myself. And this, I now triumphantly assert, has been accomplished, provided only that you are equal to the duty of the time.

And yet a great—an awful—duty has devolved on you, owing to your doubts and action, and the consequent action of the British Government. For the public prints (and you have not received, and shall not receive, a word of news, through any public source, that is not hostile to us, the most vilely hostile of all being the quasi national rags), must have made it clear to you—clear beyond any possible doubt—that the action of the Government here has been solely owing to that damnable blunder of one of your delegates. I do not wish to be hard on Mr. Meehan, and God forbid that I should be unjust to him. But the feeling here is fearful against him, and, whatever his innocence, he deserves little at our hands. But I leave you to form your own judgment of his conduct from the public prints. It is my duty, however, to add that, even since the arrests—nay, since the trials, and since his name has publicly appeared as one of your delegates—he has written a letter to one of the men in prison. This letter was very loosely written, called on the man written to to call on Mr. A. M. Sullivan (Goula!), and was signed P. J. Meehan! The letter was opened in the postoffice, and then delivered to the prisoner's wife. Even I think it strange that Mr. Meehan should still be in Ireland and free. I trust he may be able to account to you for himself. This said, I return to the essential of all essential points now—your being equal to the awful but glorious duty of the time. To be so—to save your names and souls from actual shame and remorse—you should every hour do the work of a day. Hours are now precious and mighty for good or evil. Any apparent apathy or inability on your part at present would madden men here, and even I might not be able to control all parts. Yet the madness of one district would compromise all. But if you give a fair appearance of work, I answer for everything. I answer for it, even though I should be in prison, out of which I have kept by a foresight and prudence lauded by all who know the circumstances. Don't be deceived by the apparent calmness of the friends here. It would be base to be deceived by the lying reports of our being cowed. Cowed! There never has been so true and strong a resolution to go on as now. The calmness that deceives our enemies—does it deceive them?—is the result of a discipline never before equalled by men not trained in open war. But for me—but for my express orders—Dublin City would have been captured the night of the "seizure." Some of the best men here were with me before I lay down that night and wanted orders from me. (The best men here don't come to suggest, still less to offer counsel—they come to me for orders.) I ordered them to disperse our friends and send them all home. In fifteen minutes after these orders were issued scarcely a friend of ours could be found in the streets of Dublin. And throughout the whole country the same admirable sense of discipline was, and has ever since been manifested. Outsiders cannot see this, and so it is said that we are nowhere. But that we were, and continue to be, everywhere, and with a power that, if known, would add to the ludicrous terror of the enemy, is clear from the conduct of our friends. From all parts men come to Dublin to hear from me what should be done. This enabled me to accomplish a great deal with small means. For these emissaries generally came at their own expense. And this brings me to our financial position. At the time of the first arrests I had scarcely any money. Your first large order (for £1,000) had been but a couple of days in hand. O'L. had drawn £300 of this amount. He could not well have drawn more, for, as you are aware, the bill was payable only three days after sight, and, as Rothschild has no agent here, it takes about five days to get one of his bills cashed in full. As there were heavy claims on me at the time, nearly all the £300 had been disbursed at the time of the arrests. So that I found myself compelled to borrow money again, and at such a time! Yet I have succeeded in raising enough to keep us afloat up to this, and even longer at need. But I sincerely trust you will come to the rescue soon. The remaining £700 (of that £1,000 bill), together with all the drafts since forwarded, have, with one exception (the last draft, for £1,500) fallen into the hands of the Government. Even the £1,500 draft is useless to us, the man in whose favor it was drawn being now a prisoner. But the fact of your having sent so much money (comparatively speaking), in so short a time, has done good; for it has not only shown your earnestness, but your ability also. Few true men now have any doubt that you shall fulfill your promises and realize our just expectations to the letter. This said, I must return to these intercepted drafts. They have not been forwarded according to my directions. I told our late lamented friend—McCarthy—to have all sums under £1,000 sent alternately to O'L. and his sister. All sums over £1,000 were to have been sent to my credit to Paris. In the hurry of business and the state of health into which he fell but too soon after my departure, he may have forgotten these instructions. Possibly none of you ever heard of them. * * * * * * * * *

XVII

This letter was written by O'Donovan Rossa in 1865 to John O'Mahony in New York and was carried over by Thomas Clarke Luby, who was called "Doctor" because of his degree of LL. D.

"R." 2.

My Dear Friend: As the Doctor is going voyaging, I avail of him to send you the following narrative.

On last Tuesday week a friend told me that a soldier friend of his was in difficulties. I went to see him. His name is Montague, and he belonged to the 5th Dragoons. A comrade of his was under arrest for some days. He was in his stables when a friend of his, an orderly, came to him saying: "You are to be arrested at 11 o'clock. You have only 5 minutes to spare and if you value your liberty and your life you will make the best use of the time."

Off he went. I met a friend in town just about two hours after this occurrence. He is connected with shipping and I entrusted the secret to him. He promised to do all he could, and a letter yesterday told me the soldier was in safe keeping and awaiting a favorable opportunity to go towards your country. Detectives innumerable have been scenting him here, but of course there are detectives on another side too. If this soldier reaches you, he will, in telling you what he knows, tell you something that may astonish you. And if there are amongst you any who doubt the dangerous work which we are persistently pushing, it may be well they should see Montague and hear his story.

I was in Connaught last month with another friend; we returned; the friend went again, and to-day I received a letter from him stating that he had to run from Ballymote and Ballyshannon as he was only two minutes out of the Hotel when an Inspector of Police with an escort came looking for him.

This, I believe, is partly the work of a Bishop in Sligo, who the Sunday after we were there spoke of us. There is not a county in Ireland that is not now vigorously working with a view to immediate work and we only require means from your side to accomplish the work. Many of our people are emigrating—obliged to leave, they say. I have given a few introductions against my will, to a few. My own opinion is, that the preparation cannot be given by you in the expected time, if you are not satisfied that the material is here and is being provided here.

I see a growing disaffection in the minds of men, and a determination to skidaddle shortly if there is not some appearance of Fight. I can hear them—speak among themselves, and here is the substance of their resolve. We are holding together at much personal and other sacrifice on the expectation of a fight this year, and on the promise of it. There are now but three or four months' time, there are no arms from America or means to buy them up to this. If instead of sending us the means to fight, they only send men to inquire into our condition, and report thereon the thing will never be done. This is no time for delays of such a nature, etc., etc. This is what is said, and I cannot help seeing matters in this light myself. I am almost certain the Government will shortly take alarm. I am sure of arrest myself with many others, and it is a terrible thing to have the country unarmed. This is private for yourself. If there isn't a fight this year, you will be held largely responsible and I fear inestimable harm will be done. My uncle is out through England and Scotland for the last month. He directed I would be sent for to go to see you, and I learn now that he has changed his mind. I should like to see you, as a private friend anyway, and for public reasons, with a view to hurry war. Remember me to H. O'P., Patrick, Denis, etc., etc. Yours,

ROSSA.

P. S.—Do you know what I think myself, it is this, there are parties here who write to parties amongst you saying there is little or nothing done here. This is the excuse for the cowardice here. Doubts are created in the mind of the party over there, those doubts are taken into your councils, and hence the inquiries and delay. I do not fear offending or hurting you when I give you my mind candidly. I thought to write about the soldier only, but you see how far I have gone. I suppose I'll be off again somewhere next week when my Uncle returns.

XVIII

(Printed Circular.)

War Department, F. B.,
New York, October 27, 1865.

Special Orders, No. 1.

Charles Carroll Tevis is hereby appointed Adjutant General of the Fenian Brotherhood, with the rank of brigadier general.

All communications on military matters will be addressed to these Headquarters.

(Signed) T. W. SWEENY,
Sec. of War, F. B.

Approved,
JOHN O'MAHONY,
President, F. B.

XIX

MILITARY ORGANIZATION OF THE FENIAN BROTHERHOOD.

Section 1st.—The President shall appoint, by and with the advice and consent of the Senate, a Board of Military Examination, consisting of three persons, whose duty it shall be to examine all candidates to commissions in the Army of the Irish Republic.

Sec. 2nd.—Said Board will class all successful candidates in the order of their respective merits and qualifications, as developed in their examinations, without reference to their past rank.

Sec. 3rd.—All officers who may havs passed a satisfactory examination before the Military Board will be appointed by the President, by and with the consent and advice of the Senate, said officers to be ordered upon duty at such time as the President shall determine and the exigencies of the public service demand.

Sec. 4th.—The President, by and with the advice and consent of the Senate, shall appoint one experienced military man in such State to act as Assistant Inspector General, whose duty it will be to superintend the military organization of the State, to inquire into and examine the applications of all candidates from his State for permission to appear before the Examining Board, and if satisfied as to their eligibility, he shall forward their applications to the Military Board, accompanied by such endorsement as he shall deem fit to make; Provided, that all persons whose applications may be refused by the Assistant Inspector General, may have the right to present their application in person to the Military Board for action.

Sec. 5th.—The Assistant Inspector General shall receive no

compensation for his services, but all necessary expenses incurred in the line of his duty shall be audited by the Military Board, and paid from such funds as may be appropriated for contingent military expenses or from such funds in the Treasury not otherwise appropriated.

Sec. 6th.—That all the members of the Military Board provided for in this Constitution shall receive such compensation and hold such rank as the Senate may determine.

Sec. 7th.—That the Portfolio of War establish subordinate bureaus consisting of

Adjutant Generals,	Ordnance,
Inspectors Generals,	Engineers,
Quartermaster,	Medical and
Subsistence,	Pay Department.

That the rank and pay of all officers in the military service of the F. B. of America, be based upon the system adopted for the Regulations of the U. S. A., and shall be determined by the Senate.

Sec. 8th.—The Revised Army Regulations of the U. S., so far as the same can be made applicable, is hereby adopted for the government of the military organization of the F. B. in America.

Sec. 9th.—All officers ordered for duty in Ireland or elsewhere shall be provided with transportation and receive, in addition, six months' pay, three months of which shall be in U. S. currency, and three months in bonds of the Irish Republic, in advance, according to rank; the officers to be paid as regularly, as the nature of the service will permit, monthly thereafter by the financial agent abroad. Nothing in this section shall prevent the Senate, upon recommendation of the Military Board, from increasing the allowance to meet the nature and exigencies of the service to be rendered.

Signed October 21st, 1865.

JOHN O'MAHONY, Pres. Special Congress of F. B.

PETER A. SINNOT, Sec.

XX

The following is the oath of allegiance subscribed to by the Fenians in America before the invasion of Canada:

OATH OF ALLEGIANCE, FENIAN BROTHERHOOD.

I, M........... M............, do solemnly swear that I will bear true allegiance to the cause of Ireland, and that I will serve it honestly and faithfully against all its enemies, and that I will obey all orders of the President, Secretary of War, or officers appointed over me according to the rules and regulations established for the government of the armies for the liberation of Ireland, SO HELP ME GOD.

XXI

War Department, F. B.,
Adjutant General's Office,
New York, November 7, 1865.

General Orders, No. 1.

I. In compliance with Special Orders, No. 1, War Department, F. B., the undersigned hereby assumes the direction of the Adjutant General's Office of the Fenian Brotherhood.

II. All military officers belonging to the organization will report immediately their addresses in writing to these Headquarters, giving a full history of their past services, stating the period of time served, in what arm of the service, in what corps, division, brigade and regiment or battery; if on the staff and in what capacity; the battles engaged in; if on detached service and in what capacity; what military books studied; if wounded. state how far incapacitated for active service. State age, birthplace, by whom initiated, when and where; transmit copies of all papers relative to efficiency in any branch of the service.

III. Every report must be forwarded through the Assistant Inspector General of each State, or in his absence, through the Head Centre, and indorsed by one of these officers.

IV. Any change of address will be immediately notified to these Headquarters; a non-compliance with this order will be considered as an evidence of insubordination and of an unwillingness to render service to the cause of Ireland. Any unavoidable delays will be explained as soon as practicable.

V. Tri-monthly reports will be furnished to these Headquarters by each Centre on the tenth (10th), twentieth (20th), and last day of every month, stating the number of men prepared to go into the field at a week's notice; their efficiency as soldiers, their arms and ammunition and equipments in their possession, or at the disposal of the Circles.

VI. Centres will make such necessary remarks as will enable the War Department to distinguish the most reliable men.

By order of the Sec. of War, F. B.,

C. CARROLL TEVIS,
Brig. Gen. and A. G., F. B.,
Box 3821, N. Y. P. O.

XXII

The following is in the well known handwriting of John O'Mahony, and is evidently the original draft of a letter of instructions sent or given to John Mitchel when about to proceed to France to act as financial agent for the I. R. B. in that country. It is undoubtedly one of the most important papers in the collection. The manner in which Mitchel is to act under certain contingencies, the manner in which and the names of the persons to whom he is to distribute money, are clearly given, together with instructions covering his politcal attitude and diplomatic relations toward the French government.

O'Mahony's hope that the contemplated raid on Canada might involve England in war with the United States is freely expressed, and Mitchel's personal services are to be paid for at the rate of $2,500 per year.

The letter consists of four quarto pages closely written and unsigned. There are several corrections and interlineations, and it is probable there was another page, which is missing.

HEADQUARTERS FENIAN BROTHERHOOD,

22 Duane Street, New York City.

(Box 3821, P. O.) November 10, 1865.

My Dear Mitchel:—As has been already explained to you, the immediate object of your mission to Paris is to take charge of the financial deposits of the Fenian Brotherhood and to see that they be honestly and fairly disbursed in favor of the I. R. B.

It is the intention of the F. B. that all moneys which may be intrusted to you shall be paid out from time to time to the order of James Stephens in such sums as he may require for the purpose of conducting the home organization. However, as in his present position it may be impossible for Mr. Stephens to give his receipts in his own handwriting for these sums, it will be sufficient for you to get such receipts from agents duly accredited by him. Should you not deem these sufficient safeguards against further contingencies, the payments made by you to the agents of Mr. Stephens can be certified to by J. P. Leonard or by George Doherty. Messrs. Leonard & Doherty already know one of those agents, Dr. Edmund O'Leary, who was to have taken to Ireland the last sum remitted home (£6,000 sterling). You will also find before you in Paris Dr. David Bell, lately one of the members of the Council of the I. R. B. His address is Hotel de Lesieux, No. 2 Passage Tivoli. He will inform you of the address of other parties at home with whom you may enter into relations—Gen. G. F. Millen, Col. Wm. G. Halpin and Capt. Thos. Kelly, all of whom are now in Ireland. The chief point is to keep a constant and ample supply of money to the men working the revolutionary organization of Ireland. The betetr to insure this I shall, if possible, send with a tried and trusty man, who will open a certain mode of communication between you and them.

You will also have to disburse money for the legal defense of the parties now in prison for revolutionary conspiracy In this case it will not be necessary for you to communicate with Mr. Stephens, but you can furnish whatever sums may be needed through their law agents or other parties publicly recognized as authorized to receive money on behalf of the prisoners.

Should Mr. Stephans be arrested by the time you reach Paris then advise with Col. Halpin, Capt. Kelly and Gen. Millen—James Cantwell can put you into communication with these if no other way presents itself.

These are your duties for the present as financial representative of the Fenian Brotherhood. Your diplomatic duties with the French or other European governments are left to your own judgment. You have in this respect a carte blanche. I know that you will let no opportunity be lost in advancing the interests of Ireland and injuring those of her tyrant. The

JOHN MITCHEL.

practicability of our invasion of Ireland from America must also claim your most anxious attention. Reliable information must be sought by you and conveyed to me of the amount of land and marine force of our enemies available for the defense of their domination in Ireland.

The possibility of procuring any quantity of arms and munitions of war in France previous or during our Irish insurrection is a thing most useful to be well informed on. Leonard can find out parties who may be able to give you information on this subject.

I think I have now set down all that is required with respect to your mission. Before concluding, however, I wish to repeat what I have often stated to you before, that I consider a revolutionary organization in Ireland to be absolutely essential to her liberation. It is the first grand requisite of success. Without it even an American or a French war might fail to free her. With a strong home organization even our contemplated raid upon Canada, followed up by the landing of a few thousand filibusters with arms, munitions, etc., might effect all that we desire. To keep up the home organization must then be our chiefest and greatest care. The supplies of money for that purpose should be ample and unfailing even though some of our remittances should run the risk of going astray. The Canadian raid I look upon as a mere diversion, as far as regards our present action. Unless it drag the U. S. into war with England it can only end in defeat to those that engage in it. But it is worth trying in the hope that it may lead to such a war. The money you now take with you shall be followed up closely by other and larger sums, all of which you will lodge to your own credit as soon as received in some Parisian bank to be drawn upon by you at the requisition of the C. E. I. R.

For your personal services you will receive the sum of $2,500 in gold per annum, payable quarterly in advance from these headquarters.

* * * * * * * *

XXIII

This letter contains a report of the arrest of James Stephens, C. E., and gives a description of conditions as they existed in Dublin at that time, together with recommendations regarding what should be done in the near future. The letter is in the handwriting of General Wm. Halpin and is signed "Bird," one of the assumed names under which he corresponded with O'Mahony.

Dublin, 14th November, 1865.

Col. John O'Mahony, H. C. F. B., New York:

My Dear Sir: I have the honor to report what will doubtless seem to you and our friends a great calamity, namely, the arrest of the C. E. and three others of the Council. This was affected on Saturday morning at 5 A. M. It is needless to write as to the circumstances of those arrests, as the papers will convey to you all the information on that head. The arrest of the C. E. has no other effect on the organization than a temporary depression on the public mind. This, however, will be remedied at once through the instrumentality of agents sent out to allay all fears on that account. Soon after the arrests, the Military Council called a meeting of all the Dublin Centres, when a temporary C. E. was appointed. His letter, by the bearer, will acquaint you of all that has happened. It is most important that frequent communication and a thorough understanding be kept up between the C. C. and Head Quarters here. The crisis is upon us and prompt action is absolutely necessary. The men at the head of affairs throughout the Country are strictly obedient, yet it is feared that nothing can keep the people down after this year. I would, therefore, beg that every effort be made to meet the contingency as soon as possible. Of course we will do all in our power to stay proceedings until you are ready to assist. I shall not enter further into details as the temporary C. E. will give you all the facts in the case.

I may add that strong hopes are entertained that the C. E. will be at liberty before the end of the week, arrangements are being made to effect that purpose which I think, from the lights before me, cannot fail to be successful. I would most respectfully urge again that a Paymaster be appointed to pay the American officers at stated periods. Much trouble would be avoided and much dissatisfaction prevented by this course. A full list of all men sent over should be furnished by the Adjutant General, with the rank of each, the amount furnished at starting and the date of commencement. This is necessary, for the reason that several officers have not reported to Head Quarters, in consequence of the arrests being continually made, and the fact that parties are constantly applying for funds of whom nothing is known here. I believe that I stated in my last that I exhausted all my funds on parties who had run out. Kelly is in a similar fix for the reasons I stated before. I wish it to be distinctly understood that there is no dispiriting influence in consequence of the state of affairs here. All are buoyant and anxious for the word. Permit me to suggest that some General officers of ability should be sent over at once, particularly the Commander-in-Chief, so that he might become acquainted with the Country in time to manage the forces intelligently when the hour of action arrives. Perhaps you have the ideas of the C. E. on this head, yet I venture to make the suggestion on my own account, believing as I do, that such a course would be conducive to the better understanding of all parties on this side.

I have seen several of the principal men from the country and they say that a landing from your side is confidently expected. I am certain that a force, however small, would have a great effect on the country, give confidence to the people and encourage the troops at the start. All will depend on the first effort—that successful the sun of Independence will never set on our Island again. The spirit of the people is admirable, their discipline and prompt obedience to all orders is, to my mind, the best evidence of success. There is no jealousy, no wrangling as in former days. Every man considers himself a soldier bound to obey as his first duty.

The trials will commence on the 27th inst., and, no doubt, packed juries will be got by the Government to do the work.

Every effort should be made to be prepared for that event. The red coats are being worked to perfection but I had better not say much on that subject. Some of the speeches made on your side have given much offence and done much harm. Can they not be avoided in the future. All the American officers who have been arrested have preferred claims through the U. S. Consul at this Port. An outcry should be raised over there on that subject, indignation meeting held and the Government urged to take the matter up. One such arrest of an English subject abroad, would be a Casus belli at once. Captain Rodgers and Lieutenant McNeff were kept breaking stones without any trial. Rodgers has been discharged unconditionally. McNeff is yet in Limbo. Fanning has just been released on bail.

Lt. Col. Leonard is also out unconditionally after spending 20 days in solitary confinement in Ardee jail. Every effort should be made to induce the U. S. Government to assume the offensive in relation to these arrests. A simple declaration of War by the U. S. against England would make Ireland free. John Bull is trembling lest such a state of affairs would result from his perfidy.

With my kindest regards to yourself and the members of the C. C., etc., etc., I am, my dear sir,

Yours in fraternity,

"BIRD."

Note.—"Bird" was the assumed name used by General Wm. G. Halpin.

XXIV

(Printed Circular.)

War Department, F. B.,
Adjutant General's Office,
New York, November 20, 1865.

General Orders, No. 2.

To avoid all misunderstanding, and to insure the immediate and energetic action which the necessities of the situation demand, the Secretary of War, F. B., issues the following instructions for the direction and government of the military organization of the Fenian Brotherhood:

I. Each Centre of Circle will forward to this Department on the 10th, 20th and last day of every month a roll of fighting men ready at a week's notice to take the field for the cause of Ireland.

II. In every Circle of the F. B. drills will be at once commenced, in the school of the soldier, of the company and—where possible—of the battalion. Volunteers will be divided into two classes, to be drilled separately—1st, veterans; 2d, recruits, who will be incorporated with the veterans so soon as they shall have acquired sufficient proficiency in the school of the soldier.

III. On the muster rolls will be noted the number of arms and accoutrements, with their calibre and description. Where arms are in the possession of volunteers, or are at the disposal of Circles, they will be credited to them and paid for by this Department in event of success. But it is expressly stated that muskets will be furnished by this Department in all cases where men are unable to procure their own. It is the wish of the Secretary of War that each and every patriot should share in the glory of the approaching struggle for freedom; his inability to procure an outfit must deter no one.

IV. The Inspector General, F. B., will confer with the different State Centres in the selection of suitable officers for nomination to the appointment of State Assistant Inspectors General; he will at once place them on duty and forward their names for confirmation to this Department. The Inspector General has no authority to give orders to State Centres, or Centres of Circles, but will simply advise and co-operate with them in matters pertaining to military duties. He may, however, order and direct military organizations when formed, or while in course of formation, on all matters pertaining to their military duties.

V. The duties of the State Assistant Inspector General will be: 1st. To superintend and promote, to the best of his ability, the immediate preparation of men for active service; he will select suitable officers, to whom, on his recommendation, authority will be given by the War Department to recruit regiments or companies, and who will be commissioned accordingly, subject to the rules and regulations of this Department. 2d. He will report immediately to the Board of Military Examination, through these Headquarters, the names of all officers who are applicants for commissions in the F. B., with such indorsements as an examination into their military history, qualifications and recommendations will justify, stating at what time they will be prepared to appear before the Board for examination, and, if commissioned, be ready for active service. He will also report the names with indorsements, as above, of those who have not been commissioned in any former service, and who make application to come before the Board for examination, should he deem the applicant fit, on investigation. 3d. He will inspect the arms of each Circle or military organization in the State, and report their condition and calibre to this Department.

VI. Courtesy and affability is especially enjoined on each and every officer of this Department in all his intercourse and dealings with the members of the Brotherhood.

VII. Copies of this order will be given to each State Centre, and by him transmitted to the various Circles throughout his State. Each State Centre is requested by the Secretary of War,

F. B., to address all complaints against military officers of the Brotherhood directly to this Department Headquarters.

Strict secrecy is enjoined in the promulgation of this order among the several Circles.

By order of the Secretary of War, F. B.,

C. CARROLL TEVIS,
Brig. Gen. and A. G., F. B.,
Box 3821, N. Y. P. O.

XXV

War Department, F. B.,
Adjutant General's Office,
New York, 24 November, 1865.

Special Orders, No. 13.

Col. P. F. Walsh, Inspector General, F. B., will proceed without delay on a tour of inspection throughout the Circles of the F. B. established in the different States. He will take for his guidance General Orders, No. 2, A. G. O., Nov. 20, 1865, in all matters relating to the military organization of the F. B., adding such instructions as the particular circumstances of each individual case may in his opinion demand. He will endeavor to impress upon all the well-wishers of the cause of Ireland the necessity for prompt and energetic action, and will pay close attention to the drill, particularly in the manual of arms. The simplest movements, comprising the formation of lines from columns and columns from lines, the loading and firing by company, by battalion and by file are all that will be required for our first battles.

By order of the Secretary of War, F. B.,

C. CARROLL TEVIS,
Brig. Gen and Adj. Gen., F. B.

Official,
EUGENE J. COURTNEY,
Major and A. A. Gen., F. B.

XXVI

This important and historic letter, appointing John O'Mahony Chief Agent and Representative of the Irish Republic in America, was written by James Stephens in 1865, after his escape from Richmond prison.

IRISH REPUBLIC.

To the Members of the Fenian Brotherhood, and the friends of Ireland generally in the U. S. of America, Canada, etc.

Dublin, December 23, 1865.

Countrymen and Friends: Aware that certain members of the Fenian Brotherhood, and notoriously the "Senate" of that association, have, madly and traitoriously moved to a mad and traitorous end, raise the cry of "to Canada!" instead of the cry of "to Ireland!" and aware that John O'Mahony, known as Head Centre and President of the Fenian Brotherhood, has wisely and firmly, as in duty bound, opposed this mad and traitorous diversion from the right path—the only path that could possibly save our country and our race. I in consequence hereby appoint the said John O'Mahony Representative and Financial Agent of the Irish Republic in the United States of America, Canada, etc., with ample and unquestionable authority to enroll men, raise money, and fit out an expedition to sail for Ireland and reach Ireland on the earliest possible day, and in all other ways in which, to the best of his judgment, he can serve Ireland—that land to which he has devoted life and honor—I hereby authorize and call on him

JAMES STEPHENS.
C. E. I. R.

XXVII

ESCAPE OF JAMES STEPHENS.

The story of Stephens's escape might well have thrilled the Irish people at the time. To-day it reads like a romance. His escape from Richmond Prison was startling enough, but that for four months he should have lived in Ireland, to the knowledge of large numbers of the people, and with a heavy price upon his head, and that finally he should have got clear off, despite all the detective machinery of the British Government, is still more wonderful. The dead walls of every Irish city and town were placarded with alluring offers; £2,000 was the price offered for the capture of Stephens. For private information leading to his arrest £1,000 might be had for the asking. But all in vain; and so in the early morning of March 14, 1866, James Stephens, accompanied by Colonel Thomas Kelly and John Flood, sailed from Dublin with Captain Nicholas Weldon on board a little collier, the Concord.

Captain Weldon was a native of Baldoyle and a close friend from boyhood of John Flood, a leading Fenian, who arranged with him to convey Stephens and Kelly to some port in France. The facts of that historic voyage are gleaned from an account which Captain Weldon himself gave some years ago. The Captain says:

"My narrative begins with the early days of March, 1866, when with John Flood, an old friend and townsman and as fine a specimen of Irish manhood as need be seen, and his friend, Colonel Kelly, with whom I had no previous acquaintance, I made arrangements to take Stephens and themselves to a port in the north of France. For the benefit of those who may not have a clear recollection of those stirring times, I may mention that at the period of which I am giving an account the whole available forces of the Crown of those islands was concentrated upon one object—and that object the recapture of the redoubtable James Stephens, added to which there was a reward of £2,000 upon his head. So that the taking of his body alive out of Ireland was a task of no small magnitude, more especially as the whole line of quays, north and south, was placarded with the tempting fortune of £2,000 to any person who would give such information as would lead to his capture; hence the sailors who manned the vessels that left the port were—and not unnaturally—on the alert as to strangers taking passage in any of the coasting colliers. That being the description of craft which I owned and commanded at the time, the good brigantine Concord, I may here state that the usual number of my crew was six men and a boy, and in consequence of the number of those coming, to avoid suspicion, I discharged a corresponding number of my men, including my mate, which left me but two men and the boy, and, nautically speaking, the three duffers.

"Now, it is a notorious fact, that at this time there were two revenue cutters, one at each side of Poolbeg, to board any suspicious craft outward bound. For eight or nine days after our arrangement we were detained in the Liffey waiting for a start of wind, and making whatever preparation we could for our perilous voyage. An additional filip was given to my anxiety on March 11 by a pilot, who had a vessel out of port that day, and who told me he was obliged to heave the ship to in the bay, when a search of over an hour was made, and not an inch of the ship but was overhauled, and every man on board questioned.

"After hearing this cheering news from the pilot, who little thought what an interest I had in his yarn, I retired to my cabin to think. I leave my readers to imagine what my thoughts were, if they are so minded. On the twelfth I had my vessel hauled out in the river, ready to start, and at 9 o'clock p. m., on Tuesday, the thirteenth inst., I was at the landing steps opposite Boyd's Chemical Works by appointment, when my three adventurers stepped into my boat, and I sculled them on board as quickly as possible. We cast off our moorings, and had the vessel hauled over to the north side of the river to make sail with the wind N. E.—Kelly, Flood and Stephens working manfully at the winch.

"As may be imagined, we had considerable delay owing to the want of nautical skill of my three new sailors, and it was 1.30 of the fourteenth when we hailed the revenue boat to know the time. At first we feared she would board us, but she passed up the river, merely asking what ship. I answered the Concord, of Dublin, for Cardiff. We then had to run the gauntlet of the two revenue cruisers in the bay, but we sailed gaily out innocently between them without notice, shaped a southerly course, passed the Mugglins closely, soon after Bray Head which showed remarkably beautiful in the bright moonlight. At this time we were going free with every stitch we could carry with a spanking N. E. breeze. By daylight we were off Wicklow Head, when the wind gradually died away and changed to S. E., which directly headed us on the course we were sailing, and as we were keeping close to the land so as to get all the advantage we could of the ebb tide, which had still about two hours to run, we were unpleasantly close to a very nasty lee shore. However, we beat up as far as Arklow Bay, where we put in to avoid the flowing tide.

"About midday, the wind increasing, I saw we were going to have a very bad night, as there were all the indications of a storm from the south. My position was now truly one of anxiety—the prospect of a gale right in our teeth, a dangerous shore under our lee, and two revenue cruisers in the Bay of Dublin on the lookout. About 2 o'clock p. m. I hastily consulted with my passengers as to the desirability of putting down our helm and running for a port in Scotland. After a time they agreed, and down went the helm, and we squared away to the northward, avoiding Dublin Bay by running over the Kish Bank, which in itself was no small risk, as a smart breeze was blowing and a rough see running, and slow-sailing craft as we were, we were going seven knots through the water, the wind still increasing. I was now making for mid-channel, as it was not prudent to keep too near the Irish land; also there was every likelihood of the wind becoming more easterly, which turned out so.

"It was now blowing half a gale, but I carried every stitch until 10 o'clock p. m., when we took in all our light-flyers which was most fortunate, as about 11 o'clock p. m. we were struck with a very heavy squall, which, tidy as we were, almost threw her on her beam ends. We had to let go everything and run dead before the wind until we got her under double-reefed canvas and small head-sail, which was the very most she could carry, and with that she labored and strained all night in a heavy seaway close hauled, the wind having gone considerably eastward and increased to a gale. At dawn we sighted the Isle of Man on our weather beam. How to get around the South Light was the next problem, and a difficult one, too. I could run for Strangford Lough with ease; but if I did the probabilities were strongly in favor of my being boarded and the game ended; so I clapped on sail until we could hardly stand on deck, our lee rail being almost in the water.

"I may mention that a sunken reef runs out from this island or rock for about two miles, and its termination was at that time marked by a buoy, but there is a lightship there now. This was the object I dreaded; but with the aid of the flowing tide and the heavy press of sail we were carrying I had great hopes of weathering it. It was a narrow shave, as in passing I could easily hit the buoy with a biscuit. Shortly after passing this danger a steamer hove in sight, and so overstrained were my nerves that I took her for a gunboat. This is not much to be wondered at, as the nature of my charge, the length of time I stood at the vessel's wheel—almost since we left the Liffey—

and the very disagreeable change in the weather, had their effect, and almost knocked me off my head. Flood, Kelly and Stephens, each provided with a brace of six-chambered revolvers, and setting their teeth, resolved not to be taken alive. This warlike preparation was, I was thankful to learn from one of my own men, rendered unnecessary, as the steamer turned out to be the Derry boat.

"At 2 o'clock p. m. on the fifteenth of March, we were again obliged to up helm and run for the Lough through the narrow Sound of Donaghadee into the Lough, where I let go my anchor right opposite the coast-guard station in Whitehouse Roads as dusk was setting in. At 5 o'clock next morning (March 16), weighed anchor with a fair wind and stood down the Lough, but had only got as far as Copeland Islands when the standard of the wheel broke, and the vessel's head came round and faced up the Lough again. This caused considerable delay, as tackle had to be rigged as temporary steering gear.

"We again got her before the wind, a good strong breeze S. S. E. blowing at the time, and shaped a course for Irvine, which, however, we were unable to reach, for as we stood more easterly the wind headed us again, and I decided to make Ardrossan, which we reached about 8 o'clock p. m., and run the vessel hard and fast on the ground in the old harbor. Watching a proper opportunity I launched my small boat, got my three passengers and self into her, and sculled them to the beach opposite the Eglinton Hotel, which was the deepest water, but as the boat was still some distance from the beach I had to jump into the water knee-deep and carry them one by one on shore, where our leave-taking was very short—merely a fervent shake of the hand on my part, a wish for their safe departure from the kingdom; and on theirs, a profound expression of gratitude, and that was the last I saw of the gallant old chief and his intrepid companions, one of whom was a dear personal friend of my own."

Captain Weldon died on January 5, 1905, at his residence, 2 Marino terrace, Malahide road, Dublin, in his sixty-ninth year. He was in his thirtieth year at the time of his famous exploit. The love of daring adventures in the cause of fatherland seems to have been a hereditary instinct with him, for it was his grandfather who smuggled Hamilton Rowan away to France from Howth.

XXVIII

(Printed Circular.)

War Department, F. B.,
Adjutant General's Office,
New York, January 4, 1866.

The following officers have been appointed by me to serve on the General Staff or as Inspectors General in the various States:

C. Carroll Tevis, Adjutant General with rank of Brigadier General.

John Mechan, Colonel and Chief Engineer.
P. F. Walsh, Colonel and Inspector General.
S. R. Tresilian, Major and Assistant Engineer.
Eugene J. Courtney, Major and Assistant Adjutant General.
William M. O'Reilly, Captain of Ordnance.
D. W. Greany, Clerk in War Department.

List of Inspectors General.

Major John Delahunt, State of Wisconsin.
Gen. Thos. Curry, State of Missouri.
Col. Albert P. Morrow, State of Pennsylvania.
Capt. Maurice J. McGrath, State of Illinois.
Major P. Phelan, Department of Manhattan.
George O'Neil, State of Delaware.
Col. James Doyle, State of New York.
John F. Scanlon, Department of Chicago.
Lieut. Col. John G. Healy, State of Connecticut.
Capt. Timothy O'Connor, Department of Shawmut.
Capt. John H. Daly, State of Michigan.
Capt. Andrew Mahony, State of Florida.
Col. John Balfe, State of Indiana.
Capt. T. R. Bourke, State of Massachusetts.

(Signed) T. W. SWEENY,
Sec. of War, F. B.

XXIX

This letter was written to General Halpin in New York in 1866 by Capt. Larry O'Brien, then in Paris. Capt. O'Brien is at present living in New Haven, Conn.

Paris, January 17, 1866.

Col. W. J. Halpin:

Dear Sir: I have been in Paris since the day after you left Dublin. A friend of yours, Mr. Nicholson Walshingham, is now one week here with me. You know him, he is an artist. He desires to be remembered to you all. Our friends in Dublin are in favor of Col. O'Mahony. Mr. W. desires me to tell you so. There is here a young man the name of Graney. He is from

Philadelphia. He states that he was sent here by the new Senate to see Stephens and have him go to America. He says that the reason he did not bring any letters of explanation or recommendation was because P. J. Meehan told him that he would not need them, as he, Meehan, would write to Mitchell and it would be all right, and Mitchell would recognize him, but when Mitcheil saw him he would not have anything to do with him. He was very bitter against Col. O'Mahony, but he has moderated very much and, in fact, he has not one word to say in favor of the Senate.

Is it not too bad that they do not send the money, and it needed so much? I am a witness to the proper outlay of the last amount. I have resided here since Dec. 14th and will continue to do so for another week or so. I am the agent of the Irish firm. I purchase silk very cheap and have no troubie in sending them by post. Mr. W. desires me to say to you that he has been pushing up to one of the Widows while you are absent and expects to make good progress. Every friend that comes from Ireland swears that if they get an opportunity they will have revenge on P. J. Meehan. I would call your attention to the "Irish American" of the 16th Dec. on the 2nd page, where they mention about a draft of $60,000 as if the enemy would not find out soon enough. Will you please settle with Col. O'Mahony about the checks of £19.10 which was of one amount 1st and second of bill of exchange; please to remember me to Col. O'Mahony. I have full faith that he never will do wrong and his action will be a great benefit to us and that I hope before many months pass away that I will be fighting under him defending the Green banner of Ireland. Hoping to see you in good health, I have the honor to remain,

Yours respectfully and sincerely,

L. O'BRIEN.

P. S.—Please excuse me for the liberty I take in addressing you.

XXX

24 Rue Lacepede, Paris, January 27, 1866.

My Dear O'Mahony:—I congratulate you on having got rid of the title of president, and also got rid of the constitution and of the Senate. I saw that matters were coming to that point and that there would be infallibly an open rupture. I have read your message in the Daily News and find it very satisfactory. No doubt the real and sincere Irishmen who desire the success of our cause will rally around you, and probably the organization will be as strong as ever.

In the meantime the rupture in America has greatly injured our friends in Ireland, who were expecting, if not an armed expedition, at least large supplies of money to purchase war material. I told them immediately on coming over here that

I thought they need not expect an expeditionary force, which the American Government would never allow to start, the two countries being at peace. I did not conceal my own strong conviction that an insurrection in Ireland without such aid from America must fail. But J. S. is, after all, the best judge of the exigencies of his own position, and you need not be surprised if you hear any day that a decisive movement has been made.

I have written twice in some detail to you since coming to Paris—once under cover to Mrs. Doheny in Brooklyn, and once to your box in the post office. The second letter was addressed on the outside to Mr. Killian and contained letters for him and for you. I hope those all duly arrived. If so you already know the situation of affairs as I found it, and also the rapid and constant demand for money. The sum sent out with me is now all drawn and safely sent over, except about £100, which I keep still in the bank to keep the account open. Our friends in Ireland are very eager to hear of further remittances from your side, but I suppose the unfortunate state of affairs there may have prevented that.

My constant address for the future will be as above: 24 Rue Lacepede, where I shall go to live at the end of February, and where I receive letters at present. Letters, however, addressed to me this month at 3 Rue Richer will come to hand. Address in preference to Rue Lacepede. Very truly your friend,

J. M. (John Mitchel.)

XXXI

Philadelphia, January 28, 1866.

Major Gen. T. W. Sweeny, Sec of War.

General: After a very lengthy interview and much discussion with Messrs. Jenks & Mitchell, yesterday, I have accomplished the renewal of the contract until the 28th February, that is thirty (30) days from the date of expiration of the original agreement. Mr. O'Rourke could give me but five thousand (5,000) dollars and I could not obtain J. & M.'s consent to the withdrawal of any muskets until the further payment of five thousand (5,000) dollars, when it is stipulated I shall do so. It is also understood that by payments of installments we may at any time take away the articles in a number proportionate to the amounts paid. In this arrangement I was guided by the advice of Senator Meehan in the absence of Mr. O'Sullivan.

I shall inspect to-morrow a large quantity of artillery harness to be sold at a Government sale on Tuesday, and be guided in my action by the quality and prices of the articles. During the end of the week I have opened and answered several letters to yourself and Colonel Roberts, and sent to the press several sets of resolutions passed in different circles, endorsing yourself and the Senate. I regret that the correspondence on the subject of the arms has been published; it will direct the attention of the authorities to the transaction. Colonel Roberts assured me that this part of his answer to Killian would not be made public, and I presume that in his absence some one has assumed an unauthorized responsibility. Letters from Washington and Baltimore strongly urge your visit there, and I respectfully recommend that you take these points on your return, particularly as the Baltimore Circle announces that "they have five hundred dollars in their treasury which they do not know what to do with." I wrote Gahan, the Centre, a begging letter and it may have the effect, but your presence will have a hundred fold the effect. The people are wavering, but he says "with a speech from you and Colonel Roberts two thousand (2,000) men can be raised"—my own regiment was mustered out there, and the Maryland troops, personal vanity apart, had a good deal of confidence in me. West Point reports from four hundred (400) to five hundred (500) dollars in their treasury and a similar state of uncertainty. I have written and will send them some one this week. Bryce brings an invitation from the wealthy Circle of Bordentown, N. J. I can't speak and have ordered Tresillian and Hynes there.

Colonel Doyle, our best A. I. G., has sent me a suggestion that a professional tour be made to Poughkeepsie, Malone and a number of other points along the line of the railroad and the frontier. I have directed him to visit these points; I at the same time forwarded him a commission as Colonel, 1st Regiment, I. A., with authority and instructions to recruit a regiment immediately. I will examine to-day Col. Morrow, Major Harkness and Captain Lanigan, to whom authority was given to recruit a Cavalry Regiment. If I find them fit, I shall issue their commissions and muster them in immediately. It is understood that their regiment is to act as infantry until such time as we can, or they can, mount them.

I inclose a letter from Col. Roberts.

Very respectfully,

Your obedient servant,

C. CARROLL TEVIS,

Brig. Gen. and A. G., F. B.

XXXII

This letter was written by James Stephens in 1866 in the presence of Capt. John McCafferty, who carried it to John O'Mahony in New York. McCafferty was thus enabled to certify to its genuineness, as it seems some doubts had been cast on the authenticity of a previous letter.

Irish Republic, Dublin, February 10, 1866.

To John O'Mahony,

Brother and Friend:—This note is written in presence of the bearer, Capt. McCafferty, so that he may be able to prove the genuineness of my letter at need. Is the precaution called for? It may not be, for the "Senate" faction must be very low when driven to the expedient of calling my letters of the 22d and 23d of last December forgeries. Such a faction must, I say, be very low, and may be no more by this. But I would leave nobody any excuse for affixing such a stain or any stain to your name, and whoever would attempt to do so after this I would publicly brand as a wilful slanderer and enemy to Ireland. Yours fraternally,

JAMES STEPHENS.

This letter is indorsed as follows: "New York, March 19, 1866. Read before Central Council. John O'Mahony, H. C. F. B."

Private.

Dublin, February 10, 1866.

To John O'Mahony, New York.

Brother and Friend:—I intended to have sent out by bearer an elaborate address to the friends of Ireland in America. Written as I meant to write it, this address would, I believe, have smashed all opposition and given confidence to men now sceptical enough. Unfortunately, cold began to grow on me some days ago, and yesterday this cold came to a crisis. My throat became so swollen and sore that I could take no food and could get but little sleep last night. This morning I was much worse and in high fever. However, I arose to make an effort to write. I have found it impossible to do so, and to-night I am decidedly unwell. I should not be uneasy but for my throat. But even this may be only a temporary ailment, and I trust all will be well in a few days.

Your letters since the convention have brought us all but despair. It is a miracle how we have been able to hold out since. The last money in Mitchell's hands (£160) was drawn a month and more ago. Since then we have been driven to raise money as best we could. Now, to show that we want money at present is to drive into utter despair the very class of men who could give us money. Are you aware of the number of men under pay here now? Besides those from your side, there are some thousand from England and Scotland. Then the trials demand large sums. And what of the organization? I say nothing of the needs of war. But if the real state of things were now known to all I should either consent to move at once, as we are or dissolve the organization. I had made you popular here once more and taught all in our ranks to look to you hopefully, but what can I do now in the face of facts? The heavens or the earth could not hide you if we are driven into a fight of desperation and consequent slaughter or dissolution.

I am unable to write more at present. A word of advice may be given with regard to those men just come over. We don't want privates here in this way. When such men come at all it should be with the expedition. Nor will officers, unless of a superior grade and superior ability, be worth their pay till we take the field. It is a woeful thing on your side to think that, with a few exceptions, we have not men here equal to the officers hitherto sent over. We have hundreds such.

I feel really so unwell that I must conclude here. Hoping that something of consequence has been done by this and that aid is within a few days of us, I am

Yours as ever,

JAMES STEPHENS.

The bearer has won a high opinion for himself here. I think very highly of him myself, and it grieves me to let him go. But he can do good work in various ways at your side, and you will find him specially serviceable in putting to shame or silence those treacherous runaways who are now trotted out to slander the true and brave men at home. Be very kind to bearer.

This letter bears the following indorsement: "Hd. Qrs. F. B., New York, 19 March, 1866. Read befor C. C. John O'Mahony, H. C. F. B."

XXXIII

U. S. Steamer Michigan,
Buffalo, Feb. 16, 1866.

Maj. Gen. T. W. Sweeny, Sec. of War, F. B.

Sir:—I have formed a circle on board of this ship. It numbers 17 men at present, good and true to the cause.

I gave Mr. O'Day $100 from myself to buy arms.

There is nothing new on the Lakes. We can't leave here before the 15th of April next.

I will do all I can. You may be sure that I am sorry that

I can't attend the Convention, but you can have all the means that it is in my power to give.

If you want a map of Lake Erie, I can get it for you.

I hope the President is well.

Fraternally yours,

WM. E. LEONARD,
C. F. B.

Direct.

WM. E. LEONARD, Mate,
U. S. Steamer Michigan,
Buffalo, N. Y.

XXXIV

Headquarters, F. B.,
New York, March 3rd, 1866.

Maj. General T. W. Sweeny, Sec. of War and Navy, F. B.

General:—In compliance with your instructions I have made investigations regarding the organization of a co-operative naval force, intended to capture the enemy's vessels now blockaded by ice in the Canadian waters, and have the honor to report as follows:

First. The enterprise would require from two to three hundred able seamen, divided into as many corps as there are objective points—a simultaneous movement being advisable.

Second. Each corps should be under the command of a reliable and experienced naval officer.

Third. An immediate recognizance of the position, armament and other means of defense of these vessels should be made.

Fourth. The expedition should keep open as far as possible the means of communication between the different corps, for the purpose of concentration, if necessary, for which purpose there should be a Chief of the expedition.

Fifth. The men can be raised in New York in ten or twelve days and the services of competent and faithful officers obtained.

Sixth. The expense of fitting out such an expedition at this place would be about $12,000, viz.:

Bounty or "Hand Money," $40 per man	$8,000
Two weeks' subsistence for men and officers	2,000
Transportation and subsistence	2,000
	$12,000

This amount would put the forces in the vicinity of the scenes of operation.

I think, however, that Buffalo and Chicago would afford greater facilities for fitting out such an expedition and that the expenses would be reduced. I would suggest, however, even if these points are chosen, that a few good seamen be procured here to aid in organizing.

Respectfully submitted,

J. W. BRYCE,
Captain and Naval Aid.

XXXV

26 Rue Lacepede, Paris, March 10, 1866.

John O'Mahony, Esq., President F. B.:

Dear O'Mahony: Since my last letter to you I have to report the receipt of a package of bonds of the I. R. B., which arrived perfectly safe on February 17, and of your letter dated February 20, enclosing bill of exchange on Rothschilds for 28,840 francs, of which 3,090 on my private account and 25,750 francs for transmission to Ireland, payable three days after sight, that is yesterday.

As there was a messenger already in Paris, waiting for money, with an order for £1,000, and as there was still in bank a sum of £57 15s. not yet sent over in pursuance of the last orders I had been presented with, I added these two sums together, and also the cost of procuring English money in Paris (£6) for £1,000, and remitted the whole, amounting to £1,063 16s., or, in francs, after deducting 14 francs for stamping duty, 26,576 50c.

Up to this time all moneys sent over by me have been received; but, of course, there is continual dissatisfaction at receiving so little. There is now here in bank to the credit of the F. B. something over 1,000 francs only—the precise sum I am not certain of until I settle the account with John Monroe & Co., which I shall do in a few days, and transfer our account elsewhere, for I am well watched.

With regard to the bonds of the I. R., if the society had gone on harmoniously and if the F. B. were still with strength unbroken, as when I left America, probably something could be done with them here. You are aware that to put any bonds of a foreign loan upon the market here requires previous authorization by the government. That, I need hardly tell you, was not to be expected in the present relations of France and England. But perhaps they might have sold privately. However, after the events which have happened, both in the United States and in Ireland, I see no chance of this. I have offered some to persons whom I knew to be well affected to our cause, but in vain. For the present, therefore, the whole package of bonds remains unbroken in my desk. In a few days, when I shall know precisely what balance remains in the bank (which, however, is very small, as I told you) I will send over a regular account to Mr. Killian.

Pray note my address, 26—not 24—Rue Lacepede.

Very truly yours,

JOHN MITCHEL.

PRIVATE.—I need not tell you, dear O'M., how bitterly I have been grieved by the shameful breakup of the F. B. Its worst effect was not the cutting off of money supplies—it was the deconsideration of our cause in America—which sentiment of the Americans was what encouraged the enemy to make the swoop upon all Irish-American citizens they could find in Ireland. I make no doubt that Russell had consulted Adams before doing it and that Adams told him to go ahead—they were but Irish, after all. It is very well for Mr. Killian and others to express indignation, which indeed they have a right to feel at this open abandonment of the rights of naturalized citizens who had fought for the flag and all that. But it is what ought to have been expected. And a fine situation those American Irish now find themselves in, who fought for that flag with the expectation that as soon as the war was ended they would be let loose upon England!

But it is useless to look back upon the past. The movement in Ireland is, I suppose, entirely stopped and any combined and intelligent insurrection quite impossible—though there may be local outbreaks. The last letter but one I had from him (beginning of January) was to ask my advice as to whether the outbreak should begin then, within a day or two, or be postponed for a month, when he said he was sure of being much better provided with material. Now, he knew my opinion at the time he wrote—namely, that without a considerable expedition from America insurrection in Ireland was hopeless. So in my reply I told him that I must decline to give any advice now on that point—that he best knew both what his resources were and what engagements he had taken with the multitudes of Americans he had brought over, as well as the many hundreds, perhaps thousands, of men he had induced to come from England and Scotland, abandoning their business and appearing on the streets of Dublin as strangers having nothing to do, which could not fail to attract the attention of the police—that I would have advised that matters should not be brought to such a crisis at present, but as he had brought them to such a crisis I would not recommend anything at all. All I could do was to remit the money in my hands as quickly as he called for it. Again he wrote to me, a few days later, stating that neither he nor any one else in the movement thought for one moment of settling down without a fight—that the question was only whether they should fight then or in the beginning of February. And that was all he had asked my advice upon; that he had consulted his Centres and laid everything before them, and that it was agreed to wait till the beginning of February. It is now near the middle of March, and the government has now, I suppose, made any respectable fight impossible. Stephens' friends are already laying the blame on others, especially on you for not sending an expedition, or at least for not furnishing an illimitable treasury. It was impossible for you to do, under the circumstances, more than you have done, and this I have always told them. Also the prompt action of the English government was precisely what they ought to have expected—what they ought to have been prepared for—what they ought to have anticipated, by striking two months ago if they were to strike at all.

I do not understand all this, as at present advised. But I wish to say to you that if the movement so far as immediate action is concerned be really ruined, and if the I. R. (after so many fine men have been destroyed) is to settle back into its normal form of a chronic conspiracy, I have doubts about the propriety of remaining as a financial agent in Paris. For the next three months, of course, I will remain at my post and carry out any instructions and dispositions with regard to funds that I may be entrusted with by the F. B. That will give both you and me time to convince ourselves of the real history and present situation of affairs in Ireland. I hope you will also write to me and frankly tell me what you think of all this and of the future course we ought to adopt.

I am glad to learn that you are again getting the power of the F. B. into your own hands. You know it was my opinion that you should never have shared it with others. And where you were first seriously to blame (as I thought, and think) was in permitting that Philadelphia Congress at all, or at least permitting the appointment of Senate and "Government," etc. I partly foresaw trouble before I left, and tried to impress most earnestly upon members of the Senate that their business and duty were to sustain you. But I further find you to blame, when the Senate attacked you, in retorting hard names upon them and posting them as thieves. This made the breach irreparable, provoked their friends throughout the country to sustain them through everything and added to the already inevitable scandal of an "Irish quarrel," which amused the Americans and encouraged the British to ride roughshod over the I. R.

You may have remarked that, although on quitting America I had promised Mr. Meehan a weekly letter for the Irish American, which letter I hoped to make a valuable auxiliary to the cause, I wrote him, in fact, only one before I heard of the quarrel. I came then reluctantly to the conclusion that my contributing to the Irish American under the circumstances would give me the appearance of taking part against you.

On the other hand, I did not see how I could write a public letter sustaining you without attacking the Senators, some of whom I really think good and patriotic Irishmen.

In the meantime I beg of you to consider well the present situation of affairs and give me your views fully.

With best regards to Mr. Killian I am, dear O'Mahony, very sincerely yours,

JOHN MITCHEL.

P. S.—Although the second part of my present letter is marked private, that is merely to indicate that it is not official. You can, of course, show it to any one you may think right. If you should even deem it judicious to publish the latter part of it, beginning with "I am glad to learn," I make no objection, although in writing it I did not think of this—which, perhaps, is so much the better. J. M.

Only if you do print this latter part I stipulate that you leave it as it is without retouching even the passages in which I have taken the liberty to blame yourself.

XXXVI

1334 Walnut Street, March 23, 1866.

Maj. Gen. T. W. Sweeny, Sec. of War, F. B.

General:—I am engaged in preparing, for shipment, three thousand (3,000) muskets. To-morrow I am to have an interview with the party who sent you a note offering batteries; he will then furnish me detailed specifications of his proposal. From what I have learned to-day the price of each battery complete, including harness, will not exceed ten thousand (10,000) dollars. The guns are 3-inch rifles, and are at the Phenixville foundry; they are reported to be new guns, and, to avoid the expense of a journey there, I shall direct Maj. Tressillian, who is to be there to-morrow, to make an inspection and report—the carriages, etc., I will see to myself. The best of the business is that the people will engage to deliver to us at any point we may indicate and run all risks of transportation, etc. Maj. Lanigan reports twelve hundred (1,200) men, of whom, he says, he can rely on seven hundred (700) to start with in his own regiment. They want arms and will pay for carbines or revolvers and sabres, but fear, if they once get muskets they will always be obliged to keep them. If we can secure overcoats as uniforms, money will be forwarded for them to our depot. The distribution of arms has had a good effect in the interior, and with your permission, I will store some muskets here, in charge of Major Lanigan, for issue to such circles as have contributed funds. I have terminated the answer to the N. O. people, I am not satisfied with it, however, and beg your indulgence and correction. Don't think me troublesome, but will you interest Graham about my brevet? Very respectfully,

Your obedient servant,

C. CARROLL TEVIS,

Brig. Gen. and A. G., F. B.

XXXVII

No. 28 S. 4th Street,
Philadephia, April 14, '66.

Col. C. C. Tevis, New York.

My Dear Sir:—Yours of yesterday with the papers inclosed was received this morning, and submitted to Jenks & Son, with whom I spent over an hour in the effort to convince them that they were wrong in charging for the cases. They cannot, however, be moved from the ground they have taken. Nothing, therefore, remains, but to fight them upon the point or pay the amount claimed. They accepted the $8,300, of which you will find the receipt inclosed upon upon the contract, as also a suspension of the time for the payment of the $1,871—for a week—but as they decline to permit more than 1,000 muskets to leave in cases, until the matter is settled, it would be well to bring it to a close forthwith, as Major O'Reilly may be embarassed if the matter is delayed beyond a day or two.

Inclosed you will find a letter from Jenks & Son in reply to yours.

Regretting that the circumstances have not permitted my bringing the matter to a more favorable conclusion, I am

Truly yours,

JOHN M. ARUNDEL.

The other papers I have retained subject to your order, in case there should be further use for them here.

XXXVIII

26 Rue Lacepede, Paris, April 7, 1866.

My Dear O'Mahony: I enclose account as it stands at this date. I have received, I presume, in safety all that has been transmitted. You will see the amount of my receipts, with the dates, in the account, and will know whether any have miscarried.

I am glad to say that none of the messengers carrying money from hence to Ireland have been intercepted. I have vouchers for all the disbursements, with the exception of 120 francs, $24, paid, as you will see, to destitute fugitives.

John Mitchel, in account

1865. Dr.	Francs.
Dec. 5—To amount of bill of exchange on Tapscotts, after deducting expense of commission, etc., as per Bordeau from J. Monroe & Co., cash net....	204,279.65
1866.	
Jan. 2—To interest on bank account at John Monroe & Co.'s up to this date........................	176.90
March 9—To amount of letter of cr. on Rothschilds	25,750.00
March 15—To letter of credit on same house from San Francisco, remitted by Kelly & Co., N. Y..	25,750.00
March 22—To amount of two letters of credit received same day as per my journal............	54,638.25
Total	310,594.80
By credits..	278,893.30
Balance in bank this 7th April, 1866..............	31,701.50

Mr. Stephens is now in Paris. He has drawn from me two sums of 25,000 each. He has also taken bonds of the I. R. from me to the amount of $10,000, which he says he thinks he may dispose of. I handed him the bonds to that amount, taking his receipts.

I am in receipt of letters from Mr. Killian of March 3 preparing me to receive large remittances. But since receipt of that letter only two letters of credit arrived, both on the same day, in a letter from you to the amount of £2,000, as per account. Very truly yours,

JOHN MITCHEL.

---

with the F. B., this 7th April, 1866.

1865. Cr.	Francs.
Dec. 7—Sent to Ireland by Capt. Burke £1,000 in Bank of England notes, amounting in francs, with cost of exchanging the money, to..........	25,150.00
Dec. 15—Paid to Capt. L. O'Brien, financial agent of I. R. B., by order from Kelly.................	25,150.00
Dec. 16—Do. do....................	12,575.00
Dec. 19—Do. do....................	25,150.00
Dec. 22—Do. do....................	25,150.00
Dec. 26—Paid Capt. O'Brien on two separate orders..	37.726.00
1866.	
Jan. 3—Gave Capt. O'Brien on two orders amounting to £1,800....................................	45,297.05
Jan. 16—Gave Capt. O'Brien on order for £300 only.	5,030.00
Feb. 3—Do. under same order an additional sum of..	400.00
Feb. 17—Cost of parcel from Havre, with bonds.....	13.75
Feb. 20—Gave Capt. O'Brien, still under same order.	500.00
March 3—Gave to Col. H. McConnell, who represented himself as just escaped from custody in Ireland and was quite destitute..................	100.00
March 3—To — Wrenn under similar circumstances	20.00
March 9—To stamp duty on bill of exchange at Rothschilds	14.00
March 9—Paid to Edmund O'Leary and W. O'Donovan for transmission to Ireland................	26,576.50
March 15—Stamp on letter of credit from Eugene Kelly & Co..................................	13.00
March 24—Handed to Jas. Stephens in Paris, on his receipt	25,000.00
March 30—Paid stamp duty on two bills of exchange.	28.00
March 30—Handed to James Stephens on his receipt.	25,000.00
Total	278,893.30

XXXIX

(Paris), April 7, (1866.)

Dear O'M.: Stephens leaves here, I believe, on the 14th. I wish he had gone by an earlier steamer, as his presence must be very much needed over there to give impetus to the movement and strengthen your hands. But I hope there is no intention of placing him at the head of the F. B. in America. He says he does not wish this himself and would not accept it; that he goes out chiefly to help to bring back the Senate party to reason and sustain your position. He tells me, however, that you have earnestly begged him to go over, as you are yourself worn out. It is not to be wondered at if the strain of the last few months has told heavily upon you, both in physique and morale. I trust you are to remain at the head of the American organization.

I am not sure how long my position here may be tenable, owing to the injudicious publication of my name in newspapers and speeches as a "financial agent" in Paris receiving and disbursing large sums of money. Do you know that this is advertising me as a mark to all the thieves in Europe?—besides directing the special attention of the British Government to me and all who have business with me. Accordingly I am haunted by both spies and robbers. Shortly after removing to this house three men came to lodge with a marchand du vins almost opposite the gate. The people of the house knew them to be spies at once from the way in which they dogged me. Their proceedings at first were quite unobserved by myself and had been going on in a most offensive way for two weeks without my knowing anything about it. At last I was told, and went at once to the Prefet of Police. He told me they were no agents of his and that the Frence police had never had any reason to occupy themselves about me or my movements. Then I knew the rascals must be rascals of Lord Cowley's. I wrote to him asking if it were so, and if so what his Lordship wanted with me. To this I got no reply, but the three rascals disappeared suddenly and have never been seen in the street since. Of course they have been replaced and the surveillance is kept up. The danger of this is that they may make themselves acquainted with the appearance of some of those messengers who come from Ireland to me.

But this is not all. My apartment was entered one evening in my absence, and entered by a false key, for I had the key of my room in my pocket all evening. Next morning I observed some derangement among my papers and two letters of credit gone. One was of no value, for it was a second, and the first was already paid me; but the other was a first, had been duly accepted at Rothschilds, payable three days after—and the three days expired on that very morning I discovered the loss. Luckily, it was a Sunday morning. If it had been on any week day the letter might have been presented at the opening of the bank and the money paid. As it was I had time to take my measures. Had police agents posted at Rothschilds in the morning, and also telegraphed to London, supposing that the thief might slip over there and present the letter at the London branch. But I failed to catch the thief, as he did not venture to present himself at either house. The money was safe enough and was paid to me on the arrival of the second exchange. But this gives some idea of the rascality at work around me—and all by reason of the foolish announcements. I have no doubt that gangs of thieves from London are here to rob me. Of course, I am now put on my guard and take good measures to make robbery impossible. Yet it is not pleasant to think that your room and your private drawers and all your papers may be at any time rummaged in your absence.

I asked you in my last letter to consider well and let me have your conclusions as to the present condition of the Cause. Pray write to me. Very truly your friend, J. M.

Do not make this note public, but show it to whom you please.

XL

Paris, Rue Lacepede 26,
April 10, 1866.

My Dear O'Mahony:—Received to-day yours of March 27, inclosing two letters of credit (firsts) on Rothschilds, one dated March 21, for 28,369 francs, and the other dated March 27, for 28,689.70.

Two days ago I sent you (addressed outside to Mr. Killian) a full account of my many transactions up to this date, which will enable you to see whether any remittances have miscarried. I rather think not. I will recapitulate here what I have stated in the account.

Since the first sum which I carried out with me, for which I received in cash frs. 204,279.65. I received March 9 25,750 francs; on 15th (from San Francisco through Kelly & Co.), 25,750, and on the 22d two letters of credit, amounting in all to 54,658.25. These sums, together with frs. 175.90 (interest on account current), make in all frs. 310,594.80 up to April 1.

To-day I have the additional sums mentioned above. The account which I have sent up to April 1 will show my disbursements up to that date.

I see you think it remarkable that at the date of your last letter, March 27, you had not yet received an acknowledgment of remittances contained in a letter of March 8, which was not possible. I think, however, from what you say, that one letter of mine to you must have miscarried.

For the future I beg of you to cause a clerk to send me by each letter that comes to me a statement of the remittances made before that date, with dates and amounts. This will enable me to perceive if anything has gone astray.

I wrote to you fully along with the account. Mr. Stephens goes out in a day or two.

Very truly yours, J. M.

Pray acknowledge the receipt of the account the moment it comes to hand. I carefully keep the vouchers for disbursement to be produced hereafter.

XLI

This is a copy of an interesting report made to General Sweeny showing the strength of the armed guards on the Welland Canal in Canada. It was transmitted by a U. S. naval officer, a member of the Fenian organization.

Buffalo, N. Y., April 9, 1866.

Maj. Gen. T. W. Sweeny, Sec. of War, F. B.

Sir:—William M. Andrew, being over to the Welland Canal, on the 6th of this month, reports as follows:

Total number of men stationed there is 75, consisting of some cavalry, infantry and rifles; ten regulars in all. Arms, rifles and two six-pounders placed on the dock. That is all the force to his knowledge on the Canal.

Mr. Andrews' brother lives at Welland, on the canal. He says they are drilling at night with sticks, the number true to you is 25.

The length of the canal is 28 miles, with 26 locks. Your point is the guard lock. By destroying this lock and the one below you destroy the whole canal. The feeder runs into this lock; the feeder is 18 feet high; the highest one there is. There is no lock on the feeder and the force of water from it will burst the best of the locks, as there is a great fall from this point to Lake Ontario. There are also two railroad bridges that cross the canal; one at Port Colburn and the other at Thirrell. Both are wooden bridges and swing in the centre. Port Colburn is 24 miles from Buffalo and 18 by railroad. It lies on Lake Erie and is known as Gravelly Bay. Port Delusia is at the entrance from Lake Ontario on the Canada side. There is a railroad that runs along the canal from Port Colburn to Port Delusia, which connects Lake Erie and Lake Ontario. The distance by rail from Port Delusia to Hamilton is about four hours (or to Toronto). By steamboat you can go to any point on Lake Ontaria through to Quebec by steam or sailing vessels.

General, I hope you will excuse this long letter to you; if there is anything I can do let me know and it will be obeyed.

Captain Roe, of the steamer Michigan, is dispatched from here to-day.

Very respectfully yours,

WM. E. LEONARD,
Mate U. S. Steamer Michigan.

Buffalo, N. Y.

XLII

Letter written by James Stephens in Paris in 1866 to John O'Mahony, explaining why he failed to start for America as promised.

Paris, April 12, 1866.

My Dear O'Mahony:—My intention was to have left to-day, and I sincerely regret my inability to do so. This inability is due to the limited amount of money on hand—£2,000 or so. Now, our actual weekly expense—owing to the trials, which were resumed on the 10th—being £700 to £1,000, I could not bring myself to leave till I saw enough here to make all sure for a month at least. But I don't mean to till this sum shall have been forwarded from your side. I expect to raise it here myself. Col. Kelly leaves to-day, and with his assistance you can easily have everything arranged for my reception in the States. I need not tell you how much is due to the Colonel. He has rendered incalculable service to the cause. To this I should add that no other could give so full an account of our actions and positions since the first arrests. I leave him to speak for Ireland as well as for himself. You will find him strong before friend and foe. I leave myself by the next boat—that is, on the 28th inst.

Yours faithfully and fraternally,

JAMES STEPHENS.

XLIII

In 1866 it was felt it was a serious mistake to have two rival factions of Fenians in this country, and an effort was made to harmonize their differences with a view of combining them into one strong, influential organization. With this end in view Col. O'Mahony authorized General Wm. J. Halpin to represent him in making the first overtures to the "Senate" party.

The written report made by Gen. Halpin in his own handwriting to John O'Mahony is as follows:

New York, May 4, 1866.

To Col. John O'Mahoney, H. C. F. B.

Sir:—I have the honor to report that, agreeable to your instructions of the 20th of April, I proceeded at once to open negotiations with Mr. Roberts on the subject of a union of the Brotherhood.

The following correspondence will show the result of my efforts to unite the two parties now so unhappily divided:

HEADQUARTERS FENIAN BROTHERHOOD.

April 20, 1866.

Gen'l Wm. G. Halpin,

My Dear Friend and Brother:—Relying, as you must know, most thoroughly upon your honor as a gentleman and your patriotism as an Irishman, I hereby fully authorize you to act in my name and as my representative with all parties willing to co-operate in the liberation of Ireland from English domination. Above all, you will, as I know you will, do your utmost to promote harmony of action among all lovers of freedom at this juncture.

Fraternally yours,

JOHN O'MAHONY, H. C. F. B.

In obedience to the above, I addressed the following letter to Mr. Roberts:

Wm. R. Roberts, Esq.,

Dear Sir:—I am commissioned by Col. John O'Mahony, as you will see by the inclosed document, to act for him and that portion of the Fenian Brotherhood which he represents to bring about a perfect understanding between the two sections of Irishmen who are, as they believe, working for the freedom of their native land. If we are honest in our intentions and asseverations we ought to unite for the common good and let no personal prejudices interfere between us. It will take all our united efforts to overthrow the desperate enemy we have to contend with and lift our oppressed nation up to freedom and happiness.

Mr. O'Mahony has been always anxious for this result and nothing can give him more satisfaction than a union of all good Irishmen.

I see no difficulty in the way of carrying out Gen'l Sweeney's programme if we have a perfect understanding. I much fear the result of either party attempting anything on their own account, while united they can smite the enemy at different points. Mr. Stephens will soon be here, and I think prudence would dictate a suspension of operations until he arrives.

The country looks for unity among us, and if either move and fail desperate will be our doom. I know something of the personalities bandied about by both sections for some months, and as the personal representative of James Stephens I desire to stop them.

If you appoint a committee to meet me at any time and place I shall be happy to see such a committee and confer with them on the condition of affairs.

I shall expect a reply at your earliest convenience.

I am, my dear sir,

Fraternally yours,

WM. G. HALPIN.

To that letter Mr. Roberts replies as follows:

New York, April 21, 1866.

Wm. G. Halpin, Esq.,

Sir:—I am in receipt of a communication from you with a note inclosed which purports to be a copy of one addressed to you by Mr. John O'Mahony.

Your letter is addressed to me as a private individual and as such I have to decline holding any communication with you or Mr. O'Mahony on the subject of which you treat, but any communication you choose to address to me in my official capacity as president of the Fenian Brotherhood, will receive all the attention the interests of the cause I represent requires.

Yours truly,

W. R. ROBERTS.

My great anxiety to accomplish the union so much desired by the people and so necessary to the cause of Irish freedom, and notwithstanding the studied insult conveyed in the word purports underscored lest I should not observe its meaning, I addressed Mr. Roberts again on the 24th as follows:

New York, April 24, 1866.

Wm. R. Roberts, Esq.:—

I beg to acknowledge the receipt of your favor of the 21st inst., and to say in reply that I have no objection to your assuming any title you please. Mr. O'Mahony will not stand upon points of etiquette while the freedom of Ireland is at stake. A committee can settle or suggest a plan of action that will be satisfactory to both sides.

The people demand a union, and whoever stands in the way must be prepared to receive their censure and abide the consequences of casting away the liberties of a nation.

I appeal to you as a patriot, desirous of aiding in the freedom of your country, to appoint a committee of conference that will lay the basis of a union that will be lasting and effective. Surely no personal pride should prevent this, while the whole Brotherhood requires it and the cause of suffering Ireland imperatively demands it. On your answer may depend the salvation of a generous people, who, betrayed, may not be either patient or forgiving. Those who are suffering in Pentonville and Mt. Joy, because of the division between us, will fail to understand that Ireland's holy cause should suffer, because Col. Roberts is not addressed as president of the Fenian Brotherhood or Col. O'Mahony as head centre. Union and action are demanded by every lover of Ireland, and no points of etiquette should stand in the way of their accomplishment.

Fraternally yours,

WM. G. HALPIN.

To the above Mr. Roberts gave only a verbal reply, which is embodied in the annexed note of Dr. Mahon, the agent who acted between us.

Finding that Mr. Roberts refused to act I addressed myself to General Sweeney, knowing that his name and reputation, both as a gentleman and a soldier, kept the party together. The following is the note I sent Gen'l Sweeney:

New York, April 24, 1866.

Major Gen'l Sweeney,

Dear Sir:—I am authorized by Col. O'Mahony to represent him in bringing about a union of the two sections of the Fenian Brotherhood that a concerted plan of action may be agreed upon. I wrote to Col. Roberts on the subject and wish to have your aid in accomplishing so desirable an object. The people who have been sustaining the two parties are crying out for union, and their voices cannot safely be disregarded.

Mr. Stephens will be here by the next French steamer and will find the friends of Ireland divided unless we act promptly and have an understanding with each other that will enable him to consolidate our forces.

In view of the great cause we have at heart, no private or personal differences should stand in the way of cordial union.

If the body which you represent appoints a committee to confer on the subject I shall meet such a committee at any time and place appointed.

I appeal to you, General, as an Irishman and a patriot to assist in creating this union so necessary to our success.

I shall expect an answer at your earliest convenience.

Fraternally yours,

WM. G. HALPIN.

Owing to accident, the General's reply was destroyed before it came into my hands, but I am informed that its purport was to the effect that he would receive or answer no communication except it was over the signature of Col. O'Mahony.

Thus, sir, terminated the honest efforts we have been making to cement in one great fraternity the millions of the Irish race and friends of Ireland on this continent, that we might show to the world that we could be united on one subject, however we might differ on others. And although a few men on either side may try to prevent this union, it is to be fondly hoped that the advent of our great chief and the good sense of the masses will effect the object of our dearest desires.

It is neither my province nor wish to comment on the correspondence, but submit the whole to your better judgment.

I have the honor, sir, to remain

Fraternally yours,

WM. G. HALPIN,

Brv't Brig. Gen'l.

XLIV

Bridesburg, Phila., May 3, 1866.

Maj. Gen. T. W. Sweeny, Sec. of War, F. B.

General:—I have the honor to acknowledge the receipt of your letter of the 2d inst., and in reply to state that out of the 2,000 muskets which were sent to Mr. Carey's I issued 900 as follows:

To J. F. Scanlon, Chicago, Ill	620
To J. W. Fitzgerald, Cincinnati, Ohio	100
To Philip Breen, St. Clair, Schuylkill Co., Pa	40
To Samuel Mulvill, Bergen Point, N. J	20
To Cornelius Finn	20
To Peter Higgins, Cleveland, Ohio	20
To John Egan, Elizabethport, N. J	20
To Ed. Fitzwilliam, Watertown, Mass	20
To P. J. Kelly, Newburg, N. Y	40
Total issued from New York	900
On hand in New York subject to orders	1,100
The following were issued from Bridesburg, Phila.:	
To John Nealon, Carbondale, Pa	80
To M. J. Philben, Wilkesbarre, Pa	80
To J. E. Clark, Pittstown, Pa	80
To Bryan Fallon, Archibald, Pa	20
To P. Regan, Oswego, N. Y	480
To Thomas McLean, Cincinnati, Ohio	480
To W. Fleming, Troy, N. Y	480
To C. I. King, Corry, Pa	20
To D. McGowan, East St. Louis, Ill	40
To Owen Gavigan, Auburn, N. Y	40
To P. O'Day, Buffalo, N. Y	1,000
To John Barret, Dunkirk, N. Y	480
To M. J. Cronin, Erie, Pa	840
To J. O'Farrell, Baltimore, Md	100
Total issued from Bridesburg	4,220
On hand at Bridesburg subject to orders	1,280

I will await orders from you before issuing the above 1,280, which you will see is on hand here. In the meantime I will correspond with Mr. Manix as you direct.

I deem it proper to mention that the boxes in New York, at Mr. Carey's, containing the 1,100, have not as yet been altered. I am very respectfully,

Your obedient servant,

W. M. O'REILLY,

Maj. of Ord., F. B.

XLV

Bridesburg, Phil., May 5, 1866.

Maj. Gen. T. W. Sweeny, Sec'y of War., F. B.

General:—I have the honor to state that in obedience with instructions from Colonel Mechan (by letter of 4th inst.), I visited Mr. W. R. Harmer this morning for the purpose of inspecting the batteries therein mentioned, but he informed me that it would not be convenient for him to let me see them before Monday at 1 p. m., for which time I made an appointment with him. I will report immediately after the inspection.

On opening the boxes which contain the balance of the muskets on hand here (1280) I found that there were no rammers with them and reported the fact to Mr. Jenks. He immediately started for Washington to procure them and this morning telegraphed to his partner, Mr. Mitchell, that they would have them here on Monday. If you will send me instructions where to send those arms I will lose no time after I receive the rammers. I am very respectfully, your obedient servant,

W. M. O'REILLY,
Major of Ord., F. B.

XLVI

Headquarters, F. B., 706 Broadway, N. Y.
May 6, 1866.

General T. W. Sweeny, Sec'y of War, F. B.

General:—I had a conversation yesterday with Mr. Hitchcock relative to his offer to me of 2,000,000 cartridges—58 calibre—at $14 per 1000. He informed me that officers called on him from you to inspect them and that he submitted to them the impracticability of storing at one place in New York, and inspecting in detail so large a quantity of ammunition. He also requested me to make the following suggestions for your consideration, viz.:

That the ammunition is government ammunition, purchased by him from the United States Government; that he is ready to give security for the faithful performance of his contract in any required amount.

That, being a large purchaser of the government, and known to the United States authorities, as dealing extensively with foreign nations, he proposes facilities of which you may avail yourself.

That guaranteeing the ammunition under sufficient security and inspection in detail would be unnecessary; though he is willing that it should be done at the proper depot, and

Finally, that, if purchased he will undertake to place it at a convenient depot, thus avoiding unnecessary handling and exposure.

Mr. Hitchcock desires a personal interview with you, and would be pleased to see you at his office, 48 Dey street, at any time between 12 m. and 3 p. m., or will call on you at any time designated. I am very respectfully, your obedient servant,

J. W. BRYCE.

XLVII

Philadelphia, May 7, 1866.

Colonel William R. Roberts.

Dear Sir:—Will you permit me to call your attention to a letter just mailed by me to General Sweeny in reference to the two batteries offered by Harmer.

If his new offer is now accepted while he has it in his power to carry it out it will be just as satisfactory as the other, but if more delay intervenes needlessly he may not be able to carry it through. Truly yours,

JOHN M. ARUNDEL.

XLVIII

Bridesburg, Philadelphia, May 7, 1866.

Major-General T. W. Sweeny, Sec'y of War, F. B.

General:—I called on Mr. Harmer to-day at 1 p. m., but he was not prepared to allow me to inspect the guns, so I agreed with him to call at 4.30 p. m., which I have done and received the inclosed letter from Mr. Arundel. He says he has written to you by this mail stating full particulars.

I saw Mr. Jenks this morning. He had an order from General A. B. Dyer, Chief of Ord., to Major Laidley, at Springfield Armory, for the rammers and I expect they will be here on Thursday. I am very respectfully your obedient servant,

W. M. O'REILLY,
Major of Ord., F. B.

XLIX

No. 28 South 4th Street, Philadelphia.
May 7, 1866.

General Sweeny, New York.

Dear Sir:—Mr. Harmer desires me to say that upon his going last Saturday to submit the two batteries to Major O'Reilly's inspection, he was informed through the parties through whom he was getting them, that remonstrances against their sale from the State Militia organizations had just been received, which would prevent the proposed sale from being carried out; that if the matter had gone through as at first contemplated four weeks ago there would have been no difficulty, but that the delay had afforded the opportunity for the opposition just made.

Notwithstanding this mischance, however, Mr. Harmer desires me to say that he will undertake to furnish within the time you require them, two batteries of Parrott guns, 10 and 20 pounders, precisely similar in all respects to the others, everything complete with the exception of horses, subject to the most rigid inspection, and to be delivered in Philadelphia upon the same terms, fourteen thousand dollars, payable upon delivery, provided, however, that your order to him be furnished at once, and that at the time of giving the order you deposit in my hands $3,000 to be held by me until he has closed the matter as an indemnity to him in the event of your not, from unforseen circumstances, being able to take the guns off his hands after he has obtained such as will pass your inspection.

If you see fit to give him the order and make the deposit he requires, I will hold it, of course, as much subject to your interest as to his, and will not pay it over to him until he has faithfully and to your satisfaction carried out his proposition.

If you will send on the order and draft through Major O'Reilly, I will see that the matter is put in proper shape.

Mr. Harmer desires that you allow him from the day he receives the order, fourteen days if possible, within which to deliver the batteries, although he thinks he can do it in ten days.

Truly yours,

JOHN M. ARUNDEL.

L

Quebec, May 9, 1866, 4 P. M.

General:—I have the honor to report that everything is progressing rapidly in this district.

We inaugurated the movement yesterday, and to-day I am hard at work swearing in members, etc.

I have already about 50 volunteers and nearly 100 who are not volunteers, and before Sunday the number will be largely increased.

The excitement is all over and the "loyal" inhabitants are no longer haunted in their dreams by visions of Fenian armies.

To-night we are to have a secret meeting of the leading men, when business of importance will be transacted.

There are about 1000 regulars in this garrison, including artillery. There is no cavalry, with the exception of a few volunteer companies.

If the General should have any further orders for me, my address is P. Browne, Esq., Daily Murcury Office, Quebec, C. E.

Anything addressed as above will reach me safely, and no

danger of its being opened or delayed. I have the honor to remain, General, Your faithful servant,

RICHARD SLATTERY.

Major-General T. W. Sweeny.

I have no fears for the safety of this letter.

LI

J. W. Fitzgerald, C. F. B. Detroit, Mich., May 9, 1866.

Dear Friend:—According to instructions contained in your communication of the fifth, I proceeded to Windsor, opposite Detroit, where I gathered the following information, which I most respectfully submit:

Stationed at Windsor, five companies of volunteers, aggregate probably three hundred (300) men for duty; in regard to their fighting qualities I know nothing, but are, I presume, something like we were when we first came out. There are at Windsor two (2) pieces of ordnance, almost worthless, which I ascertained from some of the volunteers. (The guns came from the Crimea.) As I went over in uniform, they were quite unreserved in their conversation. These are all of the forces that are now at Windsor.

A good many of the men joined in order to see some excitement; caring very little for their country; some Irish amongst them.

The facilities afforded for crossing at this place are very good. A small tug can take over men enough in an hour to capture the city and the companies there.

The Grand Trunk Railroad has its terminus in Windsor, I believe. Store houses in abundance and plenty of rolling stock to supply an army of ten thousand (10,000) men with the necessary supplies.

The feeling in Detroit is on the whole very good, and in my opinion many of the soldiers of the late army would rally to our standard, provided they saw a good start made.

The United States forces are stationed as follows: Major-General Ord, commanding the Department of the Ohio, comprising the following States, viz.: Indiana, Ohio and Michigan; headquarters at Detroit. At Fort Wayne, two miles from Detroit, two (2) companies of the 4th Infantry, Brevet Brigadier-General Silas Casey, commanding. Detroit Barracks, one company, Brevet Lieutenant-Colonel R. P. (D. B.?) McKibben commanding. At Fort Gratiot, two (2) companies of the 7th Infantry, Brevet Lieutenant-Colonel D. I. Montgomery, commanding.

Any further information which may be required will be furnished on application.

Very respectfully,

HENRY P. FLYNN,

"Clerk" Gen. Ord's Headquarters, Detroit.

J. W. Fitzgerald, Esq.,

Centre, Cinn. Circle, F. B. or the proper person to receive this.

LII

New York, May 13, 1866.

Major-General T. W. Sweeny, Sec'y of War, F. B.

General:—In obedience to your instructions I proceeded at once to Buffalo and as far as possible placed myself in correspondence with the parties named in said instructions. Mr. O'Day and Colonel Hoy had already opened negotiations with Messrs. Dole and Rice of the New York Central Railroad, and a few hours after my arrivel in Buffalo we had an interview with them, and after discussing the matter thoroughly, they decided they could not aid us directly, as they were rather peculiarly situated, but offered to lend us the use of tneir warehouses for the storage of our merchandise. We subsequently visited two other parties with like result. At last, Mr. Frank Gallagher and myself visited another gentleman named John S. Mundabac, a large owner of canal boats, and he has agreed to furnish us with all the boats necessary and also a sufficient number of tugs to bring the expedition to its destination.

I have this day received a dispatch from Mr. O'Day, telling me that the contract is drawn out in a legal manner by a lawyer in the following manner: That boats are chartered to go to Canada for cargoes of ashes, so that there will be no suspicion of their going over the river. None of our men appear in the business at all, so there can be no suspicion aroused by their being seen around the boats. We are to pay $25 per day for the use of the boats and the tugs are to be paid what they demand. I could not learn the price, but believe it will be moderate. The boats will be ready at our call. Our merchandise is to be packed securely in boxes and disguised as much as possible and marked to some fictitious party on Lake Superior. When our goods leave here a man is to proceed to Buffalo to claim and reship them. Mr. Mundabac will recognize him and then have the goods placed in a boat where they will remain until you are ready. I have now to inform you that the United States vessel Michigan is now lying in Buffalo harbor, it is said, watching our movements.

While in Buffalo I met a man with whom you had corresponded through his brother. This man escaped from Canada to avoid arrest for being a Fenian; his name is Patrick Andrew. He had lived at the Welland Canal some ten years. I swore him to secrecy. He will remain in Buffalo till we move. He will go ahead of the expedition and cut the telegraph and then meet the advance and act as guide. There are 90 men in Mr. Andrew's circle sworn to fight. There is no force at all at the canal, but there is one 32-pounder in charge of some pensioners living at the place, but no guard is left over it. Plenty of spades and shovels are at the canal. There are only 60 or 70 horses in the village, but plenty in the country around. There are at the following places volunteers as stated:

Welland, 1 Company; Fort Colburn, 1; Port Robinson, 1;

Allensburg, 1; Thurrill, 2; Slabtown, 1; St. Catherine's, 5; Fonthill, 1; Junction, 1; Port Dalhousie, 1; making in all, 15 companies, averaging 44 men each; making a total of 660 men now quietly residing at home unorganized. There are no regulars in those towns. The above towns are in the vicinity of the canal and extend over a space of 27 miles. Port Colburn is 18 miles from Buffalo and 8 from the canal. There are plenty of horses at Colburn. Andrews states that the people there hate O'Mahony and are eager for our movement. He believes the Irish people will rise immediately at our approach. He thinks the T. V.'s will not fight. James McMullan, of St. Catherine's, is a prominent member and should be corresponded with immediately.

The above are the results of my mission, and to my mind they are eminently successful.

I desire to inform you that Messrs. O'Day and Gallagher and Colonels Hoy and Baily rendered great service, and I would have been powerless without them. All of which is respectfully sumbitted.

A. L. MORRISON, Senator, F. B.

LIII

No. 28 South 4th Street, Philadelphia.
May 10, 1866.

Major-General Sweeny, Sec'y of War, F. B., New York.

Dear Sir:—Colonel Mechan's letter to Major O'Reilly directing an inspection of the guns and declining making a deposit has been communicated to Mr. Harmer, who states that before they can be obtained for inspection he has to lay out several thousand dollars, which he declines doing unless he has the assurance that a deposit will give him that he can be indemnified in case you do not take them and they will be thrown upon his hands, and that as the deposit is not to come to him in any sense until you are satisfied with an inspection of the guns, his request is a most reasonable one.

Mr. Harmer is obliged to obtain the guns from Alfred Jenks & Son, who obtain them direct from the United States Government. Mr. Jenks is now in Washington and telegraphs to-day that he has obtained the orders necessary to get them, but before going further in the matter requires that Mr. Harmer shall on Saturday morning at 12 o'clock make a deposit of several thousand dollars to insure the matter going through—agreeing to refund the deposit, however, should the guns not be as represented. Mr. Harmer is willing to comply with the terms of Mr. Jenks provided you indemnify him by the proposed deposit.

If you choose to go on the guns can be inspected and ready for delivery in a few days at a price nearly fifty per cent. below the price paid by the government.

Should you prefer it you can make the deposit with Alfred

Jenks & Son directly, but they will require it to be $5,000 and to be made by Saturday morning.

Truly yours,

JOHN M. ARUNDEL.

LIV

Bridesburg, Philadelphia, May 10, 1866.

Major-General T. W. Sweeny, Sec'y of War, F. B.

General:—I have the honor to acknowledge the receipt of Colonel Mechan's letter of the 9th inst., and in reply beg to submit the following statement:

Through a friend here who is a member of the City Councils I have learned that to the best of his knowledge there have been no guns of this description condemned for sale by either the State or the city authorities.

On receipt of Colonel Mechan's letter I called this morning at Mr. Arundel's office for the purpose of communicating to Mr. Harmer its contents. Mr. Arundel, who is acting for Mr. H., informs me that the payment of an instalment previous to inspection is the only condition on which the guns can be obtained. He writes you by this mail.

The ramrods required to complete the balance of the muskets have arrived and the workmen began packing this morning. I am still without directions where to send them, having received no reply from Mr. Manix as yet. I will be able to ship the entire lot on Monday morning if I receive directions on the subject. I am very respectfully, your obedient servant,

W. M. O'REILLY,
Major of Odr., F. B.

LV

May 10, 1866.

General Orders No. 3.

Colonels of regiments will immediately cause to be packed all serviceable army equipments and war material preparatory to transportation to the points of rendezvous of their command.

Colonels of regiments and commanders of detachments will immediately forward all war material to the points of rendezvous, as follows:

The troops from New York and New Jersey to Buffalo.

The troops from Massachusetts, Rhode Island and Connecticut to Dunkirk.

The troops from Pennsylvania to Erie.

The troops from Indiana and Tennessee to Sandusky City.

The troops from Ohio, Maryland, North Carolina and Virginia to Cleveland.

The troops from Kentucky and Missouri to Toledo.

The troops from Illinois to Chicago.
The troops from Iowa and Wisconsin to Milwaukee.
The troops from Michigan to Port Huron.
The orders to move will be communicated by telegraph in a few days.

By order of the Secretary of War.

C. CARROLL TEVIS,
Brig.-Gen. and Adj.-Gen., F. B.

A true copy. S. R. Tresilian.

LVI

Washington, D. C., May 16, 1866.

Major-General T. W. Sweeny, Sec'y of War, F. B.

General:—I have the honor to state that I have made a careful inspection of the batteries offered by Mr. Jenks and find them to be in every respect complete. One of them is a 10-pounder Parrott and the other a 3-inch wrought-iron rifle battery. It is now necessary that the money be sent so that the work of boxing may be commenced immediately. The packing will be done at the arsenal, and I judge will cost about $500.

I think it would be well for me to return to Philadelphia after the payment is made, and await their arrival there.

I respectfully ask that you will send me some money to defray my expenses here. I inclose a receipt for $50, which I think will be sufficient. I am very respectfully, your obedient servant,

W. M. O'REILLY,
Major of Ord., F. B.

P. S.—Colonel Benton asked if I would want ammunition, to which I replied no. If you have not make any contract as yet, I think it could be had very cheap. W. M. O'R.

LVII

May 17, 1866.

Colonel John O'Neill:—

Upon receipt of this you will immediately move your command, including all Tennessee troops, and report in Cincinnati, Ohio, to J. W. Fitzgerald (northeast corner of 5th street and Broadway) on the 25th inst., where you will receive full instructions.

By order of the Secretary of War.

C. CARROLL TEVIS,
Brig.-Gen. and Adjt.-Gen., F. B.

Same to Major A. E. Alden.

Same to Colonel Owen Starr, substituting "Kentucky" for "Tennessee."

A true copy. S. R. Tresilian.

LVIII

May 17, 1866.

Special Orders No. 58.

Brigadier-General C. Carroll Tevis, Adj.-Gen., F. B., will proceed to Chicago, Ill., for the purpose of organizing the division composed of the troops from Illinois, Iowa, Michigan, Wisconsin, Missouri and Kansas. He will communicate to the different commanding officers of districts and of regiments the instructions furnished him by the Secretary of War.

By order of the Secretary of War.

EUGENE J. COURTNEY,
Major and Asst. Adj.-Gen., F. B.

A true copy. S. R. Tresilian.

LVIX

Tremont House, Chicago, May 22.

Maj. Gen. T. W. Sweeny, Sec. of War, F. B.

General:—I have only to report so far promises of assistance from the outside world. As yet I have not seen the steamers, but Goodrich has offered to transport at $10 a head; much, however, is hoped from the contributions of a number of wealthy Irishmen whom I am to meet to-morrow. Should they not come forward sufficiently well, it can be obtained from the Circles on your order to that effect, and General Lynch suggests that you forward an order to send on to this place the funds now on hand for transportation. Including the Kansas, Missouri, Wisconsin and Iowa men, there will be about 3,000 volunteers sail from here and Milwaukee—about 1,500 to 2,000 muskets and accoutrements are needed, and, if they can be shipped at once, I shall be much more easy.

I believe that it will be politic to assign Lynch to the command; much as I desire a command, I am afraid my appointment will not be regarded with satisfaction—however, in this, as in all things else, I am entirely at your command, but will be anxious until I receive full instructions.

Very respectfully, your obedient servant,

C. CARROLL TEVIS,
Brig. Gen. and A. G., F. B.

LX

May 22, 1866.

Lt. Col. John Grace, Asst. Insp. Gen., F. B.

Colonel:—I am directed by the Secretary of War to instruct you that on the arrival of the 13th Infantry, Col. John O'Neill, of Nashville, Tenn., and the 17th Infantry, Col. Owen Starr, of Louisville, Ky., and the New Orleans company, Capt. J. W. Dempsey, at Cincinnati, Ohio, you will forward them to Cleveland, Ohio. Should existing circumstances render it unsafe or unwise to select this point, you will then send them to Buffalo, N. Y. Great secrecy and caution must be observed and you must keep this Department thoroughly posted as to the movements of the above troops.

Very respectfully, your obedient servant,

EUGENE J. COURTNEY,
Maj. and A. A. G., F. B.

A true copy. S. R. TRESILIAN.

LXI

Maj. Gen. T. W. Sweeny, Sec. of War, F. B.

General:—I have the honor to claim the following advantages for my pontoon-wagon over the ordinary pontoon boat train:

1st. It can be used for the transportation of supplies and ammunition, thoroughly protecting them from all moisture.

2nd. It can be used for hauling water to troops where it is not convenient, thereby dispensing with the tank and water barrel so often used in the late war.

3rd. That it can be used as a boat, with oars, and will safely carry 12 men, average weight 180 lbs (2,160 lbs.), while each bed has a bouyancy of 4,500 lbs.

4th. That 4 beds with the superstructure complete, will sustain a weight of 16,000 lbs., while that of a 10-pounder Napoleon, Parrott, James, smooth-bore, or a 12-pounder Howitzer does not exceed 9,600 lbs.; or a column of infantry by the flank in close order—20 men at 180 lbs., 3,600 lbs. These results I have submitted to actual test in pounds, with the model, which is constructed on a scale of one inch to the foot.

Lastly, that the saving in expense will be approximately as follows, for a bridge of 500 feet:

500 feet, complete—including 100 wagons—at $65 per foot	$32,500
50 extra wagons for hauling, ropes, tools, anchorage, etc., etc., at $245	14,250
	$46,750
36 boats, at $100	$3,600
36 boat wagons, at $300	10,800
216 horses, at $200	43,200
216 sets harness, at $50	10.800
500 feet superstructure, at $10 per foot	5,000
Extra driver's forage, etc	38,800
Total pontoon train	$112,200

Total pontoon train, which cannot be used for any other purpose $112,200
Wagon pontoon train, which can be used as above, 125 wagons of which can be used for any purpose........ 46,750

Balance in favor $65,400

All of which I respectfully submit.

Your obedient servant, S. R. TRESILIAN.

LXII

May 22, 1866.

Special Orders, No. 61.

Brig. Gen. H. T. Lynch will immediately assume command of all troops that are to embark for the different points on the Lake Erie shore for Canada. He will superintend their embarkation and retain command until further orders from me.

T. W. SWEENY,
Secretary of War, F. B.

A true copy. S. R. TRESILIAN.

LXIII

St Albans, Vt., May 23, 1866.

Gen. T. W. Sweeny.

General:—I am happy to inform you that you can ship any quantity of stores to this place, to Peter Ward; some marked "gas fixtures," and some marked "glass"; the ammunition you could send under that head. This is the best town on the line.

If the property seized at Rouse's Point remains there until we require it, I can get it at any time; or if it is sent to Plattsburg, I can get it with less trouble. I hope you will not let that sad occurrence interfere with your programme.

There are two pieces of artillery in this town that I can get at a moment's warning. They are all complete, except harness. These articles are in the charge of Mr. Ward, the man whom I have selected to receive the stores.

I saw a man from Prescott yesterday. He says that there were three companies drilling there, and to the best of his knowledge there were four hundred men there altogether. There has been nothing done at any other point to this date.

You can ship a great amount of stores to this place, but if you possibly can, hire the cars, so that it can come through without shifting it. The Custom House officers on this line are all British spies and in the pay of both Governments.

I do not think this place any too safe. Arrange it so that you can soon follow the goods.

I will go to Rouse's Point this afternoon; I wish to keep those goods in sight. Thence I will go to Malone, where I expect a letter from you. If you decide to send stores to Chautauqua, you can ship them to James Mahony. He is the Centre of the Circle and a prominent merchant.

St. Albans is the best place to send machinery. Stuff that can be marked otherwise can be sent to any other place.

I would also state that Mr. Ward is superintendent of a gas works that has lately been burned down, and he is rebuilding it. He is receiving a great quantity of material every day.

I will write again to-morrow morning.

I am, General, your obedient servant,

JOHN FALLON.

P. S.—Mr. Ward is Secretary of a Circle. I have seen the Centre, Mr. Reilly, also; he is a good man. J. F.

LXIV

Headquarters F. B., May 26, 1866.

Brig. Gen. S. P. Spear, F. B.

Sir:—You will proceed to St. Albans, Franklin county, Vermont, and take command of all troops ordered to that part of the frontier lying between Ogdensburg, N. Y., and the sources of the Connecticut River. You will superintend the forwarding of said troops and supplies into Canada as rapidly as possible.

This force will be called the Right Wing of the Army of Ireland, and will consist of the follawing regiments and battalions, viz:

1st, 2nd, 3rd, 4th and 5th Cavalry; 1st, 2nd, 3rd, 4th, 5th, 7th, 8th, 9th, 10th, 14th, 15th, 20th, 22nd, 23rd, 25th and 26th Infantry. These troops will be organized as soon as circumstances will permit into one or more divisions, the divisions formed into brigades and the artillery into a battalion.

The cavalry arm will be under the command of Brig. Gen. M. C. Murphy, and will be thrown forward in advance of the infantry on both sides of the St. Johns (or Richelieu) River and cut off or capture, if possible, the garrisons at Forts Chambley and St. Johns, and threaten Montreal by the Victoria Bridge. Should an opportunity offer, they will take possession of the bridge and hold it until the infantry and artillery arrive. Should the enemy move out of the latter place in force, the cavalry will fall back, destroying the bridges as they retire and throwing every obstacle they can in the enemy's way. A portion of the cavalry will be sent along the Grand Trunk R. R. in the direction of Quebec, and seize on Fort Levi, if not too strongly garrisoned. Should the enemy move across the river and press them, they will fall back towards Richmond, destroying the bridges, etc., and giving timely notice of the enemy's advance.

The cavalry will also collect supplies for the army, such as horses, forage, beef cattle, etc., giving receipts for the same.

In case the enemy should attempt to concentrate from Quebec and Montreal, you will draw in your forces between the St. Johns and the St. Francis Rivers and hold that country at all hazards.

You will make Sherbrook your Headquarters and place strong garrisons at Forts Chambley and St. Johns and a small force at St. Hilaire; also a strong garrison at Richmond, and small forces at different points along the lines of both rivers, taking good care to keep your communication open, etc. In case the commander of the cavalry should find it necessary to apply for a reinforcement of the other arm, such reinforcements will be sent to him by you.

LXV

Malone, N. Y., May 27, 1866.

Gen. T. W. Sweeny, Secretary of War, F. B.

General:—I have received your letter of May 24, this morning, and I must say that it makes me feel better.

I have given the bill of sale to Mr. Mannix. He understands his instructions and will work with a will.

Mr. Brown has not arrived as yet, but I will look for him to-morrow.

I need not tell you that I will do everything in my power to make everything safe here. I will go to Potsdam to-morrow for the purpose of complying with your instructions.

I was to the barracks at Plattsburg yesterday. There are two companies of the 4th U. S. Infantry there, under command of First Lieut. Miller. They have no orders that will interfere with us. There are some Fenians among them, and some old soldiers who are as true as steel. If anything turns up I will hear it at Malone.

I have talked with two deserters from the 21st Regiment, deserters say that there are 400 Irishmen, if not more, in those regiments, and that during the last two months they would not be allowed to do any but duty outside of the barracks, but the other soldiers complained so much that they were lately ordered to perform the same duty as the other soldiers. From what these two men told me, their officers could not trust them.

You must not depend on many men to fall into our ranks at this place; the cause has been neglected very much along the line. The Americans are all alive and will assist liberally when they see something taking place.

Nothing new has turned up on the other side of the line as yet; I will hear it if anything takes place.

We will do all that we can in a quiet way to get those muskets; if we do not get them, we can take them when the time comes.

If you should want a guide, there is a man here, a member of this Circle, whom I could recommend for that duty. He knows the whole country.

I am aware that my duty at this particular time is difficult to perform. I will do all in my power to have things right.

As far as the sentiment of the people is concerned, the most of them are with us.

I will write you again from Potsdam.

I am, General, your obedient servant,

JOHN FALLON,
Captain, F. B.

LXVI

War Department, F. B.,
Adjutant General's Office,
New York, 30th May, 1866.

Special Order, No. 64.

Brig. Gen. Samuel P. Spear will proceed immediately to St. Albans, Vt., to superintend the crossing of troops and supplies that may arrive at that point; and as soon as they have crossed the frontier, to organize them into a division, to be known as the Right Wing of the Army of Ireland, of which he will take command until further orders.

He will organize, on the Canadian side of the frontier, depots of supplies, which he will have properly guarded.

Col. John Mechan, Chief of Engineers, will report to him for duty.

LXVII

War Department, F. B.,
Adjutant General's Office,
New York, 30th May, 1866.

Special Orders, No. 65.

Brig. Gen. Michael C. Murphy will proceed immediately to Malone, N. Y., to superintend the crossing of troops and supplies which may arrive along that line. He will, as soon as practicable after crossing the frontier, organize the cavalry brigade, to be composed of the 1st, 2nd, 3rd, 4th and 5th Regiments of Cavalry, and carry out instructions inclosed herewith.

The cavalry brigade will be attached to the division under command of Brig. Gen. S. P. Spear, from whom he will receive further orders and instructions that any exigency may render necessary.

LXVIII

War Department, F. B.,
Adjutant General's Office,
New York, 31st May. 1866.

Brig. Gen. M. C. Murphy, Malone N. Y.

General:—I am instructed by Gen. T. W. Sweeny to direct you to move everything in the way of supplies over the border as soon as sufficient men arrive to protect them. You will establish depots, at safe and convenient points, and have them well guarded.

Hereafter, you will resist the seizure of any property of ours except the party or parties seizing show an United States warrant. Pay no attention to State or Sheriffs' writs, but do not come in contact with the United States authorities.

To Spear and Murphy.

LXIX

May 31, 1866.

Wm. J. Hynes, Esq., Buffalo, N. Y.

Sir:—I am directed by General Sweeny to inform you that Brig. Gen. W. F. Lynch, I. A., has been appointed to the command of all troops on Lake Erie, and has been ordered to report in Buffalo immediately.

You will furnish him with a copy of the instructions issued by the Secretary of War for the guidance of that portion of the Irish Army.

Very respectfully, your obedient servant,

C. CARROLL TEVIS,
Brig. Gen. and Adj. Gen., F. B.

A true copy. S. R. TRESILIAN.

LXX

Troy, N. Y., May 31, 1866.

Maj. Gen. T. W. Sweeny, Secretary of War, F. B.

General:—I have the honor to acknowledge the receipt of two letters from Captain Greany, of the 30th inst. The arms referred to in one of his letters are the Harpers Ferry rifle, calibre .54. I don't know how many there are, exactly, but will find out and ship them to-morrow morning to Malone. There has been no ammunition received for them yet. All the boxes are in a fearful condition and will have to be re-packed. I have had men working on them all day.

I have succeeded in chartering two cars for Malone and Potsdam Junction, which leave to-morrow at 12 o'clock m.

The cartridges were received from New York this morning, and will be shipped to-morrow.

I do not anticipate further trouble about getting cars, and will push the work as rapidly as possible.

I inclose a communication from Captain Bryce, whom I met this morning on the street.

I am very respectfully, your obedient servant,

W. M. O'REILLY,
Maj. of Ord., F. B.

LXXI

Troy, N. Y., May 31, 1866.

General T. W. Sweeny, Secretary of War, F. B.

General:—Major. O'Reilly and I did not meet until this morning. I believe he found everything progressing favorably. I was able to make satisfactory arrangements with the ammunition, and two carloads will go forward without delay to Potsdam Junction. Mr. Lawrence, who has it stored, has acted very friendly. He informed me that some inquiry has been made at the Arsenal as to when the balance will be taken, and I take the liberry to suggest that it may be well to have it all in his magazine, where it is safe, and can be shipped quietly. Should you determine to take the other million at once, it might be better to have Hitchcock send his order to Lawrence, who will receive it, and you can let an officer go with him to pay for it—thus save unnecessary fuss.

I am at your orders.

Respectfully your obedient servant,

J. W. BRYCE.

General Sweeny, Secretary of War, F. B.
Favor of Major O'Reilly.

LXXII

Potsdam Junction, June 1, 1866.

General:—I received your letter of the 29th this morning. My reason in not answering yours of the 24th is that I expected some news from that property at Rouse's Point. Mr. Mannix has advertised the sale of the arms and made application for them. I have not heard from him lately—that is, within a day or two. We can get them, no matter where they put them, if the men were only here to use them. Mr. Byrne, from Syracuse, N. Y., was here. I received a large case from him which I have to take care of. Mr. Murphy, from Washington, two men from Newark, N. J., and one from Rochester, N. Y., are here. Their property has not arrived yet. I have 40 teams at three different points: Potsdam Junction, Malone and Chatogue; all of the right kind. I wish you would follow up the property as close as you can.

I have received most reliable information from Canada, that you have someone at your Headquarters who gives them all the information they require. In my opinion there is nothing in your way here.

I would like to see the required amount of property here. Address me, "Potsdam Junction, St. Lawrence county, N. Y."

I will write you again to-morrow.

I am, General, very respectfully, your obedient servant,

JOHN FALLON.

LXXIII

St. Albans, Vt., June 2, 1866.

Gen. T. W. Sweeny, Secretary of War, F. B.

Sir:—In accordance with my instructions of the 29th and 30th ult., I started at once for this point, and arrived here on the night of the 31st and found Col. Brown at his post, doing everything in his power, but greatly crippled; arms, ammunition, etc., had been seized by an officer of the 14th U. S. Infantry, and next day the U. S. Marshal arrived with three companies of the 3rd U. S. Artillery and are stationed at the depot, where everything was seized at once.

Colonel Brown has buried near here about 300 arms of different calibres. We have no ammunition, not one round per man, and none can be purchased here.

Colonels Barnum, Rice, Contri, also small detachments from Boston, Springfield, etc., in all about 400 men, are here without supplies, commissary stores or anything but good comfortable clothing. Most of the men are without money or means.

Order so far prevails, but the men are getting uneasy.

If I had a few boxes of ammunition I could move to the nearest point, 15 miles, and cross; but without ammunition it would be destructive to the cause and the loss of good men.

I send this by Major Lyons, who will more fully explain all. Please send me instructions what to do.

Ammunition is the principal want.

I send a clipping from last evening's paper, which is correct relative to the conference with the committee of citizens who called on me.

Everything will be done to intercept the trains and prevent further loss.

With high respect, your obedient servant,

SAML. P. SPEAR,
Brig. Gen. Com'dg Div.

P. S.—I move at once with what men I have, and will beg, borrow or take such ammunition as can be found, avoiding the U. S. troops as much as possible. S. P. S.

I move through Fairfield to Slab City, and endeavor to cut the Trunk R. R.

LXXIV

Headquarters R. W. A. of I., Canada East, June 7, 1866.
6 o'clock p. m.

Maj. Gen. Sweeny.

Sir:—Yours of this date was received by me per Captain Greany at this moment. After your arrest, the same authority attempted to arrest me three times, but I evaded the same, and having your written instructions in my possession, I endeavored fully to carry them out to the letter and to convey to each and every officer and member of the organization the spirit of your orders, which were fully published to all. Accordingly, I left S. Albans at 3 o'clock, a. m., this day, joined my command at Franklin at 8:30 o'clock, where I found General Mahon at his post, doing everything possible for an officer to do to keep the command in order, which, under existing circumstances, he most admirably accomplished. The rations had not arrived—the men hungry, and most of them begging to go to the destination promised them—Canada. I—acting under my orders, marched them cheering over the border—raised the Green Flag and took a strong position. The cry was still—hunger. I had but one alternative—foraging parties were sent out, and plenty of meat obtained. I mounted from ten to twelve men at once—sent my engineer officer to select a better position—and in short, General Mahon, as well as every officer, deserves my commendations for the zeal and energy with which they fully carried out the instructions published to them.

I have on hand:

Plenty meat—very little breadstuff.
250 Springfield muskets.
13,000 Springfield musket cartridges.
300 carbines (no ammunition).
And, in all, not to exceed 1,000 men.

Many have gone home, but those remaining are anxious to advance.

I have expended, in every case, the funds intrusted to my charge to the best advantage, and have now left on hand the sum of $20.15.

I entered Canada at 10 o'clock a. m., and to remove to-night would be more destructive than to remain in my present position till morning.

I have fully explained to the Commanding General the disposition of his orders, and my present position; and would urgently request a return communication by a special messenger which will reach me before daylight to-morrow.

With high respect, your obedient servant,

S. P. SPEAR,
Brig. Gen. Com'd'g, R. W., I. R. A.

LXXV

Headquarters Right Wing I. R. A., Canada East, June 8, 1866,

10:30 a. m.

Col. John Mechan, C. E., I. R A.

Sir:—Yours of midnight last has been received from Colonel Brown. I have the honor to report that from the time of crossing the border to the present, I have been very busily engaged, with the valuable assistance of Major Tresillian, to ascertain and picket all important points. I find many patriotic Irishmen here, in easy circumstances, mostly farmers, who give me all the information in their power; they even loan me horses, and the first one I received was tendered to me by one of this class; this gave me new life. I sent him home to tell others, and now I can get all the information I desire from this true class of friends to our cause. They all say: "Advance to beyond our homes and we will join you."

Last night I sent to Captain O'Hara, 3rd Infantry, with a small party to reconnoiter Frelighsburg (or Slabtown), where I was informed there was 100 cavalry, partly regulars (red coats), on picket. Captain O'Hara returned, and in a most soldier-like manner made the following report, viz:

"General:—Your orders have been obeyed. I advanced cautiously toward Frelighsburg, surprised the pickets, made a dash, and the result, Sir, is, I completely routed the enemy, and drove him helter skelter in every direction, killing 3 of his horses and wounding many of his best men. I mean, Sir, by his 'best' men, the only ones who stood. One was so badly wounded that he could not be moved, and I obtained a doctor and left him in the hands of friendly citizens; and here, General, is the first British flag captured by the Right Wing, and I respectfully request to raise it with the Green above in front of your Headquarters."

I complied with this request and publicly complimented him for this brave and gallant affair. I cordially recommend him for promotion, as such acts will encourage others and warrant our success.

Frelighsburg is now in my hands; also Pidgeon Hill, St. Armand and other valuable points (see map). I have twelve men mounted and hope to have, by "Retreat," twelve more. My commissary stores arrived; were issued, also fresh beef. Give me men, arms and ammunition and I will subsist my command sumptuously off the country. I shall require no more stores from the contractor at St. Albans, and all I have received have been paid for, and all of the receipts in my possession.

I earnestly request that a small detachment of orderlies (couriers) be organized in St. Albans and mounted by Mr. Fuller (livery stable men to act as despatch bearers, sending one at a time as occasion may require, in order that I may report twice per day to the Commanding General, and that this may be kept up till I can supply the horses. A sergeant and 6 men will be adequate.)

Hurry up those arms. Send some energetic officer with a guard to stay with them till they reach their destination, and don't let them delay en route.

I send by Colonel Brown the flag and staff. The standard bearer is "non est."

Be sure to send men that will remain with the wagons containing arms, etc.

As soon as my reconnoitering and foraging parties arrive I will send another despatch.

I feel in most excellent spirits, and if I can hold my own until the 500 muskets and 100,000 rounds arrive, I shall have no doubts of success.

The men are in excellent spirits, but the fact of the Canada militia being ordered out makes some uneasy.

I have no carbine ammunition. Has Mr. Wheeler returned? If so, send it at once. Mr. Ovitt furnishes heavy wagons the cheapest.

I have received the $500, which shall be most prudently used; and pay no hauling bills until I certify to the receipt of their load.

Officers behave excellently, with but two exceptions; I can attend to their cases in person.

I am, Sir, very respectfully, your obedient servant,

S. P. SPEAR,

Brig. Gen. Com'd'g Right Wing, I. R. A.

P. S.—Scout just returned; 400 volunteers arrived at Smith's Corner at 8 a. m. this morning. S. P. S.

LXXVI

Copy of Telegrams.

Our men isolated. Enemy marching in force from Toronto. What shall we do? When do you move?

Answer—Reinforce O'Neill at all hazards; if he cannot hold his position, let him fall back—send him and his men to Malone as rapidly as possible by the Rome and Watertown roads.

[Indorsed by Gen. Sweeny—"Hynes' dispatch and order of 1st of June."]

LXXVII

Headquarters, St. Albans, Vt., June 8, 1866, 11:30 p. m.

Brig. Gen. S. P. Spear, Commanding Right Wing, Army of Ireland.

General:—Your communication of 10:30 this forenoon is received. The General desires me to congratulate you on the success of the affair at Frelighsburg last night, and the capture of a stand of colors from the enemy on the occasion. Captain O'Hara is hereby promoted to be brevet major for his gallant conduct, and you will tender to him and the men of his command, the thanks of the General Commanding.

By order of General Sweeny. JOHN MECHAN,
Chief Engineer, F. B.

LXXVIII

OFFICIAL REPORT OF GENERAL T. W. SWEENY, SECRETARY OF WAR.

Headquarters, War Department, F. B.,
September, 1866.

Col. W. R. Roberts, President of the F. B.

Sir: I have the honor to submit my report of operations prior to and during the campaign on the Canadian frontier, as directed by me.

Soon after the adjournment of the Philadelphia Congress, in October, 1865, I turned my attention to the military organization of the Brotherhood, and the procurement of munitions of war, which, owing to the obstacles placed in my way by the Stephens-O'Mahony wing, were greatly, if not entirely retarded, up to the time of the Pittsburg Congress in February last.

At that Congress I submitted my plan of campaign and the estimates necessary for its furtherance and accomplishment to that body, which were to the following effect, viz:

1st. That the minimum force with which I would consent to invade Canada should be 10,000 men.

2d. Three (3) batteries of artillery.

3rd. Each man should be furnished with 200 rounds of ammunition.

4th. Each gun should be furnished with 500 rounds of fixed ammunition.

And furthermore, that this personnel and material be furnished in time for me to cross into Canada during that season when the lakes and rivers are bridged with ice. Otherwise, double that force would be necessary.

The estimates submitted at that time to purchase the necessary munitions and equipments were four hundred and fifty thousand dollars ($450,000.)

I found it necessary to alter the plan submitted to the Convention, in its general detail, for obvious reasons—which will appear more fully in this report—from that which was proposed on that occasion.

Having received my final instructions, I returned to New York City, arriving on the 25th of February. I immediately appointed through the Adjutant General's office field and company officers in the various States. I also continued to make the necessary purchases of arms and munitions of war, as means were furnished, but, from want of funds promised, the quantity which I was enabled to procure was wholly inadequate to insure the success of the expedition.

On the 16th of April I appeared before the Senate, when a resolution was passed urging me to immediate action; every member voting in the affirmative. Taking this action into consideration with the reckless pressure brought to bear upon me by the several Circles to hasten me into premature action, and the assurances of almost the entire organization that unless I took the field at once, the dissolution of the Brotherhood would be inevitable, I reluctantly yielded, preferring the chances of an honorable failure in the field, to the disintegration of the organization, which would have entailed on this section of the F. B. the odious reputation which has attached itself to the Stephens-O'Mahony officials.

The funds placed at my disposal were hardly one-fourth the amount promised me, and enabled me to procure not over 10,000 stand of all arms, and two and a half million (2,500,000) ball cartridges. As to artillery, I had none whatever; but trusted to the gallantry of my soldiers to capture it, or to the patriotism of the Irish people to send it to the front when the blow was struck.

On the 1st day of May, I ordered Capt. J. W. Dempsey, of the New Orleans contingent, to move to Cincinnati, Ohio, and report to Lieut. Col. Grace, Asst. Inspector General.

On the 9th I instructed Capt. John Scanlan in a method of telegraphing me the available transportation in Chicago.

On the 10th, I issued General Orders No. 3, directing colonels of regiments to pack all regimental and company property preparatory to transportation, and forwarded copies to Generals of Departments for transmittal to their respective commands.

I directed Col. John O'Neill, of Tennessee, and Col. Owen Starr, of Kentucky, to forward as freight, arms and munitions of war to Sandusky City, Ohio, in charge of the regimental quartermaster and the quartermaster sergeants from their respective regiments. These instructions were the first issued; the troops being the most remote from the border. On the same date I directed Brig. Gen. W. F. Lynch, commanding Department of Illinois and Iowa, and Brig. Gen. A. G. Malloy, commanding Department of Wisconsin and Michigan, to select points of rendezvous to which their respective commands should forward their arms and munitions of war; to be guided in their selection by the amount of transportation which could be obtained to cross the Lakes, and report the points selected to my Headquarters.

From General Lynch I received a telegram designating Chicago; from General Malloy I received no report, and afterwards learned that he had retired from the organization without any notification, accepting the position of second lieutenant in the U. S. Army.

On the 12th I received a telegram from Senator Morrison, stating that "thirty canal boats and five steam tugs were secured at Buffalo"; and on the 13th received his report as a member of the Committee on Transportation, stating that all necessary transportation at that point was procured, with other valuable information.

On the 14th, having received information that some of our

arms were seized, I directed Colonel Doyle, of Oswego, N. Y., to inform me where arms could be stored with security, on the line between Oswego and Rouses Point.

On the 16th I directed Mr. Keating, of Franklin, Pa. (?), to store the arms of the district at Erie, Pa.

On the 17th I ordered Colonel O'Neill and Major Alden, of West Tennessee, and Colonel Owen Starr, of Kentucky, to move on Cincinnati, Ohio, and report to Senator Fitzgerald for full instructions.

Having been informed by Senator Scanlan that the necessary transportation for the Western contingent would be furnished at Chicago and Milwaukee, provided I sent one of my staff officers to that Department, I immediately issued Special Order No. 58, ordering my adjutant general, Brig. Gen. C. C. Tevis, to proceed to Chicago and organize a division, to be composed of the troops from Illinois, Iowa, Michigan, Wisconsin, Missouri and Kansas, to be designated as the Left Wing of the Army of Ireland.

On the 18th I instructed General Tevis to make no movement until after the 25th, as the Queen's birthday fell on the 24th and all the troops in Canada would be paraded on that day, and should the British authorities get an inkling that our forces were in motion, the result would be plain. On the same date I communicated with Colonels O'Neill and Starr and Major Alden to the same effect.

On the 21st I received a communication from Mr. Thomas Lavan, of Cleveland, Ohio, that we could get all the transportation we needed for from four thousand to five thousand men at that point. On the receipt of this information I immediately issued Special Order No. 61, dated May 22nd, assigning Brig. Gen. Lynch to the command of all the troops that were to embark from the Lake Erie shore, to superintend the embarcation, and to retain command until further orders. Also a letter of instructions, directing him to make Cleveland, Ohio, his Headquarters, and designating Buffalo, Dunkirk, Erie, Cleveland, Sandusky City and Toledo as the points where the troops would be concentrated, and cautioning him to act with great discretion, as some of our arms had been seized at Erie, and desiring him to act in conjunction with Brig. Gen. Tevis, who would give him all the information required and furnish him with a copy of instructions given by me, so the attack would be simultaneous. On the same date I issued orders to colonels of regiments to forward immediately such regimental and company property as the men could not carry with them in the passenger cars, in charge of the regimental quartermaster and the quartermaster sergeant, to the following points, viz:

1st. The Louisiana, Tennessee, Kentucky, Ohio and Indiana troops to Cleveland, Ohio; Erie, Pa.; Sandusky City and Toledo, Ohio.

2nd. The Western Pennsylvania and the Western New York troops to Buffalo.

3rd. The Illinois, Missouri, Kansas, Wisconsin, Iowa and Michigan troops to Chicago and Milwaukee, Wisconsin.

4th. The New York, New Jersey, Virginia, Maryland, Delaware and District of Columbia troops to Potsdam Junction and Malone, N. Y.

5th. The New England troops to St. Albans, Vermont.

That the orders to move would be issued by telegraph, in the following words: "You may commence working"; and would be signed, "S. W. T."; that they should proceed by the nearest railway routes to the points of rendezvous above designated.

On the same date I directed Colonel Grace, on the arrival of the Kentucky, Tennessee and New Orleans troops, to forward them immediately to Cleveland, Ohio, to report to General Lynch; but should circumstances render it unsafe, to change the point of destination to Buffalo. I also, on this date, directed T. Barnett, Esq., to forward arms at Dunkirk, N. Y., to Buffalo.

On the 25th I ordered Capt. W. J. Hynes, of my staff, to proceed to Buffalo and superintend the movement there as my representative until the arrival of General Lynch or some other general officer, giving him copies of instructions for the guidance of that portion of the army and of the Western contingent.

On the 26th I assigned Brig. Gen. S. P. Spear to the command of all troops on that part of the frontier lying between Ogdensburg, N. Y., and the source of the Connecticut River, with full instructions.

On the 30th I issued Special Orders No. 64, ordering Brig. Gen. S. P. Spear to proceed to St. Albans, Franklin county, Vermont, to take command and forward the troops as speedily as possible across the frontier into Canada.

On the same date I issued Special Orders No. 65, directing Brig. Gen. M. C. Murphy to proceed to Malone and to take command of and organize the Cavalry Brigade, to be composed of the 1st, 2nd, 3rd, 4th and 5th Regiments, and to carry out instructions of the same date. His command to be attached to General Spear's division, from whom he would receive further orders.

On this date I issued full instructions to all officers connected with I. R. A.

On the 31st I informed Captain Hynes that Brig. Gen. Lynch was ordered to move his Headquarters from Cleveland, Ohio, to Buffalo, N. Y.; directing him to turn over to General Lynch his instructions, etc. On the same date full instructions were forwarded to General Lynch.

For copies of all of the above named orders, you are respectfully referred to the annexed file.

Orders having been issued for a general movement on the 31st of May, Brig. Gen. C. C. Tevis commanding the left wing, Brig. Gen. W. F. Lynch the center, and Brig. Gen. S. P. Spear the right wing of the army.

The following plan was designated to be carried into effect: A descent from the Lakes simultaneous with the crossing of the undefined boundary on the line of the St. Lawrence. A column of 3,000 men were to move from Chicago and Milwaukee (24 hours in advance of the movement of Lake Erie), by Lakes Michigan and Huron, seize and advance directly on London by Stratford. This difference in time was given so that the other columns could cross Lake Erie; one concentrating at Port Stanley and moving on London, the other concentrating at Port Colbourne, seizing Paris, Guelph and Hamilton. This would compel the enemy to concentrate his forces about the meridian of Toronto, uncovering Montreal. So soon as this was accomplished, our auxiliaries in Canada were organized and prepared to destroy St. Ann's Bridge, at the junction of the Ottawa and St. Lawrence Rivers, on the Grand Trunk Railroad and the Beauharnois Canal. This would effectually cut off all communication between Upper and Lower Canada. To distract the attention of the enemy while this movement was being made, knowing that wherever I was he would consider the main point of attack, I was advertised in Erie and in Buffalo and other points along the frontier, the main points of the attack being along the line of the St. Lawrence. In order to more fully carry out this design, I massed troops at Potsdam Junction and at Malone; threatening Cornwall and Prescott, which had the desired effect. The success of this movement being of vital importance, Brig. Gen. Murphy, commanding the cavalry, was ordered to move on both sides of the Richeleau River and seize the garrisons of Isle aux Nois, St. Johns and Fort Chambley, or cut them off; occupy La Prairie and threaten Montreal by the Victoria Bridge, holding it if possible until the infantry came up; if forced to retire, they would fall back, destroying the bridge and placing all possible obstacles in the way of the enemy.

Simultaneously with this movement a detachment of cavalry was to be sent forward along the line of the Grand Trunk Railroad in the direction of Quebec, seizing Point Levi, if not too strongly garrisoned. Should the enemy move across the river in force, they were to fall back on Richmond, destroying the bridges and giving timely notice of the enemy's movements and holding that point. Should the enemy attempt to concentrate his force from Montreal and Quebec, the forces were to be drawn in between the Richelieu and the St. Francis Rivers and that country held at all hazards, making Sherbrooke the Headquarters. This position can be seen at a glance to be one of the strongest in Canada for defense.

The foregoing plan of campaign would undoubtedly have been successful, were it not for the following circumstances.

The staff officer, Brig. Gen. C. C. Tevis, whom I ordered to Chicago, reported that no transportation could be procured at that point, and that one-half of the column I had assurance of could not be mustered.

Brig. Gen. Lynch did not, in accordance with orders, establish his Headquarters at Cleveland, Ohio, and superintend the movement on Lake Erie. I was then compelled to throw Colonel (Brig. Gen.) John O'Neill's men across at the only point where I could procure transportation, Buffalo.

Receiving the following dispatch from Captain Hynes, dated 9:10 P. M., June 1st, 1866: "Our men isolated. Enemy marching in force from Toronto. What shall we do? When do you move?" I sent the following answer:

"Reinforce O'Neill at all hazards; if he cannot hold his position let him fall back; send him and his men to Malone as rapidly as possible by the Rome and Watertown roads."

Having found it impossible to reinforce him from lack of transportation—sufficient in the first place having been procured for the transportation of only 600 troops—and from the extreme vigilance of the steamer "Michigan," General O'Neill being compelled to retire after gallantly fighting the battle of Ridgway—he and his whole command being seized by the U. S. authorities—I immediately dispatched orders to the officer in command at Detroit to move with what force he could muster from Port Hudson on Sarnia. By that movement we would have drawn the enemy's attention in that direction, as he would have considered it the advance of the Western contingent. This was not executed. Whether from lack of transportation or disobedience of orders I know not; I have since been led to believe it was the latter.

Thus it will be seen that the campaign opened under the most discouraging circumstances; nor did the prospect brighten when I arrived at Potsdam, Malone and St. Albans. This was the most important division of the army, that with which I intended to occupy Montreal and Lower Canada. I here ordered seventeen regiments of infantry and five of cavalry (the average number of men in each regiment according to the latest report, was 800. This would give me a force of 16,800 men, but I calculated that not more than 8,000 would arrive in time to take part in the first movement). I gave ample time for these regiments to arrive on the 2nd of June in order to cross into Canada on that day. But judge of my surprise on arriving at the front on the 4th, to find that scarcely 1,000 men had reported to the general commanding the right wing of the army.

The material of war to furnish my soldiers was forwarded in disguised cases to the different towns on the railways leading into Canada, such as St. Albans, Malone and Potsdam; and for operations on the Lakes my depots were established at Chicago, Cleveland, Erie and Buffalo.

The muskets were purchased at Bridesburg Arsenal, Philadelphia, and the ammunition at Watervliet Arsenal, Troy. Calibre, .58. The United States Government, in selling these stores to my agents, was perfectly well aware of the purpose for which they were intended, and their willingness in allowing these sales to be made, together with the sympathy expressed for us by individuals in eminent positions at Washington, caused me to be totally unprepared for the treacherous seizure of our arms and ammunition, which rendered a successful movement into Canada hopeless, at that time.

I submit the action of the Executive to the liberty-loving people of the United States, and I am mistaken in their character and generous and manly sentiments, if they award their approval to the Government having permitted its marshals and other civil officials to play the role of British detectives. The virulent and pertinacious manner in which these duties were performed at Buffalo and some other points, even before orders were issued from Washington, has raised suspicion that the benign influence of the British Treasury had extended itself across the frontier.

As to the U. S. Army, it was practically placed at the hands of the British generals, and one detachment under Lieut. Col. Bvt. La Rhett L. Livingston, of the 3rd Artillery, permitted a British force to march into United States territory, in order to cut off the retreat of some stragglers left behind after the final evacuation. After crossing United States ground, by the verbal permission of this American officer, they sabred some of the unarmed men under his very eyes.

I was arrested in St. Albans at midnight on the 6th of June, together with Colonel Mechan, my chief of staff, just as I had completed my arrangements to cross the frontier with my command at daylight the next morning. General Spear, being absent purchasing provisions for the troops, eluded the vigilance of the United States officers, and escaping arrest, crossed into Canada on the 7th in accordance with orders received before my arrest, and continued to keep up communications with me during subsequent operations, which were carried on under my orders.

Previous to my arrest, I sent Mr. Roche with dispatches to you with instructions to place at my disposal in one of the New York banks for the subsistence of the troops and the payment of transportation, a certain amount of money, to which I received no answer.

Before closing this report, I beg leave to call your attention to the operations inaugurated on the Pacific Coast:

On the 11th of February last, I ordered Col. P. F. Walsh to California, to make San Francisco his Headquarters, and organize a military movement in that Department. I made him the bearer of sealed dispatches to certain prominent persons there, belonging to our organization, with instructions to organize that contingent to act simultaneously with our movement east of the Rocky Mountains. They were to seize and occupy Victoria, in British America, from which place privateers could be sent out to prey upon British commerce in the Pacific. I received a letter from that Department, dated the 26th of April, and on the 30th of May sent him a dispatch instructing him how to act. A copy of both are herewith respectfully submitted.

The immediate cause of our failure is attributable to the

seizure of our arms and ammunition by the Government authorities; and the remote cause, to the misrepresentations made by the colonels of the regiments respecting their effective force, and their failure to report promptly when the orders were issued. However, our success would have been certain, even with the number of men that we had, if they had received their arms, ammunition and equipments, as reinforcements were coming rapidly to the front. But even this was paralyzed by the Government, as it took possession of the railroads leading to the points of rendezvous, and also the telegraph lines, cutting off all our supplies and means of communication, several of our men being turned off the cars while traveling as passengers without arms or equipments.

Our officers and men behaved admirably under the trying circumstances in which they were placed and the privations in many instances which they were compelled to suffer. To select any for special praise where all, with few exceptions, behaved so bravely, might seem invidious, but I cannot refrain from noticing the splendid manner in which Generals Spear and O'Neill carried out their instructions; being ably supported by Brigadier Generals Murphy, Mahan, Heffernan, and Colonels Warren, Eason, and many others whose names I cannot now remember.

I must also call your attention to the valuable services rendered by Lieut. Col. S. R. Tresilian, Acting Chief Engineer, Colonel Mechan, holding that position, being arrested at the same time with myself; also of Captains John Fallon and W. J. Hynes, of my staff, and Colonels O'Connor and Contri, and Captains Maguire and Lonegan.

It is now my painful duty to say that I was compelled to issue special order dismissing three members of my staff: Brig. Gen. C. C. Tevis, Adjutant General, for disobedience of orders; Colonel Arundel, Chief of Ordnance, and Major Van Brunt, for desertion in the face of the enemy.

I have the honor to remain,

Yours respectfully,

T. W. SWEENY,

Secretary of War, F. B.

LXXIX

AMERICAN NOTIONS OF NEUTRALITY.

Grave reflections spring from the dangerous move into Canada of Roberts and Sweeny, which was not merited by the ridiculous tomfoolery of O'Mahony and Killian at Campobello. Among these reflections, the most obvious regard the role played by the American Government.

If there be any such thing in international courtesy as "heaping coals of fire on an enemy's head," the performance has been achieved by our Government for the benefit of both Great Britian and her colonies. When the United States was in distress, and the standard of revolt raised against law, under the pretense of waging war—as with the Fenians in Canada—what did Great Britain do? Her Government rushed with shameful haste to declare the Union dissolved, to officially annonuce the rebellion as a success, and to brand the Republic as the "late Union," as is well known. Her flag floated henceforth in honor of the insurgent victories. In her docks was built, equipped, armed, manned and thence sailed, every ship in the Confederate cruising navy. Her Armstrong guns, which money counld not buy except for allies, were found, free gifts, in Confederate earthworks. Her powder, small arms, projectiles, her stores, supplies and manufactures, were furtively thrust into every open inlet on the Southern coast. Her Alabamas and Shenandoahs ruined our commerce. Crews from her training-ships manned the 64-pounders from her foundries over which rebel colors floated; and not content with that, her greyhounds were ready to snatch from our sailors the very captives they had won in fight. Before it was even asked, much more expected, recognition of their belligerency was profusely thrust on the rebels, and the pacific ally of a round half century was spurned in a day.

What—now when the Irish Republic "secedes" from Great Britain, proclaims itself a nation, puts 50,000 troops in the field, attacks and carries a point of operations of the enemy's soil, defeats his best volunteer troops in fair fight, and claims recognition as a successful belligerent—What does America do? Does she sneakingly complain of the inefficiency of the neutrality laws, as did Lord John Russell and the whole Government and press of England at his back? Does she argue how hard it is to be neutral, and then seek to take advantage of her own wrong and negligence? She puts her entire available army under marching orders; her cutters patrol the line of lake and river; her State police and militia force are called into requisition; her Attorney General orders his subordinates and marshals to arrest all violators of the neutrality laws (an unwarrantable stretch of authority in favor of Great Britain); her prominent generals in propinquous districts, Departments and divisions—Generals Hooker, Barry, Meade, and

Lieutenant General Grant himself, hurry to the scene; the President issues a sweeping and crushing condemnation of Fenianism. By these acts, while the Fenians are at the flood of conquest, they are checked. Their rear assailed, their supplies are cut off, their troops overcome and dispersed, all their arms and munitions captured, and the whole campaign ended—all by the United States. The Canada from which we have thus turned the tide of invasion was the same country which had, within five years, a chance to show us its notions of neutrality. It was a base of insurgent operation. There were concocted the various schemes of assassinating the Chief Magistrate of the Union and his leading generals, and there subscriptions for paying their expenses were collected. Thence came, and thither escaped again, the hellish villains who tried to fire peaceful Northern cities, without a word of warning; beginning first with hotels and theatres, because most densely packed with men, women and children. On that very Vermont line, and over the self same roads where General Meade suppressed the great Fenian invasion, occurred the St. Albans raid, and the robbing of our banks and citizens by bands organized in Canada, winked at by Canadian constabulary, and after an ostentatious arrest, set free, with all their plunder, by Canadian Justice Counsels.

We assume, of course, that it was the United States which demolished Fenianism, and not Great Britain. Canada did, indeed, put troops into the field, but at the first encounter they were whipped to pieces in two hours by an equal or lesser number of Fenians. The situation of Canada, after the skirmish at Ridgway, was really pitiable. Colonel Booker had with him two full regiments of first class Canadian volunteers in that affair, of whom one, the Queen's Own, was well known to be the best volunteer regiment in all Canada. At first they advanced very gallantly, but for the veteran Fenians—heroes of such campaigns as the Peninsula, Shiloh, Fredericksburg, Chancellorsville, Spotsylvania, and Cold Harbor—the sputtering of a few rifles only made the blood mount. Actually less in number, they cleared the field of their enemies in a trice—and some of them will repay that infliction of disgrace by a felon's death. Thenceforward little reliance was placed in the volunteer troops against the Fenian veterans. If the Queen's Own could not stand, no similar regiment could. From Toronto to Halifax went up cries of "Hurry along the Regulars," and "Send us Armstrong guns." That Montreal which was once full of maledictions and plots against "the late Union," was quivering with fear—was declaring it a shame for dissatisfied men to rise up against a good government—and hoping as far as a guilty conscience would allow them to hope, for the interference of "the late Union" against the Irish. The excitement was intense when it was rumored—not without cause—that not even all of the Regulars could be relied on. As it was, there were but few regiments in the country; very few for so enormous a line. In one word, had America exhibited British neutrality in this matter, and the Fenians had been allowed to get arms, munitions, trains and supplies up to the border; had not revenue cutters with shotted guns swept their line of communication with the rear, Sweeny could have flung his columns over the border wherever he liked, and before Autumn turned the sterile earth of Canada as red with blood as the battle-ploughed soil of Virginia.—"Army and Navy Journal," June 16, 1866.

LXXX

THE INVASION OF CANADA.

The following account of the events leading up to the invasion of Canada, together with a description of the strength of the Canadian armament, was written by Mr. William Montgomery Sweeny, son of General Sweeny, and printed in the "New York Sunday News" of June 18th, 1893.

Editor of the News: I have read with much interest Major Fitzpatrick's article entitled "Invading Canada" in the Sunday News of May 28, and beg to make a few additions.

The plan for the invasion of Canada, was not, as some may suppose, gotten up to suit the exigencies of the moment; but was the result of many years of careful study on the part of Gen. T. W. Sweeny. and to which he devoted the knowledge of military life he had acquired in the Mexican War, among the Indians of the West and in the War of the Rebellion.

As long ago as 1858, he met James Stephens, who was introduced to him as "Captain Daly," and Colonel Doheny at the home of the latter, to discuss the feasibility of an uprising in Ireland. After hearing the statement of Mr. Stephens as to the condition of affairs in Ireland, General Sweeny vigorously opposed making any attempt at revolution in Ireland. He declared that "any attempt at revolution without adequate military preparation and resources would be futile and disastrous."

Shortly after the close of the Civil War, in which Sweeny played a conspicuous part, particularly at Shiloh, where he received the thanks of Gen. W. T. Sherman for having "saved the day," he hastened to submit his plan and offer his services to the Pittsburg Convention, both of which were almost unanimously adopted. In an address written shortly after accepting the position of Secretary of War and General Commanding the Armies of Ireland, General Sweeny outlined the plan which was submitted to the convention, laying particular stress on the results likely to follow an uprising in Ireland. In this address he says:

"The most reliable accounts from Ireland have convinced me that our friends there are totally unprepared with the material means necessary to contend, with any show of success, against the British troops, and that to excite an insurrection at present would be but to provoke a wholesale massacre, in which thousands of brave lives would be sacrificed in a useless struggle.

"The seizure of the steamer Meteor in New York harbor on the mere suspicion of her being a Chilian privateer will show the impracticability of attempting to fit out in any United States port an expedition of sufficient proportions to be of any real assistance to our brothers in Ireland, and the capture during the month of January of the 21 armed Fenians who dis-

BRIG. GEN'L THOMAS W. SWEENY, U. S. A.

Photograph taken when Captain 2nd U. S. Infantry, by Brady in 1861.

embarked near the harbor of Sligo will prove the criminal folly of sending over small detachments.

"By the examination of the letter books of the late Acting Adjutant General P. J. Dowling, which are submitted for your inspection, it will be seen that no definite plan of action had been adopted, but that the policy as represented by him was, 'to wait until something should turn up.'

"Firm in my belief that we were strong enough to make the opportunity, not to wait for it, I determined to act at once, and in that quarter where victory was most vulnerable, and where victory would give us the most real positive advantage; and I determined to attack Canada.

"In order to project the plan of campaign, a full and accurate knowledge of the enemy's strength, position and resources is indispensable, and of this information I have been put in possession by the reports of my own secret agents and by those made by British officials to their Government.

"The Canadian frontier, extending from the mouth of the St. Lawrence River to Lake Huron, a distance of more than 1,300 miles, is assailable at all points. In some places this frontier is constituted by a line visible only on a map; in others it is a navigable inland sea; in others the bank of a river or the shore of a lake, and coincident with it runs the frontier of the United States. English writers admit its vulnerability, and also admit the 'the Americans of the Northern States are the only enemies whom England has to fear'—and it is through and from these Northern States, whose sympathy with us and whose hostility to England is undoubted, that our expeditionary army must march to the invasion and conquest of Canada.

"In 1862 the Duke of Newcastle, in view of the possibility of a rupture with the United States, addressed the following communication to the Canadian Government:

" 'In the event of a war with the United States, Canada will naturally become a point of attack from those zealous advocates of increased sovereignty, which they term the "Monroe Doctrine." and no body of troops which England can send to her American Colonies will suffice to make Canada safe, without the hearty concurrence of the Canadians themselves. With 150,000 local troops, joined to what assistance the Home Government can furnish, our possessions will be secure, with less, we shall be pent up, in our fortified towns and be destroyed in detail. Garrisons must be established as follows to secure our strongholds: Quebec, 10,000; Montreal, 30,000; Kingston, 20,000; Ottawa, 5,000. Thirty-five thousand more will be needed for field operations, between Lake Ontario and Quebec, and with less than 60,000 more good troops our Western District cannot be protected.' "

In consequence of this recommendation a bill was introduced by the Hon. John Macdonald, empowering the Colonial Government to enroll 50,000 men who should be called out for twelve days' annual drill during three years, but so little interest was felt by the Parliament in the matter that the bill was rejected, and instead another was adcpted giving to the Government permission to enroll all unmarried men for six days' annual drill. An appropriation was made in each of the years 1864 and 1865 to cover the necessary expenses of the measure, but, so far, the official reports show that less than 10,000 men have been in attendance on the drills, out of the 197,000 militia actually borne on the muster rolls of the two provinces. Within the last three years volunteer companies and battalions have been raised, the strength of which is, according to the last returns of the deputy adjutants general to the Governor General, Lord Monk, 25,000 men, divided into six mounted batteries, ten companies heavy artillery, two companies engineers, fourteen companies cavalry, fifteen companies infantry and eighty-two riflemen, all of whom have certified to the performance of twelve days' annual drill.

"In the arsenals are stored 50,000 Enfield rifles, seven six-pounder field batteries, four batteries of eighteen-pounders and two batteries of twenty-pounder Armstrong guns, with large supplies of ammunition and military stores, besides a large number of old-fashioned brass field pieces and howitzers, not enumerated in the above statement. But, until warned of their danger by the public discussions of the last two months, there was not a single regiment of militia or volunteers which had ever been assembled as a battalion, or drilled otherwise than by detachments.

"Canada is divided into two military districts—the Eastern, under the command of Major General Lindsay, headquarters at Montreal; and the Western, under General Napier, headquarters at Kingston. The entire force of regular troops in the Eastern District consists of five battalions and a half of infantry, three companies of engineers and five batteries of the Royal Artillery, in all about 4,500 men, who are distributed as follows: Quebec, 1,750; Montreal, 2,250; Chambly, 200; St. Johns, 150; Isle-au-Noix, 150.

"Isle-au-Noix is the point nearest to the American frontier and is considered as the advance outpost of Montreal, but on the line between St. Regis and St. Johns there is no military post. This district extends from the Gulf to the Ottawa River, comprising also the section of country south of the St. Lawrence.

"The Western District, extending from the Ottawa River to the western boundary of Canada, lies to the north of the St. Lawrence and the Great Lakes and is considered from its position, as more easily defensible than the Eastern District, which has no natural objects to oppose an invasion. Its garrison consists of 3,000 regular troops, composed of three and a half battalions of infantry, four batteries of artillery and two companies of engineers, which are stationed, in Kingston, 550; Toronto, 950; Hamilton, 350; London, 700, and in Sarnia, Windsor, Sandwich, Niagara and Chippewa, 450. Of this district, Sarnia, opposite Port Huron, Sandwich and Windsor, a little below Detroit, and Niagara and Chippewa, on the Niagara River, are the outposts.

"General Mitchell, commander-in-chief of the two districts, has his headquarters at Montreal, and can dispose, in addition to the above, of all the volunteer and militia contingents of both Provinces, the present fighting force of which is in Lower Canada: Regulars, 4,500; volunteers, 10,230; militia, 4,000; and in Upper Canada: Regulars, 3,000; volunteers, 14,780, and militia, 6,000, making a total of 18,730 in Lower Canada, and of 23,780 in Upper Canada, for the concentration of which during the summer at any given point, the enemy can use, not only the Grand Trunk Railroad, with its branches, but also the St. Lawrence and Ottawa Rivers, the Lachine, Beauharnais, Rideau and Welland canals and the Great Lakes, which can be protected and kept open by means of gunboats. During the winter he is restricted to his railroad communication only.

"The fortifications of Quebec and Kingston are the only ones admitted by the British military engineers to be in a good state of defense, and preparations have been made to strengthen them by earthworks and intrenched camps at Sarnia, London, Stratford, Hamilton, Ottawa City, Prescott and Montreal. The severity of the winter, however, has interrupted their construction, which will be resumed with great activity as soon as the spring shall have set in. It is, therefore, of vital importance to our success that we attack this winter, while the principal towns are comparatively defenseless, and when the frozen rivers will not only afford us the means of crossing, but will prevent the operation of the enemy's gunboats against us. The destruction of the Grand Trunk Railway will stop all his reinforcements now, but, should we be obliged to postpone our movement for three months we will need more than double of the means and forces now sufficient to secure our success.

"Canada is shaped somewhat like an hour-glass; the occupation of the line dividing its centre, near Montreal, will cut the provinces in two, and by isolating the Western District give us entire command of the enemy's line of communication and supplies.

"From the opposition of the people of the Eastern Province we have nothing to apprehend. They were positively neutral during the invasions of 1775 and 1812, and the arrogance of British troops has only embittered the aversion which, as Frenchmen, they have always felt toward the conquerors of their forefathers. In Canada West the garrisons are small and widely separated, and even the sympathy of their friends the Orangemen will be of little real avail when cut off from all assistance from without. They must remain in their fortified towns, until compelled to surrender in detail, or they will be cut to pieces by our troops whenever they attempt to move out with a view to concentrate in the field. It is impossible to state now precisely when and where I will commence my attack; the first will depend upon the means put at my disposal by this Congress to arm and equip my troops; the second must be modified by the dispositions made by the enemy; the vast extent and consequent weakness of his line of defense offers us the choice of fifty points, and the frozen state of the rivers every facility for reaching them, and where he is weakest and least prepared, there will I strike him first. But of the general features of the plan I can state this much.

"First. By a column from Detroit to cut the Great Western Railroad, to menace London and prevent the concentration of troops from the frontier posts at that point, and to occupy Fort Stanley, thus securing us a port on Lake Erie, where we could receive supplies and reinforcements and operate against British commerce on that lake.

"Second. By a column across the Niagara River against Hamilton, which would hold or destroy the Welland Canal, thus interrupting all naval communication between Lakes Erie and Ontario; cut off the garrisons at Fort Erie and Chippewa, and prevent the expedition of troops either westward or toward Toronto.

"Third. By a column from some point near Ogdensburgh to seize and hold Brockville and Prescott, and to move at once by the line of the Prescott and Ottawa Railroad upon Ottawa City, which is without fortifications and only defended by five companies of volunteers recruited from the Government clerks and employees, and known as the Civil Service Battalion. Here are the buildings and archives of the government, and here we shall secure a number of important personages who will serve as hostages for our brothers now lying in English jails.

"Fourth. By a column along the line of the New York and Montreal Railroad in the direction of the St. Lawrence, to threaten Montreal and to obtain possession of the point where the bridge of the Grand Trunk Railroad spans the Ottawa River at Perrot Island.

"Fifth. By a small expedition, which, crossing the boundary of the State of Maine, could destroy the Metis road and effectually stop the march of any reinforcements from Nova Scotia or New Brunswick in the direction of Quebec.

"These attacks made simultaneously on the flanks and on the centre, will prevent the concentrating of the enemy's troops and will enable me to command all his lines of communication and supply, while the destruction of his railroad hold them for our own use, will entirely separate the two provinces. The country is rich and will subsist our forces until the reinforcements, which I am sure the sound of the first gun will bring into the field, shall have assembled. With strong garrisons in my rear to cover my depots and secure my communications with my base of supplies, I shall then move eastward on Quebec, which, although a very formidable fortress, is by no means impregnable to the resources of modern artillery and engineering, provided we can attack this winter, while the garrison is numerically too weak to man all the works, and when the arrival of reinforcements, which must be conveyed from St. Johns and Halifax in sleighs over a road which for four days traverses the snows of the wilderness of New Brunswick, can be prevented by a small raid from the frontier of Maine.

"Of Canada West I say but little; it will be cut off from outward support, and left to its own resources will soon fall entirely into our hands. But, with the harbor and fortress of Quebec in our possession, and with the revenues of the Canadas to pay our expenses, we can confidently look forward to the realization of our dreams of fitting out an expedition to the shores of Ireland. We shall have won glory and credit for our cause, and silenced the cavilings of our enemies, and we shall have gained the active sympathies of thousands, who have only hesitated so far to aid us with their praises and their influence because they feared that our schemes were chimerical and without practical solution."

That the Canadian invasion plan was not considered as "chimerical and without practical solution," is evinced by an article written shortly after the battle of Ridgway by a recognized military authority, Colonel Church, of the Army and Navy Journal. It may also be interesting to note the opinion of the aged Hungarian patriot, Louis Kossuth, upon the subject of securing freedom for Ireland, as expressed to a correspondent of the Pall Mall Gazette, and printed in its issue of May 11, 1893, to whom he expressed himself as follows:

"It has been said that the situation in Ireland is comparable to that of Hungary, and some eminent Englishmen have asked my opinion in regard to that assertion. My answer is that it is false. The Austrians never conquered Hungary as the English conquered Ireland. Hungary merely made a pact with the House of Hapsburg for the sake of neighborly association. Ireland, on the contrary, was conquered by force of arms, and can only be delivered by force of arms."

Respectfully yours,

W. M. SWEEN

Astoria, Long Island, June 9, 1893.

LXXXI

THE FENIAN DEMONSTRATIONS

(Reprinted from a Dublin newspaper.)

It is now some months since the occurence of that disruption of the Fenian Society in America, the particulars of which must be familiar to our readers. Since that date the criminations, recriminations, and mutual denunciations of the rival leaders have formed a curious chapter of intelligence, and we have no doubt a painful one to thousands of Irishmen. Judging from the facts laid before the public in connection with the original dispute and secession, it seemed pretty clear that Mr. John O'Mahony and some of his adherents had long been playing a false and hollow game towards the Fenian Society; but the later news exhibits these parties in a still more unfavorable light, and has caused them to be regarded with positive disgust by men who up to this time believed that the "Head Centre," however he might have broken his oath of fidelity to the Constitution of the Society, misappropriated its funds, and impeded its action, was sincere, at all events, in one thing—that is, hostility to the power of England. Recent events tend to throw doubt upon Mr. O'Mahony's bona fides even in this respect; they induce a belief that the gratification of his own vanity, the triumph of his own party over their rivals, are the objects he has nearest his heart; and that for the attainment of them he would not scruple to bring defeat and disaster on the heads of any of his countrymen who might attempt to injure England according to any programme but his own.

Our readers are aware that the Senate branch of the organization, in which are to be found the men whose integrity and ability were the boast of the Society, formed the plan of capturing Canada from England, as the surest and wisest way of inaugurating a war for the liberation of Ireland. For this course they showed abundant reasons, from a military point of view. At war with the English power in Canada, they could claim from the American Government recognition as belligerents; in the harbors of Canada they would be able to equip privateers for such a game against English commerce as the Alabama played against the commerce of America; at war in that country, they would be near their own base of supplies while their enemy would be far from his; they would also be near a great power whose sympathies would assuredly be enlisted on their side at the first glimmer of success upon their arms; they would be near a great, free people who, in any event, might be glad to give them such practical assistance as England habitually gives to the revolutionists of other countries. Then there was a chance of involving America and England in war—a war which could hardly continue without giving liberty to Ireland, a great increase of territory to the United States, and inflicting irreparable injury on the trade, which is the basis of the power of England.

With these and with many other arguments did they support the policy of making their first stroke at England on Canadian grounds. Further, they argued that the policy of striking it in Ireland did not offer the faintest chance of success. England, being at peace with the world, could throw her whole force upon the neighboring island, which, of all places on the face of the earth, is that in which she could carry on hostilities with the greatest convenience to herself. Nowhere else could she send so large an army—nowhere else could she supply that army with every requisite so readily and so cheaply; in short, nowhere else could she fight with the same advantages on her side.

"I am ready," said General Sweeney, "to fight, and, if need be, to die for Ireland, but it must be in connection with plans that hold out a fair chance of success. I never will ask my countrymen to follow me in a movement which can result only in their defeat. I will be no party to useless slaughter. Too much Irish blood has been already shed in vain and ill-considerd projects, and I do not wish to load the conscience with one drop more drawn from the rich fountain of the Irish heart. As a military man, I believe we can strike the power of England effectively in Canada; and I believe a movement on Ireland or a rising in Ireland would be a mad endeavor. If any half a dozen generals of high professional repute, men who have characters to lose, will say that an insurrection in Ireland, with such assistance as we could render from America, would have any chance of succeeding, I will embark in it; but my own military knowledge and experience convince me that no such men would pronounce such an opinion. On the other hand, I know that they consider my Canadian plans realizable, if the Irish population in America will but give me a fair share of support."

In such words did General Sweeny lay his views before the friends of Ireland in America. The stamp of honesty and common sense was upon them; but they did not prove agreeable to Mr. O'Mahony and his party, who do not like to see themselves superseded in the management of Fenian affairs—a line of business which they had found profitable and pleasant. They gave every possible opposition to the General's project; they denounced it at public meetings and in the press; they broke in with rowdyism upon the meetings which were being held to support it; they interrupted the speakers with shouts and cries; they fought among the audience, and some of their number got taken off to prison by the police. They put into circulation, from time to time, a whole flight of falsehoods to bolster up their own position. The fighting, they said, had commenced in Ireland—were they to desert their brothers in the field? The greater part of the army were sworn Fenians—were they to let that chance slip? One-half the

British fleet might be said to belong to James Stephens—were they to allow it to revert to the British Government?

These, and a number of equally veracious statements, they set afloat for the purpose of diverting the minds of the Brotherhood from the plan proposed by General Sweeny, and inducing them to contribute their money for the "direct move" favored by Mr. O'Mahony. This opposition retarded considerably the preparations which were being made by the Senate party, but did not stop them. The month of April came on; the time fixed by General Sweeny for the commencement of his operations drew near; everyone expected from day to day to hear of their initiation, when, to the great surprise of the public, news arrived that the O'Mahony party themselves were demonstrating along the British frontier! Astonishing reports of all they were preparing to do were borne on the wings of the press. Mr. Doran Killian, who, it seems, has suddenly acquired the title of "General," was reported massing his men and holding a convention at Eastport, and a rush into New Brunswick was represented as imminent. Detailed accounts of his immense preparations for war were sent flying through the United States and into the British provinces. In the latter place they caused great alarm. Defensive measures were hastily adopted, troops were ordered to the front, British gunboats were got round to the coast, and every step that prudence could dictate to the authorities in the threatened territory was taken at once. How was this action of the O'Mahony party to be accounted for? Had they united with General Sweeny? or had they determined to take up his plans and act on them before he could move? Thoroughly as we distrust the leaders of the O'Mahony party, we wondered for a while whether something of this sort might not have been their intention; but later advice from the States put a different complexion on the affair.

The organs of the Senate branch of the Brotherhood state that the demonstrations in question were got up by the O'Mahonyites for the purpose of hastening the repressive interference of the American Government. They knew the Government would interpose for the preservation of their neutrality if once the aspect of affairs on the border became serious, and they hoped to provoke this interposition in time to prevent the Sweeny party from crossing the frontier! They have, to some extent at least, succeeded in their design. The Government has despatched General Meade with a body of troops to Eastport to enforce respect for the neutrality laws of the States. And we read that on his arrival at Eastport "General" Killian immediately took his departure. His work was done. He returned, we dare say, in high spirits to Union Square, and was congratulated by Colonel O'Mahony and Field-Marshal Stephen J. Meany on the successful accomplishment of his mission. Such is the patriotism, such is the Fenianism, of Mr. O'Mahony and his men. They will suffer no attack, if they can help it, to be made by an Irish force on the British power unless under their own auspices; they wish defeat and disaster to fall upon any body of Irishmen who may attempt to strike England anywhere except at the point which they are pleased to select, but towards which they make no advance whatever. Doing nothing themselves, except collecting money, they wish to forbid others from taking action more in accordance with the threats and the promises which the Fenian Society has for years been giving utterance.

It is not Fenians and Fenian sympathizers only who will feel ashamed of those ridiculous and disgraceful proceedings. Men who do not believe that either "wing" or both "wings" of the Fenian Society could, unaided, wage a successful war against England in any part of the world, feel conscious that as Irishmen they are touched by the exhibition of such narrow-mindedness, such stupidity, such meanness on the part of a body of their countrymen. The Fenian war projects, Irish and Canadian, might be wild and desperate, and from that point of view unjustifiable; yet they be so conducted as to bring on the Irish name no other charge than that of a hostility to England so fierce, so impetuous, as to overbear all the calculations of ordinary prudence, a hatred so intense as to send Irishmen surging up against her serried ranks under circumstances which would insure their own destruction rather than her punishment. Far different is the sort of repute which Mr. O'Mahony and his followers are, to the full extent of their power, acquiring for the Irish character. It is neither that of bravery, nor honesty, nor wisdom. We forbear to write the words by which it would be most accurately described.

LXXXII

Richmond, Va., Box 1109, February 19, 1867.

Mr. M. Moynahan:

Dear Sir: I once more decline, for the reasons already explained to you, to participate in the Fenian movement as at present organized, or rather disorganized. I disbelieve in the existence of any fighting in Ireland, and in the possibility of making any fight there while England continues at peace. This has been my opinion for many years. I have never yet joined in any appeal to my countrymen in America to contribute their money towards any such premature and impossible attempt. It is but wasting their means and, what is worse, it is wasting and rising up their patriotic enthusiasm and destroying their trust in the faith of man.

I do not wish either your branch of the organization or that of Mr. Roberts to use my name in any manner whatever.

Respectfully yours,

JOHN MITCHEL.

LXXXIII

Richmond, Va., Box 1109, November 17, 1868.

Mr. M. Moynahan:

Dear Sir: I have received yours of the 14th. In reply I can only say that I had fully considered the matter before the conversation which I had with you in New York, and I cannot perceive that any duty calls me, in the present circumstances, to put myself forward in such a manner as would be interpreted, and truly interpreted, to be a renewed appeal to our countrymen at this side the Atlantic to contribute their money for promoting an insurrection in Ireland. I consider now, as I did before, that while England remains at peace—and while all hope of effectual aid from this side is now out of the question—an insurrection must end disastrously. This opinion of mine I cannot help—it is formed upon such information as I have been able to procure—and, such being my opinion, it would not be conscientious on my part to aid in keeping up the excited expectation of immediate and decisive action.

Mr. Stephens, of course, knows what his resources are better than I do; yet even he may be partly deceiving himself, as men of sanguine temperament are so apt to do. What is more, I do believe that he does deceive himself in supposing that he has at his command for real and desperate action any such mass of men in Ireland as would give the enemy serious trouble.

It was needless to explain to me that Mr. Stephens was misreported at Philadelphia. Even if his words had been exactly as they were printed there was nothing in them offensive to me. But the incident showed me the necessity of making a kind of general statement as to what I had done with the funds intrusted to me. I never supposed for a moment that he had meant to understate the amount received through me, which very probably he had kept no account of—and as to its expenditure after it came to his hands, that was a matter of which he was the sole judge—nor have I ever said to any one that I thought it had been improperly expended.

In short, nothing of which I am yet aware would justify me in imputing blame to Mr. Stephens. But, with my present views and convictions, I cannot aid him in any way.

Truly yours,

JOHN MITCHEL.

LXXXIV

This letter was written by Col. Thomas Kelly while he was acting chief executive of the Irish Republican Brotherhood in Ireland in 1867. It was addressed to General Halpin.

---

19 Grantham Street, Dublin, March 12, 1867.

My Dear General:—I owe you an apology for not having written you specially until now; but I know that you make full allowance for the circumstances under which I have been obliged to act until lately. Little Baldy has at last given up the ghost, and acknowledged that if he came to Ireland the people would be certain to make short work of him. The rascal is in Paris, taking his ease with his wife, while the destiny of Ireland is in the balance. The money he squeezed from the men of New York, through you and others, under pretence that it was necessary "to procure a boat," he coolly pockets, together with the proceeds of the "Hopper drafts" (which I am almost certain have been drawn), he now uses to take his ease in Paris, where he denounces the Irish-Americans as "dogs, dung and devil's scum." Mur. and Cos. have left him in complete disgust, recognizing in him the most perfect sample of a renegade and traitor to a great cause. When M. denounces him as an accomplished swindler, just think, how basely he must have acted toward him. When I heard that you accompanied him to Sandy Hook I was at first disappointed, but the latest news confirms the fullest confidence I had in your devotion to the Republican doctrine as contradistinguished from the notorious "one-man power." I now state authoritatively that St. is repudiated and denounced by the entire home organization. Look out for any future vindications of himself which he may offer to an American public.

I do wish you could be in Tipperary just now. I will be plain with you. A mistake was at first made by the officer having the disposition of the forces in that locality, as well as in other parts. He, however, has now to suffer for mistakes, or rather violations of orders, and the less said about the matter the better. However, notwithstanding anything that may be said to the contrary by the enemy's press, the work is being carried out according to instructions, and if the people do not fight any big battles, depend upon it, it is all owing to the faith that has been instilled into them as to what they might expect from America. At the worst the flag will be kept flying another month, and if by that time America shall not have done its duty the name of Irishmen deservedly should be hooted at with scorn. Work heaven and earth. The flag is flying! Good God! will people any longer say they will give this or that when they see a blow struck? Are those of us who hold everything at stake any longer to be guarded against as swindlers. It is better for the Irishman who does not now throw in all he has got, or himself, that he never was born. He is a renegade—an imposter—a traitor, show him no quarter. Let the names be published. When I think of the ponderous immense work that has been done on £1,500 I have no word of patience for the rich Irish-Americans who have refused us aid. Make them contribute largely now, or let them be forever marked. I do believe that with £5,000 to begin with instead of what I had the work of upsetting the British power would be as simple as rolling off a log.

I am almost out of mind to know what could have been done with a little more money, and which was obliged to be left undone. Yet, if the means arrive in time, it is not yet, perhaps, too late. We now begin to realize fully the madness of Macle's attack on Chester. But for that unfortunate affair we would have been in a position completely to surprise the government. It was undertaken against the positive wish of the Provisional Government; and no matter what may be said in its favor, it was nothing short of an attempt on the part of that individual to make an individual reputation. When done legitimately, this is well enough; but when he undertook to force his ideas on every officer who came over here, and when they all repudiated his plans and the authority which he endeavored to force upon them, it was, to use the mildest expression, unpatriotic in the extreme. However, he is now in durance, and we must look upon the fiasco, however much injury it may have done, as in the mildest possible light.

A council of at least three ought to be in session in Paris or Brussels. If I had the advice of such a body now it would be of incalculable benefit. Have your three best men sent at once. We will give them ministerial powers to treat with foreign governments. They should, of course, be men of the highest possible attainments.

You should at once have new bond plates engraved, or the old plates will answer with your name, or that of the party appointed by a general congress as American financial agent, instead of the name of John O'Mahony; or if John O'Mahony was appointed to that position the present bonds would answer but not the old series. Authority is hereby given to a general American congress to bind the Irish Republic in sums not less than ten dollars and to any individual (in one bond) to ten thousand dollars. I will at once forward addresses to which communications can be safely sent for me. M. M. will know how to find out those addresses. Mind the brackets.

In fine, don't mind newspaper reports. It is war to the knife. Only send us the knife. I am a man of my word. Never cease until you hear I am dead. The flag is flying. Proclaim war to the knife. (Remember me to MacIntyre!) The Britishers propose now to hang our Irish-American officers. Already I see that a charge of treason is to be preferred against all our men captured. Hanging is said to be too good for Irishmen who left their homes to learn the use of arms! For God's sake send us the knife!

We will win with anything in our hands. Curses on the recreant American-Irish, those whose ambition it is to be citizens of a country, which scorns them at home and repudiates their claims to citizenship abroad. Let man, woman and child rally round the green flag while one man is in the field. If I could only transport two thousand Poles to Ireland they are at our service, and yet Irishmen remain cool-blooded, sneaking and looking for Irish news in American cities! Damn such men, who don't sell all but the clothes on their backs for dear old Ireland! Where now are the men who promised me they would give their five, ten, twenty, fifty and hundred, thousand dollar subscriptions. Remember what I said in America! Mark every Irishman who refuses! Give the fullest credit to every man who behaves well now in the day of our trial. It is almost post time and I must close.

Regards to M. M., P. O'K., O'S and the F. B.

Faithfully and fraternally,

THOMAS KELLY, Acting C. E. I. R.

LXXXV

SKETCH OF GEN. KERWIN'S MILITARY CAREER.

The following is taken from "Bates' Martial Deeds of Pennsylvania."

Michael Kerwin, Colonel of the Thirteenth Pennsylvania Cavalry, was born on the 15th of August, 1837, in the County of Wexford, Ireland, from which place his family emigrated during his early boyhood to America. He was educated in a private academy in the City of Philadelphia, and in early youth

GENERAL MICHAEL KERWIN.

learned the business of a lithographic printer. Of a studious turn of mind, he early acquired a good fund of general information. He was a member for several years of a volunteer militia company, in which he attained considerable knowledge of military organization and duty.

Three days after the call for troops, in April, 1861, he volunteered as a private in the Twenty-fourth Regiment for three months' service. This organization formed part of Patterson's Army, with which he advanced into Virginia. Before crossing the Potomac, where it was known the enemy was present in considerable force, it became very important to the Union leader that he should know what troops he would have to meet. Some valuable soldier was sought, who would enter the rebel lines and gather the desired information. For this dangerous and important duty Kerwin volunteered his services. Full well he knew that, should he be discovered, death awaited him. But he was not of the temper to hesitate when called for any duty which his country might demand. Adopting the necessary disguise he crossed the Potomac river, went freely through the enemy's camps, which he found near Martinsburg, and after making an estimate of the number of men and guns and outlines of fortifications, returned and reported to General Negley, then in command of the brigade to which he belonged.

The successful manner in which this duty was performed, and the judgment and daring which he displayed in executing it, marked him as worthy of a better rank than that of bearing a musket.

In September, 1861, after having been discharged at the expiration of his first term, he was commissioned captain in the Thirteenth Cavalry, and in July following was promoted to Major. During the 12th, 13th, 14th and 15th days of June, 1863, when Melroy's little force, in which the Thirteenth was serving, was confronted and finally routed by the advance of Lee's entire army, Major Kerwin, at the head of his regiment, rendered important service, having frequent conflicts with the over-confident rebel horse. After leaving the valley, the regiment was attached to the Army of the Potomac, when Major Kerwin was promoted to Colonel and took command of the regiment.

On the 12th day of October, 1863, while on the advance picket line near White Sulphur Springs, Va., he was attacked by a heavy force of the rebel army, Lee seeking by a sudden movement to turn the Union right. Colonel Kerwin with his own regiment in connection with the Fourth Cavalry, combated the head of Elwell's columns for six long hours, giving time for Meade to recross the Rappahannock and get his army into position to checkmate the wily scheme of the rebel chieftain. Gallantly was this duty executed, but at the sacrifice of these two noble commands, large numbers of both being killed, wounded and taken prisoners.

During the year 1864, Colonel Kerwin led his force with Sheridan in his operations with the Army of the Potomac, for a time being in command of the Second Brigade of Gregg's Division. In February, 1865, he went with his regiment from before Petersburg to City Point, where he proceeded by transport to Wilmington, North Carolina, to meet Sherman, who was marching up from Georgia. On joining the grand column at Fayetteville, Colonel Kerwin was assigned to the command of the Third Brigade of Kilpatrick's Division.

After the surrender of Johnstown, Colonel Kerwin was ordered to Fayetteville with his regiment, and placed in Command of the Post. He had seven counties under his control, and managed the affairs of his department with singular skill and ability. After the conclusion of hostilities he returned to Philadelphia, where, near the close of July, 1865, he was mustered out of service, having been on duty continuously from opening to the conclusion of the war.

NOTE.—General Michael Kerwin was one of the bravest and most skillful officers sent from America to Ireland in 1865. He served with distinction in the War of the Rebellion, rising to the rank of Brigadier-General. When he was mustered out he immediately went to Ireland, commissioned by John O'Mahony to James Stephens, Chief Organizer of the Irish Revolutionary Brotherhood. While in Ireland, he was arrested and detained in prison many months. On his return to this country he continued active in the Irish cause and even to this day is prominent in its councils. For many years he was connected with the New York Post Office, was Collector of Internal Revenue for the Second District of New York, Police Commissioner of the City of New York and is at present occupying the responsible position of Pension Agent for New York, having succeeded Gen. Franz Siegel in that office. Gen. Kerwin was also editor and publisher of the New York Tablet, and is the author of many valuable papers on Ireland and America.

LXXXVI

GEN. DENIS F. BURKE.

The following sketch of the life of Gen. Burke is taken from "Powell's Army and Navy."

Brevet Brigadier General Denis F. Burke was born in Ireland in 1841, and emigrated to the United States in 1856. He was engaged in the dry goods business in the house of A. T. Stewart & Co., and H. B. Claflin & Co., New York city.

When Fort Sumpter was fired upon he enlisted in the Sixty-ninth Militia, in the company commanded by Capt. Thos. F. Meagher, subsequently organizer and commander of the Irish Brigade. The Sixty-ninth Militia was called into the service of the United States for ninety days. He participated with his regiment in the battles of Blackburn's Ford and the first Bull Run, returning with it to New York when their time expired. Immediately after, General Meagher organized the three New York regiments of his famous brigade, viz: Sixty-third, Sixty-ninth and Eighty-eighth New York Volunteers.

General Burke was commissioned second lieutenant in the Eighty-eighth Regiment and was with it from Fair Oaks to Appomattox Court House, never missing a battle in which his regiment or brigade enjoyed participation during the entire war. He enjoyed the privilge of being the only officer of the Irish Brigade who went out with it in 1861 and remained until the close of the war.

The casualties among the officers of the brigade were very heavy. He was promoted first lieutenant at the battle of Malvern Hill, and adjutant of his regiment at Hamson's Landing, and at Antietam was promoted to the rank of captain for distinguished conduct.

He was severely wounded at Fredericksburg, Virginia, December 13, 1862, when the company (C) he commanded was almost annihilated. He returned to duty in time for the battle of Chancellorsville, where he was again wounded.

After this battle his regiment, on account of its terrible losses, was consolidated into a battalion, and he was placed in command.

He was at Gettysburg and received commendation on the battlefield from General Hancock for his conduct.

During General Meade's retrograde movement from Rapidan to Centreville, Burke commanded the flankers of the Second Brigade, First Division, Second Corps, and was the first to discover the enemy's position near Bristoe Station, and to report the facts to General Warren, then commanding the Second Corps, receiving from that officer high praise.

After the Mine Run campaign the three New York regiments re-enlisted and were sent back to recruit. The regiments were fully recruited, and Burke came back lieutenant colonel of the regiment.

He was in the Battle of the Wilderness, Todd's Tavern, and Spottsylvania, May 5, 1864. His regiment was one of the first to cross the earthworks at the "bloody angle" on the morning of May 12. He was at Cold Harbor June 3, and at Petersburg June 17, 1864.

While in command of the Irish Brigade on October 29, 1864, at Fort Sedgwick, General Burke was ordered to attack the enemy's line at night. This he did with great success, calling from Gen. N. A. Miles, commanding First Division, Second Corps, the following recommendation to General Hancock:

"That Lieut. Col. Denis F. Burke, Eighty-eighth Regiment, New York Veteran Volunteers, receive the rank of brevet colonel for gallantry in action October 29, 1864. Colonel Burke, with a party of one hundred men, attacked and captured a portion of the enemy's line opposite Fort Sedgwick, taking some prisoners and holding the line until ordered to withdraw."

Burke was subsequently commissioned colonel of his regiment, and took part in all the battles during the siege of Petersburg.

He was several times complimented by General Hancock, and previous to his departure from the Second Corps to take command at Washington, General Hancock recommended Burke for the brevet of brigadier general, which he received after the surrender of Lee.

General Hancock's opinion of Burke: "I can state that he was a gallant and faithful officer who rose from the ranks to the colonelcy by his good conduct and services in the field.

"He received his brevet of brigadier general of volunteers upon my recommendation for gallant and meritorious services during the campaign of 1864."

After the close of the war General Burke returned with his command to New York, and again engaged in mercantile life.

He was subsequently appointed assistant appraiser of merchandise at the port of New York.

Note.—Brig. Gen. Denis F. Burke was one of those men who distinguished himself alike in the service of Ireland and America. He was noted for his bravery as a soldier and his skill as a commanding officer, while from the opening to the closing of his eventful career he was always devoted to the interest of his native land, and suffered imprisonment in its cause. After his return from Ireland he published the New York Emerald, an illustrated Irish weekly of much merit, and was connected with Gen. M. Kerwin in the publication of the New York Tablet. He died in New York in 1896.

LXXXVII

CORK AND THE '67 RISING.

Interesting Recollections of a Famous Episode.

Mr. J. F. X. O'Brien, M. P., when presiding over the Manchester Martyrs' Anniversary Demonstration in London, on November 23, 1904, told his reminiscences of the Rising in Cork on March 6, 1867, and his meeting with Michael O'Brien, one of the "Manchester Martyrs." Mr. O'Brien said:

"It was my fortune on the sixth of March, 1867, to meet one of the 'noble-hearted Three'—Michael O'Brien. Perhaps it would interest you to learn under what circumstances I met him. In 1849 I was in the movement organized by Fintan Lalor, and had to leave Ireland to avoid arrest. Later I went to Nicaragua in Central America, hoping to acquire some military experience, and I met James Stephens in New Orleans, where I was a member of a Branch of the I. R. B.

"In '62 I returned to Ireland, and there joined the organization of the I. R. B. at Cork, and to make a long story short, when Stephens sent to Cork the order for the '67 Rising I was one of those called upon to vote for or against the Rising. The responsibility was very grave. It had been given out that depots of arms had been provided at certain places—Mallow, Limerick Junction, etc. But judging by what I had seen and heard, I distrusted these rumors, and I could not agree to sending unarmed men to be slaughtered. So I voted against the Rising, but I submitted to the ruling of the majority, and I need hardly tell you I was 'there' on the eventful day. It is a painful thing to say, but years after I learned that men who had voted for the Rising did not themselves turn out. The party I joined at our rendezvous numbered some 1,500 or 2,000. I gathered that altogether about 5,000 left Cork that night, two other parties going by other roads. Of our body, about a dozen had pikes of a poor sort, two had shotguns, one a small rifle, five, myself among the rest, had revolvers. That was our armament. I met Captain Mackey, and learned that of the two men appointed to command, one had been arrested, and the other was not to be found. I was told he proved to be a bad scamp. I urged Mackey, who was even then very well known, that he should take command, but he declined.

"I then met Michael O'Brien, and pressed him also to take command, but he, too, declined. Apparently, he did not feel justified in accepting the responsibility, though I need not tell you how he proved the stuff he was made of at Manchester. Eventually, I took charge of a few hundred men, and tried to organize them. We were soon stepping out bravely to a marching tune, sung or whistled as we went along, and our spirits rose rapidly. When we approached Ballyknocken, it was decided that Mackey, with fifty men, should visit the police barrack. Some of them were only boys of sixteen and seventeen years of age. One young fellow carried a knapsack which belonged to me. I mention it in order to illustrate the power of police swearing, for they swore that they were attacked by one hundred and fifty men, each carrying a rifle and knapsack (laughter). On arrival at the police barrack, we told the police to send out the women and children, which was done. We then set fire to the building. Remember, we were unarmed —and with their rifles the police might easily have repulsed us.

"After a while the stairs were burned, and the floor the police were standing on was on fire, and the police seeing the priest on the road, called to him, and asked him his advice. He asked 'Have you done your best?' and they answered that they had. 'Well, then, my men,' said he, 'you are not bound to lay down lives,' and they promptly surrendered. A ladder was then laid against the window to let them down. They were to hand us their arms and ammunition first, which was a proper precaution in the circumstances, but the first man, forgetting this, was coming down rifle in hand. This being observed by the man who carried our one rifle, he let fly at the policeman from the road, and with good effect, for he cut the chin-strap close to the policeman's ear. Of course he yelled, and I ordered the firing to cease.

"The police now immediately remembered their conditions, and handed down their rifles, and came down themselves. In addition to the fifty men, who I mentioned took part in the attack, one or two hundred now came up to see what was going on, and they got the idea the credit was due to me, for they now addressed me as Colonel O'Brien. Some of the policemen were willing to join us after the surrender, but I would not allow it. I saw that the thing was a forlorn hope, and that we could do nothing, and I did not want these men to ruin their lives. Some of our own men wanted to take them prisoners, but this also I would not have, as it would be giving the police opportunities for recognizing numbers of our men.

"Truly, this is not a cheerful tale, but the wonder of it is—and it is almost miraculous—that the story of Ireland for more than 700 years has been a terrible list of disasters, with occasional brilliant successes, and yet we have never given up the fight. Scarcely a generation rises up in that ancient land but it nourishes new hopes, forever declining to accept as final, or to be disheartened, by the disasters of the past. This is a wonderful, a really grand thing to contemplate. No other race of men in this world can show such a record. Situated as Ireland is, our people should ever be as ready—as were the men whose martyrdom we commemorate to-night, to fling their lives away, if necessary, for the salvation of our country.

"If this were so and known to all, it would, most likely, never more be necessary to make a great sacrifice. Upon this I would like to make one remark: Men ready to take up such a position, should always keep themselves ready to face the hereafter, and so,

> 'Righteous men should make our land
> A Nation once again.'

The 5,000 young men who went out unarmed from the City of Cork on the 6th of March, '67, gave an extraordinary proof of courage. Nothing I have ever read has given me a higher idea of an indomitable spirit. What could such men do and dare if only trained, armed and well led."

LXXXVIII

A writer in the "Westminster Review" said "England never legislated for Ireland except under the influence of fear; Fenianism disestablished the Irish Church; Whiteboyism is uneffected Title Reform; the Clerkenwell Explosions (we have Mr. Gladstone's own authority for saying) brought about the Land Bill and Dynamite has brought Home Rule within the scope of Practical Politics."

The series of explosions which so affected Parliamentary opinion in England occurred on the following dates:

1881.

Jan 14, Explosion at the Military Barracks, Salford.

March 16, Attempted explosion at the Mansion House, London.

May 5, Explosion at Militia Barracks, Chester.

May 16, Explosion at Police Station, Hatton Garden, Liverpool.

June 10, Explosion at the Town Hall, Liverpool.

1883.

Jan. 20, Explosion at Buchanan St. Railway Station, Glasgow.

Jan. 20, Explosion at Gasometer, Irdeston, Glasgow.

Jan. 20, Explosion at Canal Bridge, Glasgow.

March 15, Explosion at Local Government Board Offices, Whitehall, London.

March 15, Attempted Explosion "Times" Office, London.

Nov. 30, Explosion at Praed Street Station, London.

Nov. 30, Explosion between Westminister Bridge and Charing Cross Railway Station, London.

1884.

Feb. 25, Attempted Explosion at Charing Cross Railway Station, London.

Feb. 25, Attempted Explosion at Paddington Railway Station, London.

Feb. 25, Attempted Explosion at Ludgate Hill Railway Station, London.

Feb. 26, Explosion at Victoria Railway Station, London.

May 30, Explosion at Scotland Yard, London.

May 30, Explosion at Junior Carlton Club, London.

May 30, Explosion at Residence of Sir Watkym Wynn, London.

May 30, Attempted Explosion in Trafalgar Square, London.

Dec. 13, Explosion at London Bridge.

1885.

Jan. 2, Explosion between Gower St. and Kings Cross on Underground Railway, London.

Jan. 24, Explosion at Westminister Hall, London.

Jan. 24, Explosion at the House of Commons, London.

Jan. 24, Explosion at the Tower of London.

LXXXIX

The two following letters in the handwriting of John Boyle O'Reilly, editor of the Boston Pilot, addressed to O'Donovan Rossa, are interesting in showing the kindly spirit of the man and the high esteem in which he held Rossa. His determination to criticize Irish speakers, giving praise or blame as he considered it deserved, was evidently something that had not usually been done before.

OFFICE OF THE PILOT.

Boston, September 14, 1871.

My Dear Rossa:—

Thank you for writing so long a letter to me when I know you are so busy. I've been angry all morning about this same charitable affair of the two "Homes." There's a mess and a mixture, and I'm glad you said you couldn't come. Let me try to tell you what I understand about it from Donahoe. First, the Home Directors in Boston had not been consulted when Donahoe telegraphed to you. He took it for granted that they would be agreeable to anything he proposed. Now it appears that they had partly engaged a lecturer, Hon. Wm. Parsons, I think, for November to speak for the benefit of the Home; and when Donahoe put forward his idea of having a reading, half the proceeds from which should go to Ireland, the "charitable" directors reared up and became unruly. So Donahoe was frightened, and let them have their own way. He thought that if you came he could secure as much for the Boston Home as the other entertainment could. And so it is best let them have their lecture and all the profits this time; and when that is over we shall get up a better one for the Kantwell Home, if Mrs. Rossa will only rest assured that this result was entirely unlooked for, and that all her friends here are sincerely anxious to welcome her again to New England.

Now, as to your objections against a visit to Boston, I'm devilish glad you hate public speaking; I do, and I wish more men did. I mean to alter it, too—if I can. Formerly the men who spoke to Irish audiences spoke nonsense or worse, and it was praised. Nobody ever dreamt of criticizing an Irish speech. I'll do it. I'll attend every Irish lecture in Boston; and I'll praise or blame impartially. I've made one thing a specialty—to fight this confounded praise of everything Irish and hated of everything un-Irish, and try to induce other men to do the same. We must criticize our own people, Rossa, if we want to raise them. They will not bear criticism from outsiders, which is thrown to them as a bone might be to a dog—not offered them as from a man to his fellow-man with a good intent. I'm afraid that confounded Tammany will make them suspect your honest when you talk, and, if so, I'll be sorry, for

I know you will speak the truth. I saw the Star. It's a mean paper, Rossa, a mighty mean paper—on a par with the Irish Democrat, which this morning nearly gave me the cholera. Oh! damn those fellows.

I'm sorry if I wronged O'Leary; but he gave me that impression. Truly, after I wrote that letter to you I felt that I had wronged him, and that it was my own ill-temper that made me feel so badly. Serves you right about your "Prison Life;" you don't deserve a cent. I told Donahoe this morning, and he said: "If he had offered it to me in the first place I certainly would have taken it." As it is, I think the really interesting part is just commencing, and the part with the least objectionable matter for The Pilot. The "Prison Life" could be made an entire thing, and when finished the whole made into a book. If you break with the others, or before you do, write to Donahoe and offer it to him. Write and tell me same mail, and don't put your "official" envelope on that letter for me. I'll manage the matter if it can be done. Depend on it, when we get rid of our present, I'll make Donahoe offer you the N. Y. correspondentship which you can take or refuse at will. What a devil of a long letter this is!

Don't you be afraid that I will hesitate to pitch into you if you get out of the straight tracks. Man alive, there's a sort of heroism in pitching into a friend. When I do it I feel so like the Galway judge, who hung his own son, that I'm sorely tempted to be always doing a little that way. Dominus Vobiscum. Writing for The Pilot is next thing to Holy Orders, and it has brought me near matrimony—that's an after-thought—mighty good one. Faithfully,

J. BOYLE O'REILLY.

XC.

THE PILOT OFFICE.

No. 19 Franklin Street.

Patrick Donahoe, Proprietor.

Boston, September 27, 1871.

My Dear Rossa:—

I enclose you a ticket for admission to the New Home in Boston, at Donahoe's request; and I personally hope it will do you a great deal of good—which it must, if you receive it in the proper spirit.

(That's a nice paragraph—meaning nothing at all.)

Now listen, or rather read attentively, and when you have read, sit down and write an answer by telegram; address it to Patrick Donahoe. (That's a mighty good name on a bill.)

Can you lecture in Boston for the Home on Tuesday, October 17, for $100, or can you not? There now, none of your quibbling. Out with it. Can you come? If you can't, you'll get hell in The Pilot; and we never want to hear anything more about you—at least I don't. If you don't come you're kicking $100 in the mud, and if you had a due regard for your offspring you wouldn't do it. (By the way, you're an industrious fellow.).

Seriously, try and come; make arrangements in Lowell, Lawrence, and two or three places around, and you'll make piles of money. Besides, Mrs. O'Reilly (that is to be) is just crazy to see you, and she's the very nicest girl in New England. Rossa, that in itself should bring you along. Besides, again, coming under the auspices of The Pilot, I won't criticize you too hard. If you refuse to come, I'll follow you like a sleuth hound wherever you go to talk and give you ———

Now, let me tell you, this letter is all my own. But Donahoe wants you to come; it is a personal favor to him, and you'll meet friends. I tell you, Rossa, that little girl is crazy about you; she never was in Ireland, and she thinks you're a good deal of ruffian, a philosopher, and a bull. That's a gentle compliment for you, now. Telegraph "yes" at once.

JOHN BOYLE O'REILLY.

XCI.

The following letter (we withhold the name of the writer) found among Rossa's papers would seem to indicate that a turbulent meeting held at the Rotunda and not the loss of the Meehan papers attracted the attention of the government to the I. R. B. and their organ, the "Irish People."

It is probable the raid on the newspaper office and the accompanying arrests were the result of a series, or combination, of events which taken together tended to bring the movement under the notice of the authorities.

---

508 Wabash Ave., Chicago, April 15, 1903.

Dear Rossa:—Here is the letter of T. D. S., which P. W. Dunne read with interest. He was puzzled as to how the author of "God Save Ireland" got the brief for your defence. I was not puzzled, as Lawless held the Nation men in high esteem, as did also Isaac Butt. The latter defended A. M. Sullivan at Wicklow in the celebrated case, White versus "The Nation—White, you know, was the coroner who concealed the government murders in the Dublin Prisons. A. M. was inspired in relation to them by an official whose name I must conceal. White's infamy was exposed in the Nation on which he based an action for libel which was tried by an Orange jury. The trial was rich in episodes. The encounters between Butt and brutal Armstrong, and between the latter and A. M. Sullivan would prove a fascinating page in Ireland's history. Isaac transcended himself in the defence and triumphed in the verdict, and although Wicklow was not in his circuit he declined to take the fee that John Scallan tendered to him as A. M.'s solicitor. God have mercy on Butt who incarnated all the noble instincts and the vices of the Gael.

Do you remember, Rossa, the Rotunda fracas in '64? I see you now through the haze of time bursting through the northern door and leading a host of brave but misguided rebels that stormed the meeting to prevent the Dublin loyalists from insulting Irish sentiment by granting in College Green a site for the statue of the hated Albert. But for the heroic efforts of A. M. Sullivan that historic spot would not now be graced by that glorious masterpiece of Foley, the statue of the immortal Grattan. God forgive Stephens for his inspiration and agency in that unfortunate incident, which concentered the eyes of Dublin Castle upon the seat and center of Irish revolution in Parliament street. That row was a suicidal and calamitous check to the secret propaganda for national liberty, causing the death of "The Irish People" (which was a fatal adventure) followed by the capture, imprisonment and exile of a noble and heroic host of patriots, few of whom, alas! survive to-day. I must cease, for I'm not in spirit to dwell on such a painful retrospect.

Your friend,

* * * * *